Iranian Cinema and Globalization

Iranian Cinema and Globalization
National, Transnational and Islamic Dimensions

Shahab Esfandiary

intellect Bristol, UK / Chicago, USA

First published in the UK in 2012 by
Intellect, The Mill, Parnall Road, Fishponds, Bristol, BS16 3JG, UK

First published in the USA in 2012 by
Intellect, The University of Chicago Press, 1427 E. 60th Street,
Chicago, IL 60637, USA

Copyright © 2012 Intellect Ltd

All rights reserved. No part of this publication may be reproduced, stored in a retrieval system, or transmitted, in any form or by any means, electronic, mechanical, photocopying, recording, or otherwise, without written permission.

A catalogue record for this book is available from the
British Library.

Cover designer: Holly Rose
Copy-editor: Macmillan
Production manager: Jelena Stanovnik
Typesetting: Planman Technologies

ISBN 978-1-84150-470-4

To the memory of
Sayyed Morteza Avini

Contents

Table of Figures   ix

Acknowledgments   xi

Introduction   1

PART I: THEORETICAL FRAMEWORK   11

Chapter 1: Making Sense of Globalization   13
   Introduction   15
   The global field   16
   Global flows   24
   A framework of the globalization theories   34

Chapter 2: The Concept of National Cinema: Theorization and Critique   37
   Introduction   39
   National cinema as 'intertextual symptom'   40
   National cinema as cultural/economic weapon   43
   National cinema as 'the other' of Hollywood   46
   National cinema as 'cultural specificity'   51
   The relevance of 'national cinema' in the age of globalization:
   Arguments for and against   54
   Conclusion   60

PART II: IRANIAN CINEMA AND GLOBALIZATION   65

**Chapter 3: Iranian Cinema in the World Cinema Circuit: Politics,
   Economics and Aesthetics**   67
   The foundations of a 'new cinema'   69
   The emergence of Muslim film-makers   70
   Debate and controversy over international awards   73

    The economics and politics of international festivals   74
    Selecting the examples   78

Chapter 4: Mohsen Makhmalbaf's 'Transnational' Cinema and Globalization   81
    Introduction   83
    Critique of the 'transnational institution of art'   83
    Makhmalbaf: From 'the local' to 'the transnational'   85
    Banal transnationalism   91
    Sex and Philosophy   91
    Scream of the Ants   94
    The rise and fall of an 'idol'   98
    Transnational film-makers and territorial attachments   100
    Conclusion   111

Chapter 5: Daryush Mehrjui's 'National' Cinema and Globalization   113
    Introduction   115
    The complex relation of 'the national' and 'the Islamic'   116
    Iranian cinema's new wave and the early impact of globalization   121
    Mehrjui and the post-revolution circumstances   122
    The Lodgers   124
    Mum's Guests   129
    Conclusion   139

Chapter 6: Ebrahim Hatami-kia's 'Sacred Defense' Cinema and Globalization   141
    Introduction   143
    Muslim Film-makers: From Makhmalbaf to Hatami-kia   144
    The Scout: Constructing the image of the *basiji*   149
    From Karkhe to Rhine: Recognition of 'the other'   154
    Glass Agency: Return of the rebel   164
    Conclusion   174

Conclusion   177

Appendices   189
    Appendix I: Interview with Abbas Kiarostami   191
    Appendix II: Interview with Majid Majidi   199
    Appendix III: Interview with Emad Afroogh   209
    Appendix IV: Interview with Mohammad-reza Jafari-jelveh   219

Bibliography   229

Table of Figures

Figure 1 Vulgar Comedy or Political Symbolism?

Figure 2 The Inspiring Feast of Reconciliation.

Figure 3 The Carnivalesque Dinner Party.

Figure 4 The 'scientific' Operation.

Figure 5 The *Basiji* Prepared for Sacrifice.

Figure 6 Reconstructing the Image of the *Basiji*.

Figure 7 Representing the Émigré.

Figure 8 Comrades Marginalized in 'the new times'.

Figure 9 Lack of Communication.

Figure 10 Asserting Agency and Refusing to Conform.

Acknowledgments

This book is based on a doctoral thesis, which I submitted to the University of Nottingham in 2009. I wish to express my sincere gratitude to Professor Peter Brooker, for his gracious guidance, intellectual insight and critical reflection. I would also like to thank Professor Roger Bromley, Dr. Lloyd Ridgeon and Dr. Jon Simons for their valuable comments and feedback in annual review meetings and the viva voce.

I wish to thank the University of Arts in Tehran and the University of Nottingham for providing me with scholarships that made the present study possible. I am also grateful to the *Iran Heritage Foundation* for a grant that they awarded in contribution to the publication of this book.

I offer appreciation to my postgraduate research colleagues: Emilse, Matt, Luca, Mohamed, Alex, Caroline, Eireanne and Adity for their friendship and support. I should also thank my Iranian friends and their families in Nottingham, who made this journey a very enjoyable experience.

I am grateful to the participants in the following conferences and workshops for their valuable comments on papers and presentations based on the material in this book: the *Memory, Trauma and Identity in the Visual and Literary Representations of the Middle East* workshop (University of Edinburgh, February 2008); the *Global-National Media Matters* panel at the Sixth Annual Meeting of the Cultural Studies Association (New York University, May 2008); the *Visual Representations of Iran* conference (University of St. Andrews, June 2008) and the workshop *Where are the Intellectuals? Culture, Identity and Community in the Modern Middle East* (University of Edinburgh, May 2010). Dr. Gay Breyly and Mehrzad Karimabadi deserve a special mention in this respect.

A shorter version of Chapter 5 was previously published as an article in the Taylor and Francis journal *Iranian Studies* under the title 'Merhjui's Social Comedy and the Representation of the Nation in the Age of Globalization' (Vol. 44, Issue 3). I wish to thank the journal's anonymous reviewer and copy-editor for their comments and suggestions.

I should also thank the staff at Intellect, particularly the editor and assistant editors, cover design artist and copy-editor. Jelena Stanovnik, who took care of this publication project, from the first manuscript all the way to print, deserves a special mention. My thanks also go to the anonymous referees appointed by Intellect, for their useful comments and kind suggestions. I am also grateful of Yusof Shamshiri who kindly helped in obtaining the images used in the book.

Last but not least, I am deeply grateful to my family: my wife, Asemeh, for her patience and support; and my daughters, Kowsar and Tasnim, who are source of joy, hope and inspiration. Many thanks also go to our parents in Iran, for their reassurance and prayers, and for bearing our absence.

Introduction

A television game show format originally created in Britain in 1998 is acquired by over 100 television stations across the globe and is remade in a range of different languages. In India, the show inspires a first novel by an Indian diplomat. The novel, published in 2005, wins several international awards and is translated into some 40 languages. It is also adapted into a play by BBC Radio 4. Two British companies – one of which is the producer of the original television game show – buy the rights of the novel and invite a British scriptwriter and a British director to make a movie out of the novel. The project is partly funded by the investment of two American and French companies. The film's setting is in Mumbai and it involves local actors and actresses, as well as other Indian professionals including the co-director and the music composer.

The film's global profile is boosted when it sweeps seven BAFTAs, eight Oscars and four Golden Globe Awards. International reaction to the film in a wide range of formats, including press reviews, blog posts, YouTube clips and television commentary proliferates around the world. A transnational debate begins over the film's representation of India, a new globalizing economy, and of Mumbai's slum dwellers. Some critics in 'the west' accuse the film of being 'poverty porn' (Miles 2009); while in India there are protests against the use of the word 'dog' in the title of the film. In the context of the local culture this word has derogatory connotations and some inhabitants of the slums are offended. These reactions are covered by international media and 'experts on India' comment on the events and their root causes. There are also concerns about the salary paid to the young local actors of the film who actually lived in the Mumbai slums. Ethical questions are raised over the impact of the film on their lives.[1]

But the story does not end there. While in the United Kingdom and the United States people were paying to watch *Slumdog Millionaire* (Danny Boyle, 2008) on cinema screens, in Iran, where the exhibition of foreign films in movie theaters is extremely restricted, millions of people had the privilege of watching the film on national television.[2] The version they saw, however, had a number of differences from the original film since Iranian television had cut out many 'inappropriate' scenes and changed some dialogue during the dubbing process.

---

[1] For an analysis of the film as well as an assessment of the reactions to it, see David Bordwell's blog post 'Slumdogged by the Past', available at: http://www.davidbordwell.net/blog/?p=3592, last accessed April 2009.

[2] The film was broadcast on Channel One of the Islamic Republic of Iran Broadcasting (IRIB) on 26th March 2009 during the *Norooz* (New Year) Holidays.

These cuts included scenes of violence, song and dance, any content of a sexual nature, and instances where Muslim characters were 'portrayed in a bad light'. Some Iranian bloggers, however, who had watched pirated DVDs of the full film,[3] wrote scathing articles against state television in their blogs as well as described the cut scenes to their readers.[4]

Slumdog Millionaire is perhaps one of the most revealing examples in the world of cinema that expose the wide-ranging impacts of globalization on the film industry.[5] Even if we hesitate to agree with the *Wall Street Journal*'s film critic who has termed it 'the film world's first globalized masterpiece' (Morgenstern 2009), the case no doubt prompts us to rethink the relations between cinema, nation and globalization. It brings to mind many questions regarding the political, economic and cultural consequences of globalization in the realm of cinema and highlights the complexities and contradictions involved. The events around this film draw attention to the scale, the scope and the speed of global flows and counterflows, and the intensification of simultaneous transnational interactions. They also feed into the ongoing debates in globalization theory over homogenization/hybridization, similarity/difference, national culture/global culture, empowerment/exploitation, inclusion/exclusion, and end/revival of the nation state.

Slumdog Millionaire also problematizes the notion of 'national cinema'. It may not serve, therefore, as the most appropriate example with which to begin a book on a national cinema, but it highlights a number of key questions that should be addressed in any such study. In particular it encourages us to think of the 'transnational' – if not 'global' – trends in the production, distribution and consumption of film. It seems to have relaxed the boundaries between British and Indian national cinemas and, given its significant achievements at the Oscars, undermined the Hollywood–national cinema dichotomy. We have a situation where, rather than Hollywood dominating the screening space in national cinemas, the most significant event of the year in Hollywood is dominated by a British film that tells a story about India while incorporating elements of Bollywood. Some may even go further to suggest that films like *Slumdog Millionaire* indicate the arrival of a new global era in which the concept of 'national cinema' is increasingly losing its relevance and usefulness. We live in times, so the argument goes, when 'cosmopolitan' film-makers produce 'transnational cinemas' with universal themes that go beyond local/national prejudices, and address a much more diverse global audience. More generally, it may be suggested, we are witness

---

[3] Since the official DVD of the film had not yet been released at the time, this copy must have been recorded by handy-cam from cinema screens somewhere in the world, and then smuggled into Iran.

[4] See for example an article by Mazdak Ali Nazari on *Gooya News* Website titled '*ma siah namaiim ya sima: Zibaeehaye roboodeh shode milliunere zaghe neshin*' (Are we depicting a gloomy image or is it (state) television: the stolen beauties of *Slumdog Millionaire*'), available at http://news.gooya.com/society/archives/085688.php, in which the author reveals over 20 instances of censorship in the broadcasted version of the film. The blogger Somayyeh Tohidloo also criticized television authorities for cutting scenes out of the original film in her blog *Bar Sahele Salamat* (http://smto.ir/?p=1597). Both sources accessed 12th April 2009.

[5] Earlier examples include, but are not limited to, *Crouching Tiger, Hidden Dragon* (Ang Lee, 2000), *Kandahar* (Mohsen Makhmalbaf, 2001) and *Babel* (Alejandro González Iñárritu, 2006).

to the development of a 'transnational institution of art' in which artists from the most remote parts of the world can exhibit their work to 'transnational audiences', and engage in a simultaneous cultural exchange with their colleagues from other parts of the world.

In contrast to the above, it appears that the British film industry – and perhaps many among the British public – celebrated and even took pride in the global success of *Slumdog Millionaire* as a 'British film'. Was this because they thought the film presents a good image of Britain to the world, for example, as a nation that cares about the suffering of others? Or was it because this film had boosted *their* national cinema's international profile and generated a lot of money for the industry? Maybe it was simply because it had a British director. In any case, we might ask, is globalization weakening and destroying national film industries in the way it has been feared for long, or is it, on the contrary, empowering and reinvigorating them? Has 'national cinema' entirely lost its meaning in the current global climate, or has its meaning been transformed in order to adapt to the new conditions? Does a film like *Slumdog Millionaire* mark 'the end' or 'the revival' of national cinema?

We might, however, hesitate in going too far with any general conclusion based on this example. After all, a film like *Slumdog Millionaire* may prove to be an isolated example that does not amount to a major exception to the rule, that is, the global dominance of Hollywood and the patterns of local/national film production, distribution and consumption. In studying the relation between globalization and national cinema, we should thus avoid a bias toward examples that clearly have a global, international or transnational dimension. This bias could obscure and exclude bodies of film from our study that continue to be financed, produced and distributed at a local/national level. Nonetheless, if the processes of globalization are as far-reaching and all-embracing as they are sometimes claimed to be, the question is in what ways have they influenced the cinema of film-makers who primarily work within local/national frameworks? In other words, what are the impacts of globalization on local strands of film-making within national cinemas?

These are the kinds of questions I address in what follows. When I began researching for this project in 2005, however, my main concern was to comprehend how globalization, particularly with regard to its cultural dimensions, was changing the world we live in. I come from a country where resisting the 'western cultural invasion' has long been an official cultural policy. But 'globalization', I suspected, was something other than 'cultural imperialism' or 'cultural invasion'. In 2003 the National Centre for Globalization Studies was inaugurated in Iran with direct funding by the government. A number of key academic reference books such as Roland Robertson's *Globalization: Social Theory and Global Culture* (1992) and John Tomlinson's *Globalization and Culture* (1999) were translated into Farsi. Conferences and seminars were organized to explain the meaning of globalization and assess its potential impact on local/national politics, culture and, of course, the economy. In fact the first director of the newly inaugurated center in Iran was an economist trained at Georgetown University. Yet in a context where the 'cultural invasion' theory was very powerful, even Iranian economists had to take account of the cultural dimensions of globalization.

Over the recent years there has been a growing interest in globalization among Iranian academics and postgraduate students from a range of different disciplines. During the course of my research, I met or was contacted by a number of Iranian students who were either doing research, or applying to do so, on topics such as 'globalization and the cyberspace', 'globalization and national literature', 'globalization and photography', etc. We may interpret this common desire to know about globalization as an outcome of a general fear. The reasons to fear globalization were not, however, limited to religious and ideological concerns. In economic terms, the backlash of neo-liberal policies in South East Asia and Latin America in the late 1990s and early 2000s – not to mention the 2008/2009 'global financial crisis' – were surely sources of major concern for many countries in the developing world. In the field of cultural exchange, the disagreements between France and the United States during the 1993 GATT negotiations had eventually resulted in France's favor, meaning that audio-visual products were excluded from the agenda of free trade. Some Iranian leaders – and perhaps politicians in other developing countries too – considered this as further evidence that 'cultural imperialism' or 'cultural invasion' were not only *real* threats, but threats which were even being perceived in the heart of Europe. New policies and initiatives were thus implemented to control foreign imports and promote local and national production. In the case of the present research project too, the fear that globalization would result in the decline of Iranian national cinema was one of the motives involved at the beginning of the study.

In addition to these fears, however, it may be suggested that there is also another motivation – perhaps now even the stronger one – behind the growing interest in research on globalization in Iran. This has to do, in my view, with the way the word globalization has been translated in Farsi. The equivalent term is *jahani-shodan*, which literally means 'becoming global', but implies being elevated to a much higher level, or achieving a global renown or world-class status. It clearly involves positive connotations, particularly in a nation that wants to reclaim its role in the 'international community' after decades of being considered an outcast. The term *jahani-shodan* also resonates well within both nationalist aspirations to revitalize the Persian Empire as a global super power; and the Islamic – in particular Shi'a – conviction that the oppressed – or *mostaz'afan*, as they are named in the Quran – will eventually rule the world following the reappearance of 'the hidden Imam' and the establishment of a just global government.[6] This may also explain why, despite being considered a parochial fundamentalist by many in the West, President Ahmadinejad made 56 international visits in his first four-year term in office, including four to the United Nations. This number is far beyond the total number of visits by two former Iranian presidents over 16 years.

'Becoming global' may be a powerful driving force in Iranian politics and even the economy, but in terms of globalization and the realm of culture there are many unresolved

---

[6] In the Shi'ite faith of Islam it is believed that the twelfth Imam descending from the Prophet Mohammad was named Mahdi (b. 869) and he did not die but went into 'Occultation' (*Gheibah* or *Gheibat*). It is believed that he will emerge again, along with Jesus, and will bring peace and justice to the world.

questions and complex issues that must be addressed. Iranian cinema, for instance, achieved international recognition in the 1990s and was awarded many prizes in prestigious film festivals across the world. This success, however, was not always matched by an equal celebration or a sense of pride back home. Some cultural authorities were highly sceptical of the intentions of European and American festivals, and accused them of awarding prizes to films that were critical of the government or portrayed a gloomy and backward image of Iran. Other critics degraded these films by labeling them as 'festival films', which self-consciously aim to cater to a particular elite audience in international festivals and art houses. The fact that some of these films were funded by foreign companies meant that the film-makers did not have to worry about exhibiting them in Iran and facing problems of censorship. Some film-makers even migrated from Iran and began a new life and career as citizens of other countries. This begs the question of whether their work, which we may call 'diasporic' or 'transnational' cinema, can be considered a component of a national cinema. Has globalization, in this sense, been beneficial or disadvantageous to national cinemas?

In order to address the questions outlined above, and more generally to study the impact of globalization on national cinema, the structure of the present book is divided into two parts: Part I (Chapters 1–2) develops a theoretical framework, and Part II (Chapters 3–6) mounts the main case study.[7] The appendices include four interviews with Iranian film-makers and cultural authorities.

Chapter 1 presents a review of the literature on globalization with the aim of making sense of this wide-ranging process (or set of processes). Of course the literature on globalization has proliferated over the past two decades and continues to do so. Academics of various disciplines with different ideological and political perspectives have made a contribution to this debate. Any attempt to generalize a particular understanding of globalization, therefore, runs the risk of ideological prejudice and political evaluations about its cultural, social and economic consequences. Another predicament in the study of globalization is that it is very difficult to separate its economic, political and cultural dimensions and focus merely on one aspect in isolation from the others. In the case of national cinema, for instance, the economic and cultural impacts of globalization are clearly intertwined. Interdisciplinary approaches are thus perhaps best suited to the study of globalization. In this chapter, I review the work of theorists who have introduced key models for understanding the processes of globalization. The concepts of the 'global field' (Roland Robertson), 'global flows' (Arjun Appadurai) and 'global transformations' (David Held et al.) are my main points of reference, although works by other theorists are also included in the discussion. The aim of this review is to arrive at a working definition of globalization, and to provide a theoretical framework, or a set of precise questions, which will guide the rest of the study.

---

[7] It may be noted here that my doctoral thesis also involved a comparative part that examined the impact of globalization – mainly in terms of economy and cultural policy – on three different national cinemas: Argentina, South Korea and France (Esfandiary 2009).

Chapter 2 examines the different approaches in theorizing national cinema as well as discusses the critiques of this concept. Until the mid-1980s national cinema was a largely taken-for-granted and self-explanatory term in critical and academic discourse. It was generally understood as a coherent body of film in an unproblematic relation with the inhabitants of a particular geographic territory. Following the developments in literary and cultural theory, as well as further empirical and critical studies into how nations are 'imagined' (Anderson 1983) and traditions are 'invented' (Hobsbawm and Ranger 1983), some film critics began raising new questions about the meaning of national cinema. As will be demonstrated in this chapter, these theoretical elaborations were generally aimed at deconstructing essentialist views on national cinema, highlighting its historically constructed nature and diverse configurations in different contexts, and revealing the politics of exclusion and inclusion inherent in its project. In the light of these critiques, the chapter closes by assessing the arguments for and against the usefulness and relevance of the concept of national cinema in an age of globalization.

Part II of the book explores the impact of globalization on Iranian national cinema. This part begins with an introductory chapter (Chapter 3) on Iranian cinema's rise to international prominence in the 1990s, and examines the factors involved in facilitating such an unexpected accomplishment. Critical perspectives on the politics and economics of Iranian cinema's international celebration, however, are also assessed in this chapter. In the Iranian film industry, there is little evidence of the well-known consequences of globalization, such as market liberalization, foreign investment and ownership, mergers, vertical integration etc. The impact of globalization, therefore, has primarily been discussed with respect to the particular internationally renowned or 'transnational' film-makers whose films, whether in terms of their funding, production or distribution, have transcended national borders. But for two reasons this study cannot be confined in its case studies to the 'transnational' dimension of Iranian cinema: firstly, 'transnational' films and film-makers constitute a relatively small fraction of Iranian 'national cinema' and do not represent it as a whole. Secondly, the profound and complex processes of globalization, as it shall be argued, have implications that go far beyond the domains of 'transnational cinema'. Three different film-makers, who each represent one aspect or dimension of Iranian cinema, are therefore selected as the principal examples of this case study.

Chapter 4 explores the career of Mohsen Makhmalbaf as a 'transnational film-maker' and examines his most recent films and statements. Since Makhmalbaf played a significant role in the formation of post-revolutionary Iranian cinema, this chapter investigates how becoming a 'displaced' and 'borderless' film-maker has influenced his vision, his art and his politics. The reception of Makhmalbaf's 'transnational' films, such as *Kandahar*, *Sex and Philosophy* and *Scream of the Ants*, by Iranian critics is also discussed. It is argued that through the extension of his cinematic profile from the local/national to the transnational/global, Makhmalbaf has not only lost contact with the audiences who first made him famous, but also seems to have lost his creative power and cinematic vision. His latest films, therefore, have even failed to attract the attention of elite 'transnational audiences'. This chapter, therefore, presents a case against the idealization of 'transnational cinema' and argues for a more cautious appraisal of its supposedly progressive and liberating potential.

The cinema of Daryush Mehrjui, a pioneer of Iranian cinema's 'new wave' in the late 1960s, who has significantly contributed to the construction of a national cinema over four decades, is the subject of Chapter 5. Mehrjui was one of the first Iranian directors to be awarded an international prize, but unlike the 'transnational film-makers', his cinema has largely remained within national borders in terms of its funding, production and distribution. Although not necessarily a *nationalist* himself, Mehrjui's films are largely considered, within Iranian film culture, to be exemplary representatives of national cinema. The irony, however, is that Mehrjui's films do not show any similarity with the kind of 'heritage films' or 'national blockbusters' that, in many national cinemas, are proudly considered as national films. By analyzing two of Mehrjui's most praised 'national films' – *The Lodgers* and *Mum's Guests* – which, despite sharing a similar genre and theme, were made at very different times (the 1980s and the 2000s), I examine how the concept of 'the national' has evolved in post-revolutionary Iran. My aim is to highlight the changes in Mehrjui's more recent films and identify the role that globalization has played in this respect. The sharp contrast between critics' reaction to the two films will also be analyzed in the light of recent global developments.

In order to expand the narrowly defined conceptions of 'Iranian national cinema' based on works of a few internationally celebrated directors, Chapter 6 takes a little-known section of Iranian cinema, namely the 'sacred defense cinema', as its point of reference. This final case study focuses on the work of Ebrahim Hatami-kia, who is one of the most prominent post-revolutionary film-makers and a founding figure in the 'sacred defense cinema'. With regard to the growing debates on the relation of Islam and globalization in recent years, in this chapter I examine how globalization has influenced the work of a highly acclaimed Muslim film-maker, whose work has contributed to adding an 'Islamic' dimension to Iranian cinema. To this end, the chapter presents a close comparative analysis of three of Hatami-kia's films: *The Scout* (1988), *From Karkhe to Rhine* (1992) and *Glass Agency* (1997). The study of Hatami-kia's films has two main outcomes: firstly, it demonstrates that even the 'Islamic' cinema of post-revolutionary Iran is far from simply being a monolithic and unified body of 'Islamist' propaganda and ideological instruction; and secondly, it highlights the ambivalence at the heart of globalization processes. In some of these films the impact of globalization can be seen in terms of the inclusion and representation of 'the other' while other films critically reflect on the struggles, conflicts and contradictions within a society that is moving toward liberal economics and politics. In doing so, these films express strong statements against the attempts to assimilate Iran into a homogenized culture of global capitalism.

In the appendices, four interviews with the theme of globalization and national cinema, which I conducted at the early stages of this research, are presented to the reader. The interviewees include two internationally renowned Iranian film-makers: Abbas Kiarostami, the only Iranian director to win the Palme d'Or, and Majid Majidi, the only Iranian director to be nominated for an Oscar. Although I have referred to the views of these two film-makers in this book, for a number of reasons which I have already hinted at and will elaborate on further, I eventually decided to focus on the work of three other Iranian film-makers as my principal case studies. I did make attempts to interview the other film-makers too, but was not successful. I hope that the views of Kiarostami and Majidi will provide a useful insight into the context of the present study.

Given the significance of cultural policy in debates about globalization, I also interviewed two senior cultural authorities in Iran. Mohamad-reza Jafari-jelveh was the Deputy Minister for Cinematic Affairs at the Ministry of Culture and Islamic Cultivation between 2005 and 2009. The post of the Deputy Minister is the most senior government position with respect to cinema. The department that he runs not only oversees all aspects of film production, distribution and exhibition, but also has a massive role in funding film projects. Before being appointed as the Deputy Minister under President Ahmadinejad's government, Jafari-jelveh had served at the state-owned radio and television organization (IRIB) for over 25 years in posts including that of the Controller of Channel One. The second Iranian official I interviewed was Emad Afroogh, a sociologist and Member of Parliament between 2003 and 2007, who chaired the Iranian Parliament's Cultural Committee. Neither Jafari-jelveh nor Afroogh belong to the 'liberal' or 'reformist' side of the Iranian political spectrum. Some of their views on globalization, culture and film policy may thus surprise readers in the West. Apart from elaborating on the theme of globalization and national cinema, I think these interviews have the potential to facilitate an understanding of the other that goes beyond the usual stereotypes and prejudices. It should also be noted here that the author has translated all the interviews.

It may be clear from this introduction that drawing out a general conclusion in terms of the impact of globalization on national cinemas is a very difficult task. The interdisciplinary approach adopted here indeed confirms this complexity. Also, although an attempt is made to diversify the case studies, there is no claim of a comprehensive representation of, or a grand conclusion about 'the whole' of Iranian national cinema, even if we were to believe the validity of any such claim.

PART I

THEORETICAL FRAMEWORK

Chapter 1

Making Sense of Globalization

Introduction

Advocates of what has come to be known as 'globalization theory' and their opponents both agree on the point that globalization was the *buzzword*, if not the Zeitgeist, of the 1990s (Rosenberg 2005; Tomlinson 2003). There is of course an extensive literature on this debate with contributions from scholars of various disciplines such as economics, politics, international relations, geography, sociology, communications, media studies and cultural studies. Even within each of these disciplines globalization has been explored and theorized from various philosophical, ideological and political perspectives. Clearly the unparalleled and frequent appearance of this term in academic discourses in the 1990s – a decade that some have named 'the decade of globalization' – has not come to a terminal decline. Tomlinson (2003: 11–15) has interestingly suggested two 'real events' that can be identified as signposts of this decade: the fall of the Berlin Wall in 1989; and the attacks on the World Trade Center in September 2001. The rich symbolism of these two events, which provided platforms for delivering political and cultural messages and expressing identities, is for Tomlinson indicative of an inherent 'dimension' of globalization: that it involves 'the proliferation of cultural identities'. The popular media coverage of issues related to globalization has probably been more extensive than is usually received by other academic concepts. Even 'Postmodernism' – the buzzword of the 1980s – falls far behind in this regard. In the case of globalization, Tomlinson argues, 'the empirical reality' and the events that were driving the process demanded a conceptual response, while the debates over postmodern theory were more rooted in 'epistemological and ontological meta-propositions' (2003: 11).

The different disciplines and standpoints from which globalization has been theorized make it extremely difficult to grasp a consensual understanding of the term. Any attempt to generalize a definition of globalization runs the risk of ideological prejudices and political evaluations about its social and economic consequences, which influence how the overall process (or project) is depicted. The complex, contradictory, multifaceted and multidimensional nature of globalization has even prevented theorists on the same side of the ideological and political spectrum from reaching a full agreement on the issue. As Held et al. have demonstrated none of the great traditions of social inquiry – liberal, conservative and Marxist – has an agreed perspective on globalization (Held et al. 1999: 4).

Another cause of confusion is that in studying globalization it is difficult to entirely separate its economic, political and cultural dimensions and to focus merely on one aspect in isolation from the others. Not only do these dimensions penetrate and impact upon each other all the time, but their boundaries have also become less recognizable due to the growing 'disjunctures' between these different spheres (Appadurai 1996). Therefore even when the main task is to concentrate on the cultural aspects of globalization, as in the present book, the economic and political spheres, at least to some degree, will have to be taken into account. Moreover, an interdisciplinary approach, which would have the advantage of acknowledging a variety of methods and perspectives in the study of such a complex phenomenon as globalization, would seem to be more useful in meeting the aims of this book. The main intention, however, as mentioned previously, would be to explore the cultural aspects or dimensions of globalization that are more directly relevant to the central concern of this book: the changes in the structure, function and output of national cinema in the context of globalization.

In the present chapter, I shall review the work of theorists who have introduced key models for understanding the cultural aspects of globalization. The concepts of the *global field* (Roland Robertson), *global flows* (Arjun Appadurai) and *global transformations* (David Held et al.) are my main points of reference. Robertson and Appadurai are among the pioneers of globalization theory and their work not only provides us with useful insights into the origins of scholarly work on globalization and its later evolution, but also demonstrates the impact they have had on generations of globalization theorists. Held and McGrew, who are perhaps the most prolific academics in the field, have, with their colleagues, produced one of the most comprehensive and multidimensional accounts of globalization, which has proved to be an essential text for any investigation of the subject.

In addition to these three reference points, the works of a number of other significant contributors to globalization theory such as Anthony Giddens, Stuart Hall, John Tomlinson, Fredric Jameson, Arif Dirlik and Noël Carroll have also been included in the discussion. Some common aspects of these theories as well as areas of dispute and disagreement are highlighted. The aim of this review, as indicated in the title, is to make sense of globalization in general terms, and to extract a set of potentially useful conceptual tools and methods so as to examine the impact of globalization on national cinemas. The relevant findings will be summarized as a 'theoretical framework' in the concluding section of this chapter.

The global field

Roland Robertson is widely considered to be a pioneer among the key social theorists who have contributed to the theory of globalization. His publications that directly deal with concepts such as 'globality' and 'globalization' were first published in the 1980s.[1] While firmly positioning himself within the discipline of sociology and frequently referring to

---

[1] In 1983 he published an essay with the title 'Interpreting Globality' and throughout the 1980s, he has published many papers on globalization with a special interest in its relation to issues such as religion, modernization and identity (Robertson 1983, 1985, 1987a, 1987b, 1989).

the work of classic social scientists such as Emile Durkheim, Max Webber and Georg Simmel, Robertson also attempts to distance himself – to a certain degree – from the typical 'scientific' and 'positivist' perspectives of classic sociology in order to allow more space for what he calls the 'subjective' and 'cultural' aspects of human life. His most influential and widely cited book *Globalization; Social Theory and Global Culture* was first published in 1992. Robertson explains that his main motive for investigating the concept of globalization was the increasing concern with cultural and religious identity in the contemporary world. His intention was to determine whether this new 'search for the fundamentals' should be regarded as an inherent aspect of globalization or a form of resistance to it. This point of departure, in particular, and the question of identity in general are also directly relevant to the main topic of the present book concerning the impact of globalization on national cinemas. The construction and representation of identity in national cinema productions and the way globalization influences the latter processes will be a key matter of investigation in the following chapters.

Globalization: 'out there' or 'inside the head'?

In Robertson's view the study of globalization 'under the umbrella of cultural studies' has paid little attention to 'global complexity' and 'structural contingency'. He stresses the necessity for any viable theory of the contemporary world to provide a 'systematic comprehension of the structuration of world order' (1992: 55). Yet he insists that such an approach must recognize and separate the factors that have facilitated the shift towards 'a single world' – such as capitalism, imperialism and new media systems – from what he calls 'the general and global agency-structure theme' (1992: 55). For Robertson, globalization is not just a process that is happening 'out there' but also involves people having increasingly converging conceptions of the world. On the one hand there is the compression of the world, mainly through new means of transport and communication, into a 'single space'; and on the other an 'intensified consciousnesses' of the world as a whole (1992: 8). The latter aspect that Robertson names 'globality' – others have called it the 'inside-the-head aspect of globalization' – is considered to be his main contribution to the theory of globalization (Beynon and Dunkerley 2000). What the present study can learn from such an approach to globalization is that a mere focus on recent developments in the economic and institutional aspects of national cinemas, or the new cultural policies employed in response to globalization, would not allow for the study of its 'inside-the-head' impact. The latter would require an in-depth analysis of relevant films and need also to take account of the critical discourses and audiences' response to them.

In Robertson's theory, universalism and particularism are not seen as totally separate and opposing tendencies. Rather, the two are considered as being 'tied together as part of a globewide nexus'. For Roberson, 'contemporary globalization in its most general sense [is] a form of institutionalization of [a] two-fold process involving the universalization of particularism and the particularization of universalism' (1992: 102). The latter he explains, provides the idea of the universal with 'global-human concreteness', while the former diffuses the idea that there is no limit to particularity and uniqueness. The international (almost universal) dispersal and appeal of the idea of nationalism (itself a version of particularism) is the main example that Robertson uses to flesh out his argument. Another area, we can suggest, where Robertson's articulation of the universal–particular nexus can be applied is the history of cinema. The technology of film production swiftly travelled around the globe and found universal appeal in many different countries. Yet this universalism was followed by a particularism: the establishment of diverse national film industries, which began producing films that would appeal to local tastes and represent particular cultural characteristics.

The 'global field' and processes of relativization

Following Louis Dumont's anthropological model for a community (Dumont 1979), Robertson introduces a theoretical model for understanding globalization in its contemporary phase. His model of the 'global field' is based on four major reference points: *national societies*, *individuals* (selves), *relationships between national societies* (or *the world system of societies*) and *humankind* (Robertson 1992: 25–29). Stressing that this model is 'based upon both epistemic and empirical observations', Robertson further expands on his scheme by arguing that between the above reference points there are a number of 'relativization' processes going on, namely relativization of societies, social identities and citizenship. Such processes, he adds, increase the challenges to the stability of perspectives on, and participation in, the overall globalization process. There is therefore for him an 'inexorable' trend toward the 'unicity of the world' (1992: 26). While admitting that his scheme involves a 'totalizing tendency', he suggests that this model is flexible in the sense that each of the four main components of the global field enjoys a degree of autonomy. This implies that his model recognizes the possibility of different 'responses' to globalization by different national societies and individuals who may challenge and even change the overall shape of globalization. Referring, for example, to the history of Islam and its 'general globalizing thrust', he emphasizes that 'had that potential form of globalization succeeded, we would now almost certainly comprehend contemporary "globality" differently' (1992: 28).

For Robertson, the 1960s youth movement in numerous parts of the world was a clear example of 'globality', that is, a global consciousness of the world as a whole. In his view even anti-global gestures are encapsulated within the discourse of globality and 'resistance' is part and parcel of the interactions involved in the global field that shape the processes of globalization. He contends that 'the expectation of identity declaration' is a built-in-feature of the globalization processes, and thus even 'fundamentalism' is an aspect or creation of globalization, rather than a mode of resistance or opposition to it. He goes even further to insist that there is no need to worry about this, since 'fundamentalism, within limits, makes globalization work'; in other words 'it is the particular which makes the universal work'

(1992: 180).² Although at the time of Robertson's writing the anti-globalization movement was not yet in full swing and events of 11ᵗʰ September 2001 and 7ᵗʰ July 2005 had not taken place, the significant impact that such movements and events have had in challenging the dominant – and largely utopian – discourse of globalization seems to verify Robertson's observation that globalization is an open-ended process.³ The relevance of the latter approach to the present book relates to the possibility of national cinemas becoming alternative sites of cultural production, which challenge and resist dominant modes of cinematic production in the age of global 'free trade'. In other words, the question would be whether there is any evidence of national cinemas and individual film-makers making a difference.

Globalization and the representation of cultural identity

It has already been mentioned that the issue of identity has been a key matter of concern for Robertson and that he considers the increasing concern with identity as a result of the intersection of different forms of life through the globalization processes. For him globalization involves the institutional construction of the individual; it encourages individualism and identity and increases the establishment of minority movements and other forms of identification. All in all, 'globalization in itself and of itself involves the expectation of identity clarifications' (1992: 27).

From a different perspective, Stuart Hall (1991) also arrives at a similar conclusion with regard to the relation of globalization and identity. He argues that like capitalism, globalization advances on contradictory terrain. Rather than creating a homogeneous global culture based on 'Englishness' or 'Americanness', global mass culture recognizes and absorbs differences: 'it does not attempt to obliterate them; it operates through them' (Hall 1991: 28). Hall refutes the idea that globalization is 'a non-contradictory, uncontested space in which everything is fully within the keeping of the institutions, so that they perfectly know where it is going' and stresses that global capital always needs to negotiate in order to maintain its global position (1991: 32–3). Through the process of negotiation, he adds, global capital has to 'incorporate and partly reflect the differences it [is] trying to overcome. It [has] to try get hold of, and neutralize, to some degree, the difference' (ibid.). Yet the latter process, by

---

² From a different standpoint Hardt and Negri have gone further in this respect arguing that fundamentalism – even without limits – can be seen to serve the 'Empire' and its global networks of multinational power. Through its acts of global terrorism, they argue, fundamentalism produces a permanent state of war and creates an unknown, uncertain and unexpected enemy that would justify a permanent 'state of exception', thus providing the Empire with the pleasure of extraordinary powers that easily undermines the civil and human rights of its citizens (Hardt and Negri 2004: 3–7).

³ In their introduction to the second edition of *The Globalization Reader* (Lechner and Boli 2004), the editors state that nearly half of the content of the first edition (2000) has been changed in response to the new voices and contributions to the debate over globalization, particularly from the 'anti-globalization' and 'cultural resistance' viewpoints. In 2008, the third edition of the book was published with further revisions and new sections.

enabling 'the margins' to come to representation, has paradoxically resulted in what Hall terms 'the most profound cultural revolution':

> Paradoxically in our world, marginality has become a powerful space [...]. The emergence of new subjects, new genders, new ethnicities, new regions, new communities, hitherto excluded from major forms of cultural representation, unable to locate themselves except as de-centered or subaltern, have acquired through struggle, sometimes in very marginalized ways, the means to speak for themselves for the first time. [They] can only come into representation by, as it were, recovering their own hidden histories. They have to try to retell the story from the bottom up, instead of from the top down.
>
> (Hall 1991: 34–5)

Tomlinson echoes this view in an article where, referring to the events in the Balkans after the collapse of the former Yugoslavia and also the 9/11 attacks, he stresses that 'far from destroying it, globalization has been perhaps the most significant force in creating and proliferating cultural identity' (Tomlinson 2003: 16). Bearing in mind the topic of the present book, the main question that arises from the debate is whether globalization has also intensified the concern with national cinema – as a major site of identity construction and cultural expression – and how the 'expectation of identity declaration' is dealt with in national film productions.

David Morley and Kevin Robins have also explored the relation of globalization and identity and examined the ways that globalization – and particularly the new global media – influences local cultures and identities (Morley and Robins 1995). They argue that by constructing new electronic landscapes, global media in effect weaken old cultural boundaries. The authors identify a shift in the principles that governed the regulation of broadcasting 'from regulation in the public interest to a new regulatory regime – sometimes erroneously described as "deregulation" – driven by economic and entrepreneurial imperatives' (Morley and Robins 1995: 10–11). The political and social concerns of 'the public service era' with democracy, national culture and identity, they argue, have come to be regarded as factors restraining the development of new media markets. In 'the new media order', therefore, the principal objective is to dismantle such barriers to trade (1995: 11).

For Morley and Robbins, in this respect, globalization is not merely a threat to non-western cultures and nations, but a threat to Europe itself:

> Europe and its members are no longer [...] at the centre of the world, no longer the source of universal values [...].Whereas once [Europe's] project was about universalism, now it is about recovering a sense of European particularism [...] it is about 'the Europeanization, not of the rest of the world, but [...] of Europe itself'.
>
> (1995: 20)

The latter observation is clearly in line with Robertson's notion of 'universalization of particularism' discussed above, as well as his anticipation of the impact of globalization in intensifying the search for and the expression of identities. Morley and Robbins recognize a growing interest in the 'embeddedness of life histories in the boundaries of place' as well as a desire for the 'continuities of identity and community through local memory and heritage', and argue that the particular relation of place and culture is something unparalleled, which we may never be able to transcend (1995: 116). Whilst maintaining that we should not 'devalue the perceived and felt vitality of local cultures and identities', the authors stress that the significance of the latter 'can only be understood in the context of a broader and encompassing process' (1995: 117).

Globalization and modernity

One significant aspect of Robertson's theory of globalization is that it does not consider globalization simply as a 'consequence of modernity'. He dedicates a whole chapter of his book to a fierce critique of *The Consequences of Modernity* (Giddens 1990). He criticizes Giddens for failing to register the already available literature on globalization theory and accuses him of fighting a straw man. Giddens considers modernity as a 'western project' but insists that globalization is more than a diffusion of western institutions across the world in which other cultures are crushed (Giddens 1990: 175). Robertson questions the very use of the term 'other cultures' here, since he deems that in Giddens' theory, not only is no 'other' recognized but the significance of 'culture' is also completely neglected. Overlooking the importance of culture has also been considered a shortcoming in Giddens' work by other scholars (Featherstone 1995: 145; Tomlinson 1999: 59). The universal–particular dialectic is for Robertson a basic feature of human life and has a history at least as old as that of the 'world religions'. Contemporary globalization, he argues, is a form of institutionalization of the two-fold processes of universalization and particularization. While recognizing the significant and unique features of contemporary globalization, he avoids regarding globalization as something completely new or exclusive to the modern era. This is a position that Held et al. (1999) have further elaborated in their comprehensive study of globalization, which will be reviewed later in this chapter.

For Robertson resistance to globalization – which at the time of writing he has only seen in the example of 'radical Islam' – is more indicative of *anti-postmodernism* rather than *anti-modernism*. He explains that resisting globalization is not just about opposition to a homogenized world but rather opposition to 'the conception of the world as a series of culturally equal, relativized entities or ways of life' (1992: 102). Considering the history and legacy of the anti-globalization movement, we might disagree with Robertson's suggestion today. Far from being 'anti-postmodern', the latter movements have themselves been considered as symptoms of the postmodern era (Esteva and Parakash 1998). Even 'fundamentalist' groups are seen by some analysts as having a postmodern nature (Hardt and Negri 2000). By assuming that the problem with globalization for radical Islamist groups is mainly globalization's inherent processes of relativization, Robertson ignores the material, political and economic conditions in Muslim countries – including poverty, social and political repression and western-backed authoritarian regimes – that are also involved in the creation and appeal of fundamentalist movements. Moreover, it is also possible to question Robertson's claim that globalization involves or results in 'a series of culturally equal, relativized entities or ways of life'. Again it seems that Robertson is neglecting the unequal power relations that prevent certain nations from having an equal stance for promoting their different 'way of life'.

The culture-economy relation

Robertson shows great enthusiasm for the case of Japan, which is for him a vital and unavoidable topic: a 'new comer' to the 'world system' that nonetheless has become significantly modernized and globalized (1992: 85). His main argument is that in all the literature on the 'miracle of Japan', little attention has been paid to the role of Japanese culture and religion (1992: 90). The latter can explain, Robertson says, Japan's capacity to 'adapt selectively' and 'import systematically' from other societies. Japanese identity, he stresses, is formed by encounters with the outside world, and its syncretism together with the infrastructural significance of Japanese religion (polytheism and purification rituals) has played a great role in the 'decontamination' of foreign ideas (1992: 95).

Despite its attractiveness and unique attributes, even the case of Japan does not depart from the hegemonic model of global capitalism in the view of some other scholars in the field. Jameson, for instance, argues that 'fresh cultural production and innovation […] are the crucial index of the centrality of a given area and not its wealth or productive power' and thus 'whoever says the production of culture says the production of everyday life' (Jameson 1998a: 67). For Jameson the latter can explain why the global distribution of Japanese industrial products and even the ownership of major American studios by Japanese firms has not resulted in 'the global diffusion of Japanese culture or a Japanese way of life' (Jameson 1998a: 67).

While some cultural analysts have suggested that 'when Japan's export exceeds American export […] the spectre of western consumer imperialism is an out-dated myth' (Classen and Howes 1996: 187–8), Arif Dirlik maintains that 'the apparent end of Eurocentrism is an illusion' (1996: 30). For Dirlik 'capitalist culture as it has taken shape has Eurocentrism built into the very structure of its narrative' and therefore 'even as Europe and the United States lose their domination of the capitalist world economy, culturally European and American values retain their domination' (Dirlik 1996: 30). Mike Featherstone has also addressed this issue pointing to the fact that Japanese consumer goods – unlike the American – do not seek to sell on the back of Japanese culture. Although he acknowledges that this could be related to (the foreign) attempts to mute Japanese national identity (*Nihonjinrom*) after

World War II, he prefers to consider it as a result of Japan's marketing strategy *dochaku*, or what Robertson has named 'glocalization' (Featherstone 1995: 9). In other words, Japanese corporations use western icons to advertise their products because they want to sell them in western markets. But the remaining question here is why have the Japanese also used such icons for selling their products in their own markets and those of other parts of the world?

This debate about Japan and its similarity with or difference from 'the west' is also relevant to the concerns of the present book. There are, for instance, similar questions about recent developments in non-western national cinemas where institutions, financial practices, methods of production and styles of film-making similar to those in American and European film industries are adopted. The rise of vertically integrated media conglomerates, the multiplex and what may be called 'national blockbusters' are examples in this regard, and they have triggered extensive debates concerning similarity/difference, mimicry/authenticity and culture/economy. A comparative analysis of such developments in different national contexts would be useful in obtaining a clearer image of the impact of globalization on national cinemas. Such an endeavor is clearly beyond the space and scope of the present book.

On the relation of culture and economy, Robertson maintains that the cultural impact of capitalism on different cultures, by means of consumerism, should not be considered a one-way process. On the contrary, he suggests, local cultures have in many cases played a significant role in forcing such corporations to tailor their products for specific regional and local markets. This is the standpoint from which he introduces the term 'glocalization' to refer to the dialectical relation of the global and the local. In another chapter published a few years later, Robertson goes further to propose that it may be better to use 'glocalization' as a substitute for 'globalization' altogether, given the increasingly negative connotations of the latter, which is mostly understood in terms of being opposed to, and in constant tension with localization (Robertson 1995).

While Robertson's 'glocalization' theory gives recognition to the local marketing strategy of global corporations for respecting and reproducing diversity and cultural difference, Dirlik argues that these processes manipulate people and appropriate the local for the global. Glocalization is thus for him 'to admit different cultures into the realm of capital, only to break them down and to remake them in accordance with the requirements of production and consumption' (Dirlik 1996: 32).[4] Dirlik goes even further to suggest that global capitalism requires the inhabitants of the local to be 'liberated from themselves (stripped of their identity)' and 'homogenized into the global culture of capital (their identities reconstructed accordingly)' (1996: 35). He emphasizes, however, that the struggles against Euro-American and capitalist oppression should not lead us to 'sweep under the rug' the pre-modern forms of oppression. Dirlik reminds us that localism may also produce oppression and parochialism, which can be disguised by its promise of liberation. He therefore calls for a 'critical localism' instead of a 'nostalgic or romantic localism' (1996: 39).

---

[4] Fredric Jameson has also commented on Robertson's theory of globalization. In Jameson's view, Robertson's two-fold process (universalization of particularism; particularization of universalism) offers a 'utopian vision of globality' and needs 'a dose of negativity' (Jameson 1998b: xii).

The potentials of local and national cinema in reflecting critically on local and national culture will be further investigated in the following chapters.

Another critique of Robertson's theory can be found in the work of Holton, for whom the largely cognitive nature of global interactions in this model is problematic (Holton 1998: 188). Holton acknowledges the multidimensionality and the dialectical character of Robertson's model, yet identifies a number of weaknesses and limits within it. His first point is that there is almost no mention of political economy in Robertson's schema. Not only does Robertson reject the idea that capitalism is the main driving force behind globalization, or that the logic of capitalism directs culture, he also neglects the disproportionate relation between multinational power(s) and the powerless consumers. Holton argues that Robertson's exclusive focus on cognitive issues – that is, consciousness of the world as a single place – downplays the existing patterns of institutional power and inequality within the global field 'especially those installed after the Second World War' (1998: 195). For Holton, 'general programmatic statements' – such as the 'global field' model – are 'little more than broad orientations to analysis', and they are no substitute for the 'fine-grained analysis of particular global processes, events or historical transformations' (1998: 196). He concludes that we should try a 'middle range approach', which 'seeks specific explanations of particulars and looks for the broadest possible patterns, but does not seek to force the complex, paradoxical and sometimes contradictory phenomena of globalization into a single Procrustean bed of general theory' (1998: 196). 'It may be preferable', he thus suggests, 'to think in terms of globalizations rather than globalization' (1998: 198).

Global flows

Arjun Appadurai is another pioneer in globalization theory whose most significant contribution to the field was an article published in 1990 with the title 'Disjuncture and Difference in Global Cultural Economy' (Appadurai 1990). As an Indian-American with a background in area studies and anthropology, his theory of globalization pays particular attention to the subject of migration. Maybe it is this engagement that has inspired him to base his model for globalization on notions such as 'flows' and 'scapes'.

For Appadurai – unlike Robertson – globalization involves 'a general break with all sorts of pasts'. He describes globalization theory as 'a theory of rupture that takes media and migration as its two major and interconnected diacritics and explores their joint effect on the *work of imagination* as a constitutive feature of modern subjectivity' (Appadurai 1996: 3, emphasis in original). Yet in a way similar to Robertson's cognitive approach, which emphasizes 'consciousness of the world', Appadurai also contends that 'the work of imagination' plays a crucial role in the processes of globalization, although he puts more weight on the collective and social forms of imagination.

Referring to American social science's narrative of modernization, which was claimed as 'the theory of the true, the good, and the inevitable' (1996: 11), Appadurai acknowledges that the idea of a dramatic rupture between the past and present has already been put forward about modernity. But he argues that globalization theory, in contrast, is not a 'teleological recipe' or a 'social engineering project'; it is different in being an open-ended and trans- or even post-national theory. Distinguishing globalization theory from the ill-fated American modernization theories of the 1960s and defending its merits over the latter is a common task in both Roberson and Appadurai's work. The idea that globalization *is not* a controlled top-down project moving the world toward a predetermined destination is also one of the premises of the 'transformationalist' standpoint in globalization theory (Held et al. 1999), which shall be discussed below. Giddens, for instance, has even used the term 'Runaway World' to emphasize the out-of-control nature of the globalization processes (Giddens 2002).

Global cultural flows and the 'scapes'

Appadurai's central argument is that the new global cultural economy has a complex, overlapping and disjunctive order that cannot be explained in existing models such as: the center–periphery model; the push and pull model (in migration theory); surplus and deficits ideas (as in trade); or consumers and producers models (as in neo-Marxist theories). He emphasizes that this complexity is largely a result of some 'fundamental disjunctures between economy, culture and politics' (1996: 32). He introduces a framework for exploring such disjunctures by investigating the relationship between five dimensions of global 'cultural flows', which, according to Appadurai, consist of:

– *Ethnoscapes*: The 'landscape of persons who constitute the shifting world in which we live' (1996: 33). In other words the flows of people via migration, travel, exile, etc.
– *Technoscapes*: The 'global configuration [...] of technology and the fact that technology [...] now moves at high speeds across various kinds of previously impervious boundaries' (1996: 34).
– *Financescapes*: The flows of global capital.
– *Mediascapes*: This refers both to the 'distribution of the electronic capabilities to produce and disseminate information' and to the 'images of the world created by these media'. The importance of the latter scapes, he stresses, is that they provide (especially in their television, film and cassette forms) 'large and complex repertoires of images, narratives, and ethnoscapes' to viewers throughout the world. They mix the world of commodities and the world of news and politics and thus 'lines between the realistic and the fictional landscapes are blurred'. In a nutshell, they are 'image-centred, narrative-based accounts of strips and bits of reality' (1996: 35).
– *Ideoscapes*: These are also 'concatenations of images', but they are often 'directly political' and frequently have to do with the 'ideologies of states' (1996: 36). For Appadurai, 'ideoscapes' are composed of elements of the Enlightenment world-view, which consists of a chain of ideas, terms and images such as freedom, welfare, rights, sovereignty, representation and democracy.

The suffix '-scape', Appadurai argues, allows us to acknowledge the fluid and irregular shapes of these landscapes, since they are 'deeply perspectival constructs' (1996: 33). He states that current global flows occur in and through the growing disjunctures among ethnoscapes, technoscapes, financescapes, mediascapes and ideoscapes. This formulation is the core of his model of global cultural flows. He admits that many of these flows have occurred before in history, yet maintains that 'the sheer speed, scale, and volume of each of these flows are now so great that the disjunctures have become central to the politics of global culture' (1996: 37).

As mentioned earlier, migration and media play a central role in Appadurai's articulation of global flows. He has already signaled the significance of film along with other media in creating 'large and complex repertoires of images, narratives, and ethnoscapes' for viewers throughout the world. In other words, cinema, whether as an institution, art form or body of textuality, is not just passively influenced and impacted upon *by* globalization; rather it has been, and will continue to be, actively involved in the processes that we have come to call globalization. 'Cinemascapes', to adopt Appadurai's terminology, have been largely responsible, long before the recent 'age of globalization', for the global dissemination of images and narratives about the world. By reaching even the most remote local communities in different countries, films have facilitated the creation of new transnational cultures.

The issue of migration and the concept of 'ethnoscapes' is also relevant to the present study, given the fact that, for a variety of reasons, many film-makers today live and/or work outside there homelands. Some film-makers have gone further to consider themselves as 'borderless artists' who practice film-making across different national boundaries. 'Accented cinema' (Naficy 2001) or 'transnational cinema' (Ďurovičová and Newman 2010; Ezra and Rowden 2006; Higbee and Lim 2010) have thus increasingly become the subject of critical attention and cultural analysis in debates on globalization and 'world cinema'. Today we even have an academic journal titled *Transnational Cinemas*.

Theorists like Noël Carroll have elaborated on Appadurai's theoretical model and gone further to suggest that today a new 'integrated, interconnected, transnational artworld' has emerged (Carroll 2007: 139). This 'transnational institution of art', Carroll argues, is 'a culturescape with its own language games and networks of communication, distribution, and reception' (Carroll 2007: 141–2). Art and cultural products did of course travel across borders and influence other cultures prior to this stage, but in Carroll's view their 'canons' and 'artworlds' usually remained discrete. While the artworlds of different cultures were 'segregated by virtue of their diverse traditions of making and meaning, of articulation and interpretation', today artists and critics from different parts of the world, says Carroll, 'share a number of conceptual frameworks and hermeneutical strategies that facilitate understanding transnationally' (2007: 140–1). For Carroll, these themes, forms and strategies together create 'a worldwide discursive framework', a 'toolkit' for accessing and interpreting 'if not all then at least a very great deal of ambitious art from all over' (ibid.). He thus concludes that today we witness a 'unified' transnational institution of art: 'a *culturescape* with its own language games and networks of communication, distribution, and reception' (2007: 141–2). Carroll's rather rosy description of the 'transnational institution of art' will be further examined in Chapter 4 where the case of the Iranian film-maker Mohsen Makhmalbaf will be discussed.

Globalization and Americanization

Like some other theorists of cultural globalization such as Robertson and Tomlinson, Appadurai is not so enthusiastic about the 'cultural imperialism' thesis. He contends that 'the United States is no longer the puppeteer of a world system of images but is only one mode of a complex transnational construction of imaginary landscapes' (1996: 31). The fear of Americanization, he adds, is the kind of fear that the politics of smaller scale have always had of being culturally absorbed by the politics of larger scale. He maintains, therefore, that there can always be alternatives to America, since one person's imagined community can be the other's political prison (1996: 32). Despite such a view, later in this chapter Appadurai strongly criticizes 'the transnational movement of martial arts', which he believes is mediated by the Hollywood and Hong Kong film industries. His assessment is that they create new cultures of masculinity and violence, which are the fuel for increased violence in national and international politics. He goes even further to suggest that such violence has triggered a rapid increase in the arms trade, which penetrates the entire world (1996: 41). Such a critical perspective seems to share a basic component of most cultural/media imperialism theories that Appadurai rejects, namely that they take for granted a passive and victimized audience whose attitudes and behaviour are directly shaped by the global media and the products of major culture industries. Moreover, Appadurai seems to imply that Hollywood is not just 'one mode of a complex transnational construction of imaginary landscapes', but rather a hegemonic and dominant one, as referred to in the theory of Americanization. In any case, it is clear that the different sites of production and distribution of 'imaginary landscapes' do not operate on the same level and in equal terms, and this, at least in the case of many national cinemas, can be a cause of major concern.

Globalization and the nation state

Appadurai's view of the nation state in his 1991 article is close to that of neo-liberal strategists who had, in the 1990s, predicted or even proclaimed *The End of the Nation State* (Ohmae 1995). He too asserts in his book that the nation state is on its last legs, even that 'the very epoch of the nation-state is near its end' (1996: 19). In search for alternatives to the nation state however, Appadurai admits that 'the road from various transnational movements to sustainable forms of transnational governance is hardly clear' (1996: 22). His aspiration – in line with Benedict Anderson's theory on the role of print media in facilitating new 'imagined communities' (Anderson 1983) – is that the new electronic media and the increasing levels of migration can play a significant role in the imagining and emergence of a 'post-national' political world (1996: 22). He stresses that the 'relationship between states and nations is everywhere an embattled one', adding that the latter is a 'battle of imagination' (1996: 39). Using an over-dramatized rhetoric, he adds that 'state and nation are at each other's throats […] seeking to cannibalize one another, and the hyphen that links them is now less an icon of conjuncture than an index of disjuncture' (1996: 39).

Despite his prediction about the nation state and the 'embattled' relations between the state and the nation, Appadurai acknowledges that the states are still capable of exercising a degree of control over the global flows: 'too much openness to global flows, and the nation-state is threatened by revolt, […] too little and the state exits the international stage […]. [T]he state has become the arbitrageur of [the] *repatriation of difference*' (1996: 42). However, for him the production of locality – or what he names 'neighbourhoods' – is often at odds with the projects of the nation state for a number of reasons: the commitments and attachments of local subjectivities are more vital and wide-ranging than the nation state can afford; their memories and attachments often collide with the nation state's attempts to regulate public life; and the production of 'contexts of alterity which distinguish neighbourhoods from each other, may not be compatible with projects for social standardization carried out by nation-states' (Appadurai 1996: 187).

Two decades after the first publication of Appadurai's article on globalization, there seems to be little, if any, sign of 'the end of the nation-state'. Not only are the regulations, protections and superior actions of nation states still firmly in place, the ideology of nationalism also continues to enjoy a strong and popular status in many parts of the world, inciting separatist movements and leading to the creation of more and more smaller nation states. Other events such as the war on Iraq have even been described by some commentators as a vigorous re-affirmation of the nation state and its interests in the global arena (Rosenberg 2005). In their view this war has undermined utopian aspirations about globalization and global governance. Justin Rosenberg goes as far as declaring globalization theory 'dead', and offers his 'post mortem' account on its fate (ibid.).

Appadurai himself has acknowledged a slight change of view with regard to the nation state in a more recent interview:

> Now, unlike in 1996 when I was more convinced that the nation was in a kind of terminal crisis – and that may still prove to be true – I often say to people that there is no reason the nation is more eternal than any other form, but what is certain is that we have many other forms of sovereignty. That to me is clear. Whether or not the nation is in crisis, there are many competitors in the sovereignty business. That's what I'd say now, as opposed to 10 years ago.
> (Rantanen 2006: 18)

Appadurai's rather harsh appraisal of the relation between nations and states, which he deems is an 'embattled' relation *everywhere*, also seems to need some further scrutiny. It is clear that due to the homogenizing and unifying project of nationalism, states have always been engaged in masking and marginalizing some aspects of cultural difference within their territories, and there has always been resistance and opposition to such unifying projects on the side of minority groups within the nation. Nevertheless, there are also instances where the fear of an even greater cultural intervention or influence from outside the national territories can create strong alliances within the nation and encourage the unity of the state and the nation on matters of mutual concern. The important point, as Jameson has argued, is 'the level at which a malign and standardizing or despotic identity is discerned' (Jameson 1998a: 74). If it is from the state, 'a more micro-political form of difference' will be affirmed against it. But when the threats of identity come from a higher global level, things can change. At this stage the enemy of difference, in Jameson's view, is 'the transnational system', not the state. At this point the 'nation-states and their national cultures are suddenly called upon to play the positive role' against such systems (ibid.). This, as it shall be argued in the following chapter, is one of the reasons why national cinema continues to have relevance in the age of globalization.

Global transformations

Global Transformations (1999) is the title of a volume that includes one of the most comprehensive studies on globalization and offers a multidimensional analysis of its processes. This sophisticated account not only introduces a theoretical model for the study of globalization, but also provides a great deal of historical and empirical evidence from different political, economic and cultural spheres to support the main argument. The authors, David Held, Anthony McGrew, David Goldblatt and Jonathan Perraton are based in the different disciplines of politics, international relations, sociology and economics and have aimed to provide an interdisciplinary theorization of globalization. Although they have dedicated a full chapter to the subject of 'national culture' and discussed the main debates in the field at some length, their analysis of cultural globalization is more sociological than culturalist. The authors, therefore, are more interested in theorizing the larger transformations and explaining their dynamics than engaging with the analysis of cultural texts and artifacts and their meanings. Their illustration of the big picture of globalization does nonetheless involve some insights for anyone interested in exploring the finer details and the smaller changes at the local level. One of the merits of this account is that it offers a credible working definition of globalization, which is helpful in understanding this process (or set of processes), as well as useful for those involved in making decisions on how to respond to it.

Three standpoints in globalization theory

In their review of the literature on globalization, the authors categorize three broad schools, which they label as 'hyperglobalists', 'sceptics' and 'transformationalists'. The 'hyperglobalist' thesis, Held et al. contend, is generally based on an economic logic and emphasizes the emergence of a single global market (Held et al. 1999: 3). It argues that globalization is not only bringing about a 'denationalization' of economics but is also 'constructing new forms of social organization that are supplanting or will eventually supplant traditional nation states' (1999: 3). Held et al. distinguish two variants in this thesis: the neo-liberal variant, which celebrates this situation and believes that it will be advantageous for all the states and societies; and the neo-Marxist variant, which, in contrast, maintains that it 'creates and reinforces structural patterns of inequality within and between countries' (Held et al. 1999: 4). They cite the work of Luard (1990), Ohmae (1995) and Albrow (1996) as references of the 'hyperglobalist' standpoint.

For the 'sceptics' like Hirst and Thompson (Hirst and Thompson 1996a, 1996b), on the contrary, globalization is 'essentially a myth' and national governments in the form of three major regional blocks (North America, Europe and Asia-Pacific) continue to remain very powerful. They refer to the significant flows of investment, trade and labor in the late nineteenth century to argue that contemporary levels of economic interdependence are by no means historically unprecedented (1999: 5). Some 'sceptics' consider global governance a 'western project' that helps sustain 'the primacy of the west in world affairs' (1999: 6). Again Held et al. suggest that within the 'sceptics' we can identify theorists from both sides of the ideological and political spectrum: Hirst and Thompson, for instance, on the Left and Samuel Huntington on the Right (1999: 6).

The 'transformationalists', whom Held et al. identify with, argue that the current phase of globalization is 'historically unprecedented', yet maintain that its outcome is uncertain. Theorists with this standpoint (Castells 1996; Giddens 1990; Scholte 1993) consider globalization as the central driving force behind the rapid social, political and economic changes that are shaping modern societies and the world order but emphasize that globalization is a contingent and contradictory process, with pulls and pushes, fragmentations and integrations, universalizations and particularizations. Rather than asserting the end of the nation state, the 'transformationalists' maintain that a new 'sovereignty regime' is today complicating the relation between sovereignty, state power and territoriality. They encourage a more 'activist state', which employs new strategies to 'reconstitute and restructure' itself in response to the new global conditions (Held et al. 1999: 9).

Defining globalization

In an effort to provide a precise definition of globalization, Held et al. criticize previous definitions such as 'accelerating interdependence' (Ohmae 1995), 'action at distance' (Giddens 1990) and 'time-space compression' (Harvey 1989) for being compatible with other processes in smaller scale, such as localization, nationalization or regionalization (Held et al. 1999: 15). They stress the need for a definition that would take into account the stretching of social relations and interactions; the intensification of global interconnectedness; the speeding up of the global flows; and the growing impact of distant events (ibid.). They therefore propose the following definition for globalization:

> A process (or set of processes) which embodies a transformation in the spatial organizations of social relations and transactions – assessed in terms of their extensity, intensity, velocity and impact – generating transcontinental or interregional flows and networks of activity, interaction, and the exercise of power.
>
> (1999: 16)

This definition is complemented by the definition of *flows* as 'movements of artefacts, people and information across space and time'; and of *networks* as 'regulated or patterned interactions between independent agents, nodes of activity or sites of power' (1999: 16). Although Held et al. do not acknowledge Appadurai's work – which is also based on the notion of flows – they do at one point criticize what they call 'an exclusive focus on flows' for failing to recognize 'the importance of the enduring relationships established by such flows and the experience of participants at either end of the flows' (Held et al. 1999: 329).

The significance of Held et al.'s account of globalization is that it proposes certain criteria or 'dimensions' for analyzing globalization and comparing its processes in different periods of history. They argue that the 'dimensions' of globalization can be sorted into two main categories: 'spatio-temporal' and 'organizational' dimensions. The 'spatio-temporal dimensions', the authors explain, consists of factors such as the *extensity, intensity* and *velocity* of global flows and transnational interactions, as well as their *impact propensity*. The 'organizational dimensions', on the other hand, include *infrastructures* that facilitate or carry global flows, networks and relations; the level of *institutionalization* of the patterns of transnational interaction; the degree of *stratification* in terms of the hierarchies and unevenness of globalization processes; and finally the *modes of interaction* in global relations (such as imperial/coercive, competitive/conflictual, military/economic) (1999: 19–20). With the help of these conceptual tools, the authors are able to provide a systematic analysis of the 'typology of globalization' in different periods of history, as well as making sense of the contemporary global developments.

Another merit of Held et al.'s work, which distinguishes it from the above-mentioned theories, particularly from Robertson's notion of an apparently *even* 'global field', is that their theory does not present globalization as a 'neutral' or 'even' process, and does not neglect the crucial matter of inequality in the processes of globalization. The authors of *Global Transformations* clearly emphasize that, although involving both enablement and constraint, globalization is 'a highly stratified structure, profoundly uneven, with existing patterns of inequality and hierarchy which generates new patterns of inclusion and exclusion or new winners and losers' (1999: 27). In theorizing and analyzing the processes of globalization, therefore, they take account of the notion of power and its significant impact on the outcome of globalization processes.

In order to bring the globalization theories discussed above closer to the main topic of the present project, the following section will examine one part of Held et al.'s study that mainly deals with the impact of globalization on 'national culture'.

Globalization and 'national culture'

In Held et al.'s historical analysis, 'national cultures' are considered as one of the main agents of globalization in the modern industrial era (1850–1945).[5] Drawing upon the vast literature on the history of nationalism, they define the nation as

> a cross-class community, whose shared sense of identity, solidarity and interest is rooted in an ethnic identity and common historical experience (real, imagined or interpreted) and whose central project is the possession of a distinctive state in a bounded territory.
>
> (1999: 336)

The creation of national culture, the authors argue, was a core project in the nation state in which state organizers and government officials were deeply involved. They used institutions such as national/official language, national schooling system, national press, national post service, national telecommunications and national broadcasting to create a sense of national identity and belonging. The contribution of the project of nationalism to cultural globalization, in Held et al's view, is that it helped expand the spatial and social reach of networks and institutions that transmitted cultural messages. 'Forging the nation', the authors write, 'required cross-class communication rather than intra-elite communication', which dominated the previous eras (1999: 337). In this sense nationalism can be considered as a catalyst, or a preliminary step toward globalization.

In the contemporary phase of globalization (1945–present) however, Held et al. argue, new information technologies and institutions of mass cultural production have challenged the centrality of nation states and national cultures. They consider the role of language (particularly the English language) and telecommunication as the key infrastructures of globalization in this phase. They refer to some of the significant changes in the fields of media and communications that have taken place since the 1970s: 'the increasing concentration of ownership'; 'a shift from public to private ownership'; 'the increasingly transnational structure of the corporations'; 'general corporate diversifications across different types of media products'; and 'an increasing number of mergers of cultural producers, telecommunications corporations and computer hardware and software firms' (Held et al. 1999: 347).

The rise in the production and consumption of popular cultural products, and the emergence of consumerist and materialist cultures, Held et al. maintain, has made it extremely difficult to assess the accurate impact of cultural globalization on national cultures in the contemporary era (1999: 328). The authors stress that 'cultural globalization is transforming the *context* in which, and the means through which, national cultures are produced and reproduced' (1999: 328, emphasis in original). While acknowledging that the characteristics of a 'national culture'

---

[5] The authors also identify Socialism, Liberalism and Science as three other major 'transnational ideologies' that shared a secular orientation and a universal perspective and acted as agents of globalization in the 'modern era' (1999: 339).

or its changes cannot be easily – if at all – defined and charted, they summarize the political impacts of cultural globalization on national cultures under two broad categories: 'decisional and institutional impacts' and 'distributional and structural impacts'.

With respect to the former, the authors argue that cultural globalization has significantly altered the 'institutional context', in which local or national projects develop. Therefore the costs and benefits of national policies of cultural autonomy or political control and censorship have increasingly changed (1999: 370). They assert that those states that have applied a closed cultural policy to minimize foreign influences are more threatened by contemporary cultural globalization. Held et al. mention that even some 'western' governments have introduced policies to preserve their 'cultural identity' by limiting or controlling external influence. Tomlinson and Miller have discussed these cases in more detail with reference to the GATT and NAFTA negotiations where France and Canada actively challenged the United State's demand for free trade in media and cultural products (Miller 1996; Tomlinson 1997).

Regarding the 'distributional and structural impacts', Held et al. underline the fact that the ratio of foreign to domestic consumption of cultural and media products in most countries indicates a shift toward the foreign. '[W]estern cultural industries', the authors stress, 'have even eaten into areas of consumption where domestic production has some foothold and strength', thus resulting in 'local producers being squeezed out of the market' (1999: 372). The import of films from Hollywood has been a major concern in this respect and a range of policies have been adopted in different countries toward ensuring a screening space for national productions. Held et al. remind us, however, of some exceptions such as the Indian film industry that still dominates the vast majority of its domestic market. The authors also mention the particular case of Iran and suggest that the 'power of the Iranian state' and the 'cultural hegemony of Islam' ensure that home consumption is 'overwhelmingly domestic in origin' (1999: 372).[6]

Held et al. also point to the counter movements and alternative possibilities in the global media market, that exist in spite of the dominant media systems of the West. They refer to the research by Tracy (1988) and Sinclair (1996) that indicate some reverses in the global flows of television programs, such as Brazilian television programs that have found audiences in Portugal. Joseph Straubhaar has discussed the case of Brazilian television, its national development and the regional and global reach of its programs in more detail (Straubhaar 2001). Highlighting the significant role that the state plays in forming and maintaining

---

[6] This judgment on cultural production and consumption in Iran fails to acknowledge that in Iran, apart from a state policy that blocks foreign imports, there is also a long history of film and media production. This means that the necessary institutions, infrastructures and human resources that facilitate local cultural production are available and can – as far as the regulations allow – cater to public demands for art and entertainment. Moreover the 'hegemony of Islam' is not exclusive to Iran and does not always have the same impact in terms of cultural consumption. It may be argued that such hegemony is in many ways much stronger in Saudi Arabia, for instance, where we do not see much evidence of domestic consumption of culture. It appears instead that, in the Saudi case, the 'hegemony' of a particular reading of Islam (Wahhabi), rather than guaranteeing domestic consumption, has increased the consumption of foreign cultural products, mainly via satellite television.

national television systems, he suggests that in Latin America 'there is still a tendency toward preferring cultural proximity, that is, preferring cultural products from a culture similar to one's own' (2001: 135). In Straubhaar's view globalization has had different effects in different regions:

> while most European and African countries continue to import most television programs from the Unites States and relatively little from each other, that is less true in Latin America and the Middle East, where cultural trade within cultural-linguistic regions is large and growing.
>
> (2001: 136)

In addressing the political impacts of globally distributed popular culture on national cultures, Held et al. acknowledge the concerns about the homogenization of mass cultural consumption, mostly among young people. Yet following Tomlinson's critique of cultural imperialism (1991), the authors maintain that 'simple notions of homogenization, ideological hegemony or imperialism fail to register properly the nature of the encounters and the interplay, interaction and cultural creativity they produce' (1999: 374). Overall, they do not agree that nationalist cultural projects are in terminal decline. 'Hollywood, Microsoft, and AT&T', the authors write, 'are in the business of making money – not funding alternative centres of political identity and legitimacy' (1999: 374). But they emphasize, once again, that national cultural initiatives and policies should be modified and adapted to the new conditions of the global context.

A framework of the globalization theories

The review of different theoretical standpoints within globalization theory not only provides us with a general understanding of globalization and its complex processes, but also offers insights into identifying the ways that such processes impact upon the cultural sphere in general, and local and national forms of cultural production in particular. At this point I want to draw out a theoretical framework of the globalization theories discussed above, which can guide the direction of the rest of this study. Some relevant aspects of the theories have already been indicated and they are identified more systematically here.

1. Robertson's model emphasizes the cognitive or 'inside the head' aspect of globalization: the way globalization changes our understanding of the world we live in, and of our 'neighbours' and the issues we have with them. This theoretical view would suggest an approach to the study of national cinema that takes account of those 'inside the head' changes. Textual analysis of different films by the same directors, particularly comparing those that have been made before and after the intensification of globalization processes, could be one possible approach.

2. One feature of Robertson's model of the 'global field' is that it acknowledges the possibility of different responses (including resistance) to globalization by individuals and national societies, and predicts that the latter would result in globalization – or 'glocalization' to be more precise – producing different outcomes in different contexts, rather than having unified universal consequences. To examine this view with regard to national cinema, it would be appropriate to compare and contrast the ways in which different film-makers of a national cinema have responded to globalization, whether in terms of their film-making practices, or in the content and style of their films.
3. With respect to the issue of identity, the key question is how globalization has influenced the representation of identity (ethnic, gender, racial, class and religious) in national cinema productions, and how the very idea of the nation and that of national identity are reinforced or deconstructed in films. Stuart Hall's observation that globalization ironically bring the margins into representation and enables them to 'retell their hidden histories' can also be examined through the analysis of films that represent marginalized sections of the society and minorities within the nation.
4. The significance of the case of Japan and its globalized economy raises questions about recent developments in different national cinemas where certain institutions (such as media conglomerates, the multiplex, exhibition chains, etc), modes of production (such as efficiency-optimized 'planned' projects) or even film genres (such as the blockbuster) have been appropriated from Hollywood. Should the latter developments be denigrated as mere cultural mimicry and criticized as evidence of global capitalist expansion, or, alternatively, celebrated as signs of a revival of national cinemas and examples of glocalization, hybridity and the empowerment of the margins?
5. Appadurai's conceptualization of mediascapes and ethnoscapes are directly relevant to the study of globalization and national cinema. The former involves both the worldwide diffusion of media (including film) production technologies, and the creation of 'large and complex repertoires' of images and narratives about the world. In this respect, the ways in which what we might term 'cinemascapes' are involved in creating and exhibiting images of the world and of other nations and cultures can be investigated. The issue of migration and the concept of ethnoscapes are also relevant with regard to the growing interest in the work of 'transnational', 'diasporic' and 'exilic' film-makers. Whether and how the work of such film-makers can be related to a national cinema is a matter that deserves further examination. The economics and politics of transnational cinema, and the reception of 'transnational films' in the film-makers' homelands are other topics for investigation.
6. The debate on Americanization and its relation to globalization is perhaps more relevant to film than any other art form. Given the tendency in some theoretical accounts (such as that of Appadurai and Tomlinson) to put less emphasis on the 'fear of Americanization' and draw attention to other more positive aspects of globalization (such as hybridity, cosmopolitanism and grassroots globalization), it would be useful to examine whether there is any sign of decline, or transformation, of the 'fear of Americanization' among and within different national cinemas.

7. Many theorists of globalization have associated the process with new challenges posed to the centrality and authority of the nation state, if not its total dismantling. Neo-liberal economics of the global age, so the argument goes, have forced nation states to relinquish many of their powers to the 'free-market' and withdraw their involvement and intervention in the economy. The question is whether this observation would also apply in terms of national cinemas. In other words, is there any evidence to suggest that government intervention, protectionist cultural policies and state support for national film industries has witnessed a significant decline in the age of globalization?
8. Held et al.'s recognition and periodization of the history of globalization brings to the foreground questions about the history of cinema and whether the contemporary phase of globalization in film history is substantially different from events in the early decades of cinema when films and film-making technologies rapidly travelled around the world. Some authors have even suggested that film was at first a more 'global' artifact and it was only at later stages – particularly following the introduction of sound – that it found 'national' attachments (Williams 2002a). What, therefore, has changed in the recent era?
9. Held et al. have charted a number of developments in telecommunications and broadcast systems over the recent decades. These include concentration of ownership; a shift from public to private ownership and the appearance of transnational corporations that spread their dominance across different sectors through mergers and takeovers. The question raised with respect to the topic of the present book is whether similar developments have appeared in all national cinemas and, in cases where they have, how this has influenced the outcome of national cinema in terms of themes and forms.
10. In assessing the impact of cultural globalization on national cultures, Held et al. formulated two broad categories: 'decisional and institutional impacts' and 'distributional and structural impacts'. These categories are clearly relevant to the aims of this study in terms of assessing: how have the costs and benefits of national film policies changed in the new context; how has the ratio of foreign to domestic cultural consumption changed over the past few years; and what are the cultural implications of these developments.

Clearly addressing all the above questions and examining the globalization theories across different regional and national contexts, which requires a sufficient number of case studies, is far beyond the scope of this book. With these questions in mind however, the present book is focused on a corpus of diverse examples from Iranian cinema so as to illuminate parts of the broader picture. Before moving on to the case study and the examples, however, it is necessary to reflect critically on the concept of 'national cinema', which so far in this discussion has been taken for granted. What exactly constitutes a national cinema and how can such a concept be defined? Does it really make sense and is it still relevant in the age of globalization to speak of national cinema? These questions will be explored in the next chapter.

Chapter 2

The Concept of National Cinema: Theorization and Critique

Introduction

Up until the mid- to late 1980s, 'national cinema' was for many critics and film scholars a largely taken-for-granted and unproblematic concept. Within the worldwide circuit of film distribution dominated by Hollywood, the term national cinema was generally used as a marketing strategy to distinguish the limited number of films in circulation that were not from Hollywood. In such contexts, national cinema was by definition contrasted with, or seen as being opposed to, Hollywood. As Thomas Elsaesser (2005) has argued in the case of European cinemas, national cinema was 'the other' against which Hollywood was defined. 'Hollywood' was also largely defined through this binary opposition. As if describing a unified and coherent body of film, which was seen to be in a stable and unproblematic relation with the inhabitants of a particular geographic territory, the term national cinema did not seem to require any further scrutiny. Such a view of national cinema has nonetheless continued to maintain a relatively strong presence around the world, particularly within journalistic discourses and cultural policy.

From the mid-1980s, however, the concept of national cinema has increasingly been the subject of critical examination and theorization. In line with the developments in literary and cultural theory, and new conceptual frameworks for comprehending how nations are 'imagined' (Anderson 1983) and traditions are 'invented' (Hobsbawm and Ranger 1983), film scholars began raising new questions about the long-held assumptions on national cinema. These critical debates have generally aimed at deconstructing essentialist views of national cinema and exposing the politics of exclusion and inclusion, which are inherent in the process of defining and promoting it. In doing so, these accounts have been highly influential in expanding 'the limited imagination of national cinema' (Higson 2000) and have encouraged more attention toward neglected or marginalized sectors within national film industries. Some scholars, however, have come to conclude that, given the developments involved in processes of globalization and regionalization, national cinema may no longer be a useful concept in discussing world cinema. They argue that the vast number of transnational networks, institutions and corporations that are now involved in the co-production and transnational distribution and exhibition of films have rendered national cinema a less relevant term, particularly in regions like Europe (Elsaesser 2005). Others have gone further to suggest that instead of calling for the protection or renewal of national cinema, it would be more meaningful to call for a 'socialist cinema', a 'green cinema' or a 'feminist cinema' (Higson 1995).

Despite such skepticism, both theoretical elaborations on national cinema and fine-grained academic studies of particular national cinemas have somewhat flourished over the past decade. Susan Hayward, a key advocate of the term, and author of *French National Cinema* (Hayward 2005), edited the *National Cinema Series* for Routledge, which, apart from her own book, involved 12 volumes on different national cinemas. Wallflower Press, a younger publisher, specializing in film, has over the recent years also published a series of books, each dedicated to the study of a particular national cinema or a number of national cinemas within a region. More recently Intellect has also commissioned a series of World Cinema 'Directories', each dedicated to a particular national cinema.

Moreover, a number of essay collections that include both theorization and individual case studies of national cinemas have also been published since the 2000s. *Cinema and Nation* (Hjort and MacKenzie 2000), *Film and Nationalism* (Williams 2002b), *Theorising National Cinema* (Vitali and Willemen 2006) and *Traditions in World Cinema* (Badley et al. 2006) are key titles in this respect. A major research project titled 'Dynamics of World Cinema', led by Dina Iordanova and Stuart Cunningham, is underway at the University of St. Andrews in Scotland that deals with many issues relating to this. Despite some counter arguments and alternative perspectives that appear to have made national cinema less fashionable in recent years (Ďurovičová and Newman 2010; Ezra and Rowden 2006), the subject does not seem to show much sign of exhaustion and new publications continue to demonstrate a growing interest in the field. All this can be interpreted as sign of a growing attention toward the relation between film and nation in the age of globalization.

This chapter sets out to examine a number of different ways in which the concept of national cinema has been defined and theorized. After examining how national cinema has been conceptualized and reconceptualized, the chapter concludes by addressing the question of the relevance of this concept or otherwise in a world that has witnessed unprecedented levels of transnational and global movement, communication and interaction.

National cinema as 'intertextual symptom'

In a pioneering essay that was first published in 1984, Philip Rosen applies theories of textual analysis to scrutinize film history and historiography. In doing so, he challenges some of the generally accepted notions and principles in the study of national cinema:

> The discussion of national cinema assumes not only that there is a principle or principles of coherence among large numbers of films; it also involves an assumption that those principles have something to do with the production and/or reception of those films within the legal borders of [...] a given nation-state. That is, the intertextual coherence is connected to a socio-political and/or socio-cultural coherence implicitly or explicitly assigned to the nation.
>
> (Rosen 2006: 18)

In order to explain how such coherences are 'constructed' by film historians, Rosen builds up on notions of 'containment' and 'dispersion' in semiotics and textual analysis. He considers 'nationality' as an 'intertextual symptom' and argues that the dialectic between the two counter processes of containment and dispersion should be taken into account in the study of national cinema. The former process works to maintain the unity and coherence of a text or body of textuality, while the latter, exposes its gaps and contradictions. Rosen's main emphasis is on the ways in which intertextual coherence is constructed among groups of films. In other words he aims to describe 'how a large number of superficially differentiated texts can be associated in a regularized, relatively limited intertextuality in order to form a coherence, a "national cinema"' (Rosen 2006: 18). To address this question, he presents a critique of two influential historiographies of national cinemas: Siegfried Kracauer's *From Caligari to Hitler* (1947) on the German cinema; and Noël Burch's *To the Distant Observer* (1979), which analyzes Japanese cinema.

Rosen summarizes Kracauer's central argument as follows: 'generally and compulsively repeated motifs appearing throughout all levels of a nation's films – from a self-consciously "artistic" cinema to the most mass-oriented – are symptoms of a "collective mentality", a shared "inner life"' (2006: 19). Kracauer, following Freud, treats a diverse national population (the German middle-class) as if it bore exactly similar characteristics with that of an individual. This approach, says Rosen, has been criticized for its massive unification of the nation; for its simplistic reflectionist presumptions, which assumes that it is possible to read the deep mental structures of a nation in its films; and for its teleologism, which interprets almost everything in post World War I German cinema as leading to Nazism and the rise of Hitler (2006: 21). In his analysis of German films of the 1920s Kracauer aims to explore the 'mental preconditions' that facilitated the rise of National Socialism. For Rosen, this approach implies that 'the pertinent coherences (textual, national) of the period are defined by what followed it' (2006: 21). He argues that although Kracauer's analysis is not a psychoanalytic one, it uses methods that are common in the practice of psychoanalysis. For instance he treats films as if they are discourses of a patient and thus projects individual characteristics onto a collective entity such as the nation (2006: 24). Rosen finds the latter problematic and points out that Kracauer's account cannot be accepted as an 'overarching historiographic principle' but only as 'one possible form of understanding a differentiated, local, conjunctural historical phenomena' – in his case the mentality of middle class German society between the two World Wars. In this sense, Rosen concludes, Kracauer's approach could be useful as a method that is not necessarily applicable in any individual case, but is sometimes useful for 'organizing historical temporality in relation to specific kinds of questions' (2006: 21).

Noël Burch's semiotic analysis of Japanese cinema and his attempt to demonstrate its difference in form, style and narrative from western modes of cinematic representation also raises questions for Rosen. He criticizes Burch for drawing upon a 'certain strain of western theory from Brecht through Derrida and Barthes in order to explain the significance of the Japanese difference' (2006: 22). Interestingly, Burch does identify a number of similarities between the two modes of cinematic representation, for instance between Japanese cinema and western avant-garde cinema. Yet he maintains that unlike western film-makers who were vanguard and subversive, the Japanese artists were masters of a 'unified cultural practice' that had been formed over centuries: 'What was a mass cultural attitude in Japan was a deeply subversive vanguard practise in the Occident' (Burch 1979: 115, 148; quoted in Rosen 2006: 22). For Rosen the latter observation implies that the major Japanese film-makers were not 'original artists in the western sense' (ibid.). Burch's analysis of Japanese cinema, Rosen indicates, involves a celebration of the 'supreme refinement and systematization of those traits which are most specifically Japanese' (particularly in the work of Ozo and Mizoguchi during the 1930s and 1940s), while it also credits other masters such as Kurosawa – who have applied more western-style modes of cinematic representation – for engaging in an 'active deconstruction' of the western codes of film language (ibid.).

'What would be at stake in the study of national cinemas', Rosen writes in his conclusion, 'is not the nation as a concrete and automatically unified producer/reader of films, but as an appeal to a general ego-function by means of specific configurations of textuality' (2006: 25). He suggests that '[i]f there is something particularly "national" about a set of films, such as German films of the early 1920s or Japanese films of the 1930s, the nation would appear as a construction of that cinema's discourse, and its address' (2006: 25). In Rosen's view, Kracauer and Burch attempt to 'construct' and 'explain' certain types of 'intertextual coherence' as being especially forceful during certain periods of film/national history (2006: 26). This kind of diachrony, he adds, can be associated with the play of an 'intertextual dialectic between containment and dispersion' in order to analyze 'historically specific national identities'. In this sense:

> The national identity of a group of films becomes, neither the realization of some hypothetical notion of *Geist*, nor a trivial tautology (these films were made in Germany therefore they are part of a German national cinema), nor the catchwords of patriotic claptrap. National identity becomes an entity more or less realized precisely as a readable discursive coherence which is unstable and whose terms and/or intensity may well shift to the point where it becomes at least theoretically possible for a historian to argue that the cinematic output of a given nation during a period does not embody that particular kind of intertextual address one would call national cinema.
>
> (2006: 26)

Rosen's article was a major step in deconstructing essentialist views of national cinema. It clearly highlighted the differentiated, conjunctural and historically constructed nature of national cinemas and usefully applied the processes of containment and dispersion from theories of (inter)textuality to explain how national cinemas are constructed and maintained and how they may be challenged and even subverted. However, in considering the national identity of films as 'a readable discursive coherence' Rosen tends to put more weight than is necessary on the idea of 'coherence'. He does not mention, for instance, the possibility of competing or contradictory 'readings' of a national cinema even at the same historical moment. Kracauer's account of German cinema between the two World Wars, for instance, may be challenged by other critics and scholars who may not see the same kind of coherence that he has identified in 'all levels of [the] nation's films'.

The other point, which can be raised here, is that Rosen does not acknowledge the impact of power relations and government policies that promote and privilege 'preferred readings' of national cinema at the stake of others. Some readings of national cinema can thus be repressed or marginalized while others become dominant. As in the practice of 'narrating the nation', we inevitably face processes of inclusion and exclusion when reading/constructing 'coherence' in a national cinema: certain examples, which support the argument, are usually brought to the foreground while others that do not fit so well are neglected or marginalized. In terms of state policy, the latter process usually leads to censorship and/or channelling government funds toward the production of particular films that are considered to be 'more national'.

The study of national cinema should therefore be based on an awareness, not only of its historically constructed and differentiated nature, but of the limitations and contradictions in reading/constructing a single and unified notion of national identity from among a very large and heterogeneous group of films.

National cinema as cultural/economic weapon

In the introduction to his collection of essays entitled *Cinema and Nationalism* (Williams 2002b), Alan Williams refutes the assumption that the relation between cinema and nationalism has only recently become destabilized under the impact of globalization. He maintains that this relation has always been a problematic one. In fact in its silent era, he writes, 'the cinema appeared to many observers to be the first truly global, transnational medium, for this simple reason: it has no, or very little, language' (Williams 2002b: 1). In other words cinema was in its early years a more 'global' or 'transnational' art form and it was only later, particularly with the introduction of 'talkies' and the recognition of the power of film by governments that the national aspect of cinema came into focus. For Williams, it was the struggles in defining and maintaining 'the nation' that engaged cinema with the nationalist project: 'Rather than simply being related to the nation, the cinema [was] an essential part of a process of defining the nation, [it was an] arena for conflicting interest groups to quarrel over the definition of the nation' (2002b: 4). In this sense cinema's status and function shifted from being merely an art form or a means of entertainment to taking on the new mission and responsibilities as a 'cultural weapon'. National cinemas, Williams argues, are not therefore 'things-in-themselves' but part of a 'complex dynamic in which they do things *to* and *for* nations' (Williams 2002b: 6, emphasis in original).

From this point in history national cinema becomes significant for the nation state in different ways. In economic terms it is important for creating jobs; for keeping the nation's money at home; and for performing as an export industry that brings in dollars (ibid.). But it is also a weapon of cultural nationalism that can be used to promote 'national values' and 'national heritage' and mould mass opinion. This is why, Williams reckons, propaganda film is usually the first example when we think of film and nationalism. But he questions the effectiveness of fiction films on audience attitudes:

> [T]here is virtually no evidence that the fiction film is an effective medium for changing audience attitudes. Fiction films can, probably, change *behaviours* – make people more violent, more inclined to go shopping, more sexually active – more effectively than they can change *ideas*. Nonfiction films, or 'documentaries', might be somewhat more effective at this.
>
> (2002b: 7, emphasis in original)

As evidence Williams refers to the fact that very few fiction propaganda films were made under the Nazis. They rather preferred short 'culture films' that were shown along with fiction films in cinemas. He points out that even most of these non-fiction films were 'preaching to the converted' rather than inviting conversion. Williams does acknowledge however, that both fiction and non-fiction films have a significant role in the '(re)creation and maintenance' of nationalism: '[They] *reflect* and keep *in circulation* values and behaviours associated with a particular nation' (2002b: 8, emphasis in original).

Williams also discusses the history of global film distribution, mentioning the pre-1915 era where the French cinema was the dominant supplier of films even in America; the between-the-war period where nation states asserted control over their film industries; and the post-World War II era when Hollywood consolidated its control. He refers to the active involvement of the US government and its diplomatic missions in producing market research reports for Hollywood and promoting the export of films as means of encouraging the consumption of other American products around the world. 'Unfortunately', Williams writes, this 'campaign of covert, international espionage by government and the industry working together' has largely been neglected in film histories (2002b: 11). By overlooking the latter, he adds, critics have usually considered the success of Hollywood as a result of its 'intrinsic advantages' (right-wing analysis) or because of its 'addictive poisons' (left-wing analysis), while the aid of 'mercantilist-minded American governments' was nonetheless crucial. Williams refers to the role of the Republican politician Will Hays, 'best known as Hollywood's chief censor' (ibid.), who was the director of the Motion Picture Producers and Distributors of America (MPPDA) between 1922 and 1945.[1]

In his conclusion Williams proposes that we distinguish between global, international and national films. For him, the first category marks big-budget Hollywood action movies, which are the only films to be distributed and exhibited on a truly global scale. The second category refers to the low-budget art-house films that are 'self-consciously national' but are usually aimed at foreign film festivals. The 'ideal' ones, Williams states with a hint of irony, 'are those that go against the grain of its own national cinema or national state apparatus' and the most exciting examples are 'those banned, denounced, or commercially discouraged in their domestic markets' (2002: 18). His final category 'national films' are medium-budget films designed for a home or regional audience. In this category, unlike the 'international' category, films are 'national' in a less conscious and less manipulated way. 'It is in this type of production', Williams maintains, 'that national differences are to be observed on various levels – most obviously, of film genre' (2002: 19). Yet he is quick to acknowledge, following Altman (Altman 1999), that the question of genre is no less complicated and problematic than the question of nationalism and thus warns that 'any generic approach to national filmmaking is anything but easy' (2002: 20).

It seems that in his categorization Williams tends to privilege the third category as somehow being a more reliable or authentic source in the study of national cinema. It is certainly the case that in some instances the production of what Williams terms 'international films' – or 'festival films' – becomes a business of manipulating, commodifying and exoticizing national culture for the pleasure of an elite audience based in the great metropolitan centres of world art. This topic and its relation to national cinema will be discussed in more detail in the next chapter. Yet it can be argued that the boundaries between 'national' and 'international' cinema are not as clear cut as Williams seems to suggest. There are many

---

[1] It may be noted that between 2004 and 2011 the CEO and Chairman of Hollywood's trade association – now named Motion Picture Association of America (MPAA) – was Dan Glickman, the former US Secretary of Agriculture (1995–2001). One of his achievements in lobbying for the interests of Hollywood has been to persuade the Swedish government to crackdown on the *Pirate Bay* website. Originally created by a group of young anti-copyright activists, *Pirate Bay* became one of the world's most popular websites, mainly for providing links to files of music and film that were shared on numerous computers around the world. The Swedish police initially launched a controversial raid on the location of the website's servers in Stockholm in 2006 and confiscated their servers. The raid, however, only caused the website to be offline for three days as it restarted its normal operation from elsewhere. A copy of a letter by the MPAA to the Swedish Minister of Justice was later revealed in which the MPAA demanded action against *Pirate Bay*. The date of this letter (17th April 2006) indicates that the raid took place 44 days after it had been sent. The letter is available on the blog *TorrentFreak* which specializes on news of file sharing on the Internet: http://torrentfreak.com//images/pirate_mpa.pdf, accessed 19th April 2009. In April 2009 a court in Sweden sentenced four co-founders of the website to one year in jail and a fine of $3.6 million. For the full story of the verdict and a review of the website's history see: 'The Pirate Bay trial: Guilty Verdict', *The Guardian*, 17th April 2009, available online at:
http://www.guardian.co.uk/technology/2009/apr/17/the-pirate-bay-trial-guilty-verdict.

films that initially were made to address local audiences but were subsequently celebrated on the international stage. Majid Majidi's *Children of Heaven* (1996) is one example in the Iranian context. On the other hand Majidi's *Colour of Paradise* (1999), which was made following the international success of the previous film, and was seen by some critics as an exotic image of Iranian rural life made primarily for international audiences, surprisingly became a box office hit *inside* Iran. Im Kwon Taek's *Sopyonje* (1993) is another prominent example of a national production that broke box office records in South Korea and was also critically acclaimed and celebrated in international festivals. A more recent example is Asghar Farhadi's *A Separation* (2011): a realist film intended for local audiences that stood second among the top box office hits of the year in Iran, while simultaneously sweeping prizes in international festivals such as Berlin. Williams' suggestion that films that are made for local audiences are national 'in a less conscious and less manipulative way' may also seem problematic when we take into account the often state-sponsored 'heritage films' in different national contexts, which despite aiming at a local audience are no less conscious or less manipulative than 'international' films in their deliberate construction of a privileged image of the nation.

Overall, however, we can agree with Williams that, whether officially stated or not, national cinema is conceived of by many governments as a cultural or economic weapon in the current global economic and cultural wars. State-sponsored initiatives and development plans for film industries are in most countries largely justified in terms of such conceptions of national cinema. The powerful enemy, in fear of which many of the above justifications are made, and the significant 'other' against which many 'national cinemas' are defined, is of course Hollywood. While Hollywood cinema is already historically, though perhaps ambiguously, the national cinema of a hegemonic world power, the question is whether the conceptualization of national cinema as 'the other of Hollywood' continues to have meaning and value in the age of globalization.

National cinema as 'the other' of Hollywood

In his influential essay 'Reconceptualising National Cinema/s' (first published in 1993), Stephen Crofts critically reflects on the fact that 'national cinema' is usually defined against Hollywood. He argues that in theorizing national cinema we need to move beyond this 'self/other model', which ironically, hardly ever speaks of Hollywood as a national cinema (Crofts 2006: 44). Crofts reminds us, like Williams, that Hollywood's superior position in world film trade was not fully realized until the late 1920s: 'whereas in 1914, 90 per cent of films shown worldwide were French, by 1928, 85 per cent were American' (ibid.). From its early days of global dominance, Crofts argues, Hollywood has always attempted to 'naturalize' its forms, narratives and modes of address in different regional and national contexts in order to avoid being identified as 'the other'. Yet the context of unequal exchange – both in cultural and economic terms – has constrained most national cinema producers to operate on the ground rules set by Hollywood. Rather than assuming a single definition for national cinema, Crofts proposes seven taxonomies that would better explain how national cinemas are formed in relation to the different political, economic and cultural contexts of different nation states. These are:

1. Cinemas that differentiate themselves from Hollywood but do not compete directly, since they target a distinct, specialist market sector. 'European-model art cinemas' are Crofts' main examples of this category. This model is 'elitist' – if not bourgeois – in the sense that it attempts to reach domestic and export markets through specialist distribution channels and venues usually called 'art houses'. 'National pride' and 'national cultural identity' are key terms in the arguments in defense of such cinemas, which usually depend on state subsidies or television channels for funding. Crofts does acknowledge that since the 1960s Hollywood has developed its own art cinema and in the course many borrowings and interchanges have happened between European and American cinema. The latter processes have made it more difficult to draw neat lines between art cinema and Hollywood. Crofts also mentions the politics of art cinema and the limitations that follow accepting state funding. He cites Elsaesser (1980: 44, quoted in Crofts 2006: 46) who has suggested that state policies in favor of a 'cultural mode of film production' encourage difference from Hollywood, but discourage biting the hand that feeds them.
2. Cinemas that differ from Hollywood and do not compete directly but oppose Hollywood in their theme and form. 'Third Cinema' is Crofts' main example in this category: a term introduced in the late 1960s by Fernando Solanas and Octavio Getino. The Argentinean film-makers described Third Cinema as an 'anti-imperialist cinema' with 'distinct aesthetic models from Hollywood and European art cinema' (cited in Crofts 2006: 47). For the theorists of Third Cinema, says Crofts, what Hollywood and European art films have in common is 'bourgeois individualism': 'the existentialist-influenced "universal" humanism of much 1960s art cinema […] shares a western individualism with the achieving heroes of Hollywood who resolve plots within the global-capitalist terms of a US world view' (2006: 47). Third Cinema, Crofts reminds us, also stands in sharp contrast with popular genre films of the Third World. Domestic censorship in the 1980s and 1990s and lack of funding, however, has shifted some Third Cinema film-makers from their previous standpoints. Some of them have sought to finance and distribute their films through art cinema's international distribution and exhibition channels. The boundaries between Third Cinema and art cinema thus have also become blurred. This situation, Crofts adds, also raises 'vital questions about the cultural role played by First World financing of Third World cinemas' and the possibility of 'distortion' (2006: 48). The latter topic will be discussed in more detail in Chapter 4 in a case study of the Iranian film-maker Mohsen Makhmalbaf.
3. European and Third World entertainment and commercial cinemas, which struggle against Hollywood with different degrees of success. Crofts recognizes the differences

within this category – for example between European and African cinemas – yet maintains that in most of these cases local films share only a small proportion of a market dominated by foreign films. Another point raised by Crofts is that Third World popular cinemas are largely unknown to, and hardly discussed in, European and Anglophone critical film cultures (2006: 49). Given their significant share in the overall production of a national cinema, this highlights the necessity of paying more attention to locally popular films in any study of national cinema.

4. National cinemas that manage to 'ignore' Hollywood. For Crofts 'large domestic markets' and 'effective trade barriers' play the key role in the success of this kind of national cinema. India and Hong Kong (before its reunion with mainland China) are Crofts' only examples for this category: cinemas that outsell Hollywood not just at home, but also in some regional markets.

5. Cinemas that attempt to imitate Hollywood. By these Crofts refers to film productions in Anglophone countries (mainly Britain, Canada and Australia) that have attempted – and in his view overwhelmingly failed – to target the US market. One problem of this strategy, Crofts reckons, is that these countries have already had their indigenous cultural bases modified by Hollywood's influence. As Geoffrey Nowell Smith has put it, American cinema 'is by now far more deeply rooted in British cultural life than is the native product' (quoted in Crofts 2006: 51). One other problem, Crofts says, is that many directors from these countries have moved to America and taken on careers in Hollywood. It could be added that beyond the Anglophone world, French cinema has also become engaged in the production of English-language blockbusters that aim at entering the US market (Danan 2006: 177).

6. 'Totalitarian cinemas', according to Crofts, are cinemas that work within a wholly state-controlled and often state-subsidized industry. Fascist cinemas in Germany and Italy, Chinese cinema between 1949 and the mid-1980s and the Stalinist regimes of the Soviet bloc are the examples that Crofts mentions under this category. He acknowledges that in some instances art cinemas with elements of political and social critique have also been produced under totalitarian regimes, due to reforms in cultural policy or as a matter of cultural diplomacy. Examples of the latter are the work of Andrei Tarkovsky in the Soviet Union, Andrzej Wajda in Poland or the Chinese Fifth Generation directors such as Zhang Yimou and Chen Kaige.

7. Regional and ethnic cinemas whose culture and/or language distinguish them from the nation states that enclose them. The Quebecois cinema, Afro-American cinema and Black British cinema are Crofts' examples.

Crofts argues that while Hollywood relies on star, genre and production values in its export strategies, other national cinemas are largely marketed abroad through highlighting aspects such as 'nation of production', 'authorship' and 'less censored representations of sexuality', which are 'modes of differentiation' defined against Hollywood (2006: 52). In addition, he raises questions on the politics of inclusion/exclusion in situations when certain films

The Concept of National Cinema: Theorization and Critique

get selected for distribution in other countries. He describes international film festivals as places where 'the dominant film-critical discourse is the depoliticising one of an essentialist humanism ("the human condition") complemented by a tokenist culturalism ("very French") and an aestheticizing of the culturally specific ("a poetic account of local life")' (2006: 53). The important debates surrounding the role of European festivals and critics in defining national cinemas will be further discussed in the case of Iranian cinema in Chapter 3. It should be emphasized that taking account of the politics of national cinema – both within the framework of the nation state and on the international stage – is one of the merits of Crofts' elaboration on national cinema.

In his conclusion Crofts emphasizes the 'continuing power of the nation-state' and draws attention to the significance of 'national developments' that 'can occasion specifically national filmic manifestations' such as Italian Neo-Realism, Latin American Third Cinema and Chinese Fifth Generation. In this sense he is arguing for the relevance of the concept of national cinema but at the same time demanding its reconceptualization, as well as historicization. He is clearly cautious of possible pitfalls such as neglecting the 'cultural hybridity of nation-states'; buying into 'fantasies of irrecoverable cultural roots'; and advocating 'unitary, teleological and usually masculinist fantasies in which nationalisms represent themselves' (2006: 55). While acknowledging that 'the struggle of many national cinemas has been one for cultural, if not also economic, self-definition against Hollywood' (2006: 55), Crofts tends to favor the 'abandonment of the self/other model as an adequate means of thinking national cinemas' (2006: 57). He rightly stresses that in theorizing differences between national cinemas, what Homi Bhabha calls the 'exclusionary imperialist ideologies of self and other' are inappropriate, because '[t]his dualist model authorizes only two political stances: imperial aggression and defiant national chauvinism' (2006: 57). Such thinking cannot take account of new hybrid film cultures and transnational modes of film production in the contemporary age.

Despite its informative and innovative approach in drawing attention to a range of different meanings that the term 'national cinema' may imply, one problem with Crofts' categorization of national cinemas is the ambiguity of the criteria by which national cinemas are categorized across seven types. In fact we may say that the subject of his categorization is not entirely clear. He has himself admitted that the above categories are 'highly permeable' and therefore some individual films or national cinemas could 'straddle these groupings' (2006: 45). Yet he seems to consider certain strategies within a film industry (imitating Hollywood), or particular styles and modes of film production within national cinemas (European art cinema), as a category, along with other categories that refer to a national cinema as a whole ('Totalitarian cinema'). Similarly, while under the title of 'ignoring Hollywood', Crofts is directly making reference to Indian and Hong Kong film industries as a whole, his category of 'regional and ethnic cinemas' refers to different strands *within* a national cinema such as Black British cinema.

The category of 'imitating Hollywood' also brings to mind an increasingly fashionable trend in a number of national cinemas to produce 'national blockbusters'. Needless to say, considering such productions as mere 'imitation' can prove problematic, given the processes of appropriation and negotiation through which 'the national' (or 'the local') makes strategic uses of Hollywood (i.e. 'the global') for its own specific purposes. Highlighting the similarities between blockbusters made in different national contexts, however, should not cause us to neglect the differences that distinguish those national cinemas from each other.

In his book on British cinema *Waving the Flag: Constructing a National Cinema in Britain* (Higson 1995), Andrew Higson uses an approach similar to that of Crofts to demonstrate the different strategies that were adopted within British cinema between the 1920s and 1940s to confront Hollywood's domination of British screens. 'Competing with Hollywood', 'differentiation from Hollywood' and 'genre films with local specificity' are the strategies that Higson discusses. The advantage of Higson's account is that he combines analysis of films with a discussion of the status of the film industry, and what he calls the 'intellectual film-culture' of the time. In other words he does not merely base his own reading of 'the national' on a set of films, but also pays attention to the way these films were read by critics of the time and the kind of arguments made for or against the films in terms of their representation of 'the nation'. In Higson's work, therefore, we notice a shift in studying national cinema: from previous views that focused on production to a new perspective that takes account of consumption. 'Instead of thinking how films work as vehicles for the articulation of nationalist sentiments', Higson argues, 'we should analyse how audiences construct their cultural identity in relation to various products of the national and international film and television industries' (Higson 1995: 278). This approach will be applied in this research in Chapters 4, 5 and 6, which present analyses of the works of different Iranian film-makers.

The relation between Hollywood and national cinema, as well as between the national and the transnational, are however more complicated and problematic than presented in the work of Crofts and Higson.[2] Thomas Elsaesser, who has contributed to the debates on national cinema since the 1980s, sheds lights on some other contradictions in the Hollywood–national cinema dichotomy in his book *European Cinema: Face to Face with Hollywood* (2005). He argues that the term 'national cinema' disguises a binary opposition within its own framework, namely between 'auteur' and 'commercial' cinema. Citing examples such as the film-makers of the French *Nouvelle Vague* (François Truffaut, Eric Rohmer and Claude Chabrol) and the second generation of New German film-makers (Wim Wenders and Rainer Werner Fassbinder), he draws attention to auteur directors whose vision was based on 'a decided preference of Hollywood over their own national cinema' (Elsaesser 2005: 37).

Another paradox that Elsaesser brings to the foreground is that most national cinemas rely on Hollywood to maintain a healthy exhibition sector: 'without Hollywood, no national exhibition sector; without a national exhibition sector [...] you cannot have a national cinema' (2005: 38). In some instances national film-makers (such as Werner Hertzog and Wim Wenders in the case of Germany) have only become recognized by their own nation

---

[2] For a recent critical investigation of the national–transnational binarism, see Higbee and Lim (2010).

after their films had been picked up for distribution by Hollywood majors. In Elsaesser's ironic words 'they had to become Hollywood (or at least Miramax or Buena Vista), before they could return home to Europe as representatives of their national cinema' (2005: 39). Elsaesser goes even further to assert that 'national cinema' is a 'displaced category': one that 'can only be recognized from without' (2005: 40). He suggests that national cinema is a label that has to be attached on films by others: 'either by other national or "international" audiences, or by national audiences, but at another point in time' (ibid.). In his view these 'mirror images' are considered to be the tokens of a national identity as far as the other who defines them is a 'significant other' (2005: 41).

The mirror metaphor is perhaps Elsaesser's particular contribution to this debate, and he uses it further in order to explain the Hollywood–national cinema relation. He believes that 'both the old Hollywood hegemony argument (whether justified on economic or stylistic grounds) and the "postmodern" or "pragmatic" paradigm ("it is what audiences make of films that decides their identity and value")' are inadequate in describing this relation (2005: 46–7). Apart from 'communicating vessels', he suggests, Hollywood and national cinemas can be seen as 'existing in a space set up like a hall of mirrors, in which recognition, imaginary identity and mis-cognition enjoy equal status, creating value out of pure difference' (ibid.).

While the above metaphor does not reflect on the unequal power balance between Hollywood and most national cinemas, Elsaesser does express concern about the failure of European cinemas to produce films that are widely popular at home and can also appeal to audiences abroad. He emphasizes that 'a cinema that does not have the assent and love of a popular audience and cannot reach an international public may not have much of a future as cinema' (2005: 52). Refusing to buy into the kind of explanations that conspiracy theory, media imperialism or colonization theorists have offered for the global appeal of Hollywood, Elsaesser maintains that Hollywood's success and European cinemas' failure have roots in the 'mythic dimension' of cinema. From his viewpoint, Hollywood's main attraction lies in its recycling and reproduction of myths and 'the lack of European films to be able to embed these myths in the contemporary world' is why European cinema does not enjoy the loyalty of the masses (2005: 51). As we shall see throughout this study, the dilemma between 'being different' and 'being popular' resurfaces in many debates on national cinema.

National cinema as 'cultural specificity'

In a recently revised version of an article first published in 1994, Paul Willemen takes account of some of the problems in theorizing 'national cinema' and attempts to offer an alternative approach (Willemen 2006). For Willemen, the project of nationalism aims to 'bind people to identities through modes of address carefully nurtured, reproduced and policed', and it is therefore 'a question of address, not origin or genes' (Willemen 2006: 30). Stressing that 'subjectivity' always exceeds 'identity', he argues that although '[s]ome aspects of our subjectivity may be occupied or hijacked by the national identity modes of address […] there are always dimensions [...] that exceed any such identity straitjacket' (Willemen 2006: 31). The main contribution of his approach is the notion of 'national and cultural specificity', which is offered as an alternative to 'national identity'. With respect to cinema, he suggests that the boundaries of 'cultural specificity' are defined by government actions through its various institutions. 'Specificity' is therefore a 'territorial-institutional' issue that 'coincides with the boundaries of the nation-state' (2006: 33). As an example he refers to Black British cinema, which, in comparison with Afro-American cinema, is 'strikingly British' but cannot be seen as part of British nationalism. As mentioned earlier both these examples were labelled as 'regional and ethnic cinemas' in Crofts categorization of national cinemas.

Willemen, however, goes further to suggest that the discourses of nationalism and the construction and analysis of 'national specificity' are not only essentially different, but are also in a state of conflict, since nationalist discourses always try to colonize and cover the complexities within specific national formations (2006: 34). '[A] cinema addressing national specificity', he contends, 'will be anti- or at least non- nationalistic' (2006: 36). For Willemen, such a cinema critically engages with the complex and multidimensional tensions within the nation, and this distinguishes it from the homogenizing view of a nationalist approach. He too acknowledges the irony, already discussed above in the work of Williams and Elsaesser, that this kind of cinema is usually a 'marginal and dependent' cinema: 'dependent for its existence on the very dominant, export and multinationally oriented cinema it seeks to criticize and displace' (2006: 36).

In a second argument Willemen calls for a new self-critique on the part of western film and media scholarship, for paying insufficient attention to the 'determining effects' of national specificity, thus encouraging 'a kind of promiscuous or random form of alleged internationalism' (2006: 34). National boundaries, he stresses, have a 'significant structuring impact' on social and cultural formations and should be taken into account when scholars attempt to analyze works of art and culture from 'elsewhere'. Otherwise, he writes:

> [R]eading a Japanese film from within a British film studies framework may in fact be more like a cultural cross-border raid, or worse an attempt to annex another culture in a subordinate position by requiring it to conform to the raider's cultural practice.
>
> (ibid.)

Despite the above statement, Willemen uses Mikhail Bakhtin's theory of dialogics to discuss the different ways in which scholars can frame relations with other sociocultural networks. Following Bakhtin he argues that when engaged in dialogue with texts or artifacts from other cultures, we should use the understanding of another cultural practice to 're-perceive and rethink one's own cultural constellation' (2006: 38). The critical study of other national cinemas, he therefore insists, should also be aimed at modifying 'our Euro-American notions of cinema' (2006: 38). In this sense what actually happens through dialogue is a 'double outsideness': 'the analyst must relate to his or her own situation as an other, refusing simple identifications with pre-given, essentialist socio-cultural categories' (2006: 40). Willemen's advice to western scholars is clearly a noteworthy one, although, one might say, many non-western scholars, in their endeavour to understand the West, have been familiar with 'double outsideness' for a long time.

The distinction between identity and specificity in Willemen's account, and the results that follow can also be subject to further scrutiny. It appears that what distinguishes 'national identity' from 'national specificity' in his view is that the former is essentially fixed, unified and homogeneous while the latter is socially constructed, complex (even contradictory) and diverse. Such a dichotomy fails to acknowledge that some pragmatic advocates of national identity have also clearly acknowledged that national identity is not a fixed or homogeneous entity and may transform in time, while insisting on its continuing relevance in contemporary societies. David Miller, for example, writes in his book *On Nationality* that '[n]ational identities are not cast in stone [...] they are above all "imagined" identities' (Miller 1995: 127). Miller's 'ideal' situation is that national identities emerge through open processes of debate and discussion to which every member can contribute, rather than being 'authoritatively imposed by repression and indoctrination' (1995: 39). He even criticizes 'conservative nationalism' for moving from 'a valid premise' – the advantages of 'nationality' – to 'a false conclusion' – that 'nationality' can be preserved 'only by protecting the present sense of national identity' (Miller 1995: 129). Other ways of theorizing the processes of identity construction, such as applying Judith Butler's notion of 'performativity', have also been discussed by theorists of nationalism to develop non-essentialist notions of national identity (Edensor 2001).

Willemen's assertion that in terms of cinema 'specificity' coincides with the boundaries of the nation state also seems to neglect the emergence of 'transnational' cinemas and what Naficy has named 'diasporic and exilic' modes of film-making (Naficy 2001). Such films are produced outside territorial borders but in many cases, they embody elements of what Willemen calls 'national and cultural specificity'. The boundaries of 'national specificity' therefore, may at times transcend the boundaries of the nation state.

Finally, Willemen's observation that 'a cinema addressing national specificity will be anti- or at least non- nationalistic' may also prove inaccurate under certain conditions. These include times of imperial or foreign occupation of a national territory or internal hegemony of non-nationalist (e.g. Communist, religious) ideologies. In these circumstances even the distinction he draws between 'identity' and 'specificity' may be difficult to maintain, since films addressing national specificity may well lend support to a nationalism that they see as being potentially liberating. More generally, it is sometimes very difficult to draw a clear line between films that would fit in Willemen's 'national specificity' category, and those that reinforce a sense of 'national identity' in harmony with the ideology of the state. Im Kwon Taek's *Sopyonje* (1993) in South Korean cinema and Daryush Mehrjui's *Mum's Guest* (2004) in Iranian cinema are examples that may resist such easy categorization.

In his conclusion Willemen makes two final remarks. Firstly, he advises western intellectuals who engage with 'other' cultural practices, to keep an eye on the 'potential effects of their discourses' upon their object of study. In the case of Indian cinema, he refers to the fact that some Indian film-makers secure production finance, partly on the strength of their reputation in the West. He therefore suggests that 'western intellectuals must be careful not to lend inadvertent support to work which, in India, obstructs the very positions they are trying to support' (2006: 41). Bearing in mind the significant role that western festivals and critics can play in privileging particular films, auteurs, styles and themes within a national cinema, Willemen's point is clearly a valid and noteworthy one. In the case of Iranian cinema, for instance, following a number of awards at the Cannes festival in the 1990s, making films *for* Cannes became epidemic among young film-makers and subsequently many pseudo-Kiarostamies and pseudo-Makhmalbafs were created.[3]

Willemen's second point is of crucial importance too. He argues that in the same way that 'the nation' is constructed through modes of address and geographically bounded systems and institutions, 'so "cinema" is an "object" that emerges in the interactions between a loosely bounded industrial sector and that sector's complex relations to a national institutional configuration' (2006: 42). In this sense 'what may be cinema in one country may not be so in another one' (2006: 42). As an example, Willemen refers to the subordination of the film industry in Britain to television after World War II. He compares this example with the status of cinema in France or the United States where unlike Britain, 'it would be absurd to write a history of cinematic production dominated by telefilms' (2006: 42).

The relevance of 'national cinema' in the age of globalization: Arguments for and against

It is quite clear from the theoretical standpoints discussed above that arriving at a grand theory of national cinema or providing an overarching definition for the term is a futile, if not an impossible, task. Not least because 'nation' and 'cinema' are themselves historical constructs and their meanings vary in different times and different sociocultural contexts. The transnational developments and transformations in recent decades, which have destabilized the authority of the nation state, have also brought to the foreground further questions regarding the relevance and usefulness of the concept of national cinema in the age of globalization. In a recent chapter that proposes a 'typology of transnational cinemas' and examines different categories in transnational film-making practices, Mette Hjort initially questions 'whether the very cinematic phenomena currently being described in 2009 as transnational would not, just some ten years previously, have been discussed in terms of a now allegedly outdated national cinema paradigm' (Hjort 2010: 12). The final

---

[3] In 2006 when none of the Iranian films submitted to Cannes were admitted in any of the official sections of the festival, the news was so shocking for some in the film industry that they suggested Iranian cinema should punish Cannes festival by not submitting any films in the future.

section of the present chapter will thus examine some of the arguments for and against the continuing relevance of national cinema.

In their introduction to the anthology *Theorising National Cinema* (2006), Valentine Vitali and Paul Willemen address 'the question of how to speak of cultural "identities" in an academic landscape that appears to have shelved as resolved debates about national specificities in the name of vague notions of "globalization"' (2006: 13). It seems that Vitali and Willemen fail to acknowledge that many globalization theorists, as demonstrated in Chapter 1, have considered the intensification of quests for national/cultural identity as an outcome of the globalization processes, and thus emphasized the importance of taking such concerns seriously in academic research (Morley and Robins 1995; Robertson 1992; Tomlinson 2003). Vitali and Willemen argue that cinema can be thought of in terms of a 'national configuration' because films 'are clusters of historically specific cultural forms the semantic modulations of which are orchestrated and contended over by each of the forces at play in a given geographical territory' (2006: 7). In other words, because the 'forces at play' in any given nation state influence the production of films within that territory, it is important to take that 'national configuration' into account when studying and analyzing the films. Referring to the impact of government policies – ranging from censorship to taxation – on film production, the authors add that 'the functioning of cinema as an industry and a cultural practice […] is overdetermined by the institutions of the state' (ibid.). They are, however, cautious in taking this observation too far in the direction of a classic Marxist infrastructure–superstructure analysis by acknowledging that 'the economic forces sustaining any given film do not necessarily mobilize the available narrative stock in the directions preferred by the state', therefore 'films may and may not reflect the ideological dominant within the nation at one time' (ibid.).

Andrew Higson, whose 1989 article in *Screen* (Higson 2002) was among the first critical assessments of the concept of national cinema, expresses doubts on the usefulness of the concept in a more recent chapter entitled 'The Limiting Imagination of National Cinema' (Higson 2000). Below I shall examine his arguments and assess the strength of his critique of 'national cinema'.

Higson begins by criticizing Benedict Anderson's notion of 'imagined communities' and the widely held view that the mass media and their ritualized events play a determining role in re-imagining the nation. Referring to various examples in the British context – ranging from Princess Diana's widely watched funeral to the popularity of soap operas like *EastEnders* and *Coronation Street* and the success of 'typically British' films such as *Four Weddings and a Funeral* (1994) and *The Full Monty* (1997) – Higson asks whether such media events can unproblematically be considered as being national. His first objection is that many Britons did not participate in such allegedly national media events; many of them do not watch soap operas; and not all of them share the sense of national identity represented in films like *Four Weddings and a Funeral* or *The Full Monty* (Higson 2000: 65). Here Higson seems to be implying that we can consider an event 'national' only when every single citizen of a nation has participated in it, or expressed consent about its national significance. Clearly by this definition the adjective national cannot be applied in case of any event at all, regardless of the size of the population that had participated in it.

Higson's second point is that some of these media events had audiences beyond the national audience in Britain. In other words, they were transnational events, where participants from different origins made different meanings of their experience according to their cultural backgrounds and social contexts. This is a valid point, it should be said, but rather than rejecting the *national* aspect of these events, it is drawing attention to their additional *transnational* dimensions. His third point is that the same national audience that watches a film like *The Full Monty* also watches Hollywood films. Thus the 'imagined community' of a nation can have a collective transnational experience, which may equally – if not more than through 'national' experiences – influence the construction of its identity. Higson fails to acknowledge that apart from films, there are many other processes and institutions, such as education and the family, which influence an individual's sense of belonging to an imagined community. Moreover, even the practice of collectively watching a 'foreign' film in a movie theater, can be seen as a rite that reinforces the 'imagined community'.

Higson rightly argues that the 'imagined community' of national viewers is an unstable, contingent and even fragmented community, which involves many other communities based on generation, gender, class, ethnicity and politics. The members of each of these communities, he emphasizes, also share a sense of collective identity that the 'imagined community' argument fails to acknowledge (Higson 2000: 66). It seems that Higson is expecting too much from Anderson's argument, which was basically a way of explaining how nations are imagined. The fact that citizens of a nation may also belong to other communities of identity within or outside 'the nation', does not mean that they cannot, at the same time, consider themselves as being part of a national 'imagined community'. The national and the transnational are not necessarily mutually exclusive. As Higbee and Lim have stressed, 'the national continues to exert the force of its presence even within transnational film-making practices' (Higbee and Lim 2010: 10).

Higson also examines the arguments advanced by John Hill (1992, 1996) in support of the relevance of national cinema. For Hill the significance of a national cinema results from the 'value of home-grown cinema to the cultural life of a nation and, hence, the importance of supporting indigenous film-making in an international market dominated by Hollywood' (Hill 1992: 11, quoted in Higson 2000: 70). Yet the key question, which remains unanswered for Higson, is: what exactly is the value of a home-grown cinema? Higson reminds us of the role that Hollywood has played in 'ensuring a populist diversity' and thus 'broadening the British cultural repertoire' (ibid.). Hill, on the contrary, downplays the potential in Hollywood films to democratize British culture and maintains that national cinemas can play a greater role in this respect.

In an argument that resembles Willemen's views on national cinema discussed above, Hill suggests that it is possible for a national cinema to be critical of 'inherited notions of national identity'; to avoid assuming a 'unique, unchanging "national culture"'; and to reflect 'social divisions and differences' (Hill 1992: 16, quoted in Higson 2000: 71). Such a national cinema, he proposes, is 'characterized by questioning and enquiry' (ibid.). Hill's example for the latter is British cinema in the 1980s and the work of directors such as Ken Loach. In this period, he believes, the 'Britishness' of the films was 'neither unitary nor agreed but dependent upon a growing sense of multiple national, regional and ethnic identifications which characterized life in Britain in this period' (Hill 1999: 244, quoted in Higson 2000: 71). His main concern is that the forces of the film market must not limit the range of varied cultural representations available to audiences.

Higson finds a number of problems with the above arguments. Firstly he points out that Hill's statements tend to be more in favor of a critical or radical (implicitly leftist) cinema rather than a national one. The second point is that a critical cinema does not necessarily need to be based on national grounds in terms of its funding, its content or its reception. Thirdly, as hinted earlier, Higson maintains that cultural diversity within a national film-culture may also be achieved by a range of imports as well as by supporting local films. And finally for Higson the description that Hill provides of British cinema in the 1980s does not account for all British films made in that period but only for those that involved radical themes and critical approaches. In other words Hill is only including under the rubric of 'British cinema in the 1980s' films that cater to his ideological preferences. Hill even makes value judgments by contending that

> the most interesting type of British cinema, and the one which is most worthy of support is not a cinema that exemplifies the virtues and values of Britain but a cinema that involves the provision of diverse and challenging representations adequate to the complexities of contemporary Britain.
>
> (Hill 1992: 18–19, quoted in Higson 2000: 71)

Higson reads the latter as a call for a very specific type of film, namely 'social dramas set in contemporary Britain, attending to the specificities of multiculturalism and employing a more or less realist mode of representation' (Higson 2000: 71). This for Higson is the reason why in Hill's book *British Cinema in the 1980s* (1999) costume dramas and heritage films have 'less relevance' than the work of directors like Ken Loach. Higson, on the contrary, takes a different approach in his own book on British cinema (Higson 1995), and includes in the corpus of his study a range of different genres, styles and themes that existed within British cinema in the period that he investigates. He ends the book with the following conclusion: 'in the present climate, I would rather call for a socialist cinema, or a green cinema, or a feminist cinema than for the renewal of British cinema' (1995: 279).

In his overall assessment of Hill's arguments, Higson suggests that by calling for a critical cinema that ensures cultural diversity, Hill has actually weakened the case for supporting national cinema rather than strengthening it. Unlike Hill he maintains that 'to argue for a national cinema is not necessarily the best way to achieve either cultural diversity or cultural specificity since 'the contingent communities that cinema imagines are much more likely to be local or transnational than national' (Higson 2000: 73). Higson does recognize that in some 'political circumstances' a national cinema could 'advance the struggle of a community for cultural, political and economic self-definition' (ibid.). He thus admits that while 'in some contexts it may be necessary to challenge the homogenizing myths of national cinema discourse; in others, it may be necessary to support them' (ibid.).

While Higson's point about both Willemen's and Hill's preference for a 'critical cinema' is noteworthy, he tends to neglect the fact that being British and being critical – as the case of Ken Loach demonstrates – are not incompatible. Even a 'green cinema', 'socialist cinema' or 'feminist cinema' will have significant differences when made by film-makers of different origins in different national contexts. How can we explain and analyze these differences, if not by acknowledging the national configurations and cultural specificities that cause them? Moreover, an abstract 'critical cinema' that is entirely detached from the national in terms of its funding, distribution and exhibition – as the case of Mohsen Makhmalbaf examined in Chapter 4 will demonstrate – risks becoming an alienating and uprooted cinema, which may end up compromising its critical edge.

Higson is not alone in his skepticism about the continuing relevance of national cinema as a concept in the contemporary age. Thomas Elsaesser has also expressed reservations about the usefulness of the term in his analysis of the current condition of 'European cinema' (Elsaesser 2005). He highlights a new mode of film-making in Europe, which he calls the 'European post-Fordism' model. The mode is based on 'small-scale production units, cooperating with television as well as commercial partners, and made up of creative teams around a producer and a director' (2005: 69). These production units are supported and partly funded by the new institutions and funding pools created by European legislation to support the production of 'European' films. However, they also cooperate with Hollywood in some of their productions. This is a good example of a film-making practice that goes beyond the national, even the regional.

For Elsaesser, 'what used to be nationally specific protectionism has now become European protectionism' (2005: 70). In these circumstances 'national cinema' 'has become a floating designation, neither essentialist nor constructivist, but more like something that hovers uncertainly over a film's "identity"' (2005: 76). In a world where binary oppositions such as art–commercial cinema, fiction–documentary and independent–mainstream are no longer working, Elsaesser believes 'there hardly seems any space, recognition, or identity left at all [for national cinema], when looked at from the audiences' perspective' (ibid.). He concludes that 'the debate around national cinema may have exhausted its usefulness for the study of contemporary cinema in Europe', yet he remains hopeful that

> both the essentialist and the constructivist notion of national cinema can be superseded by a new cognitive mapping of the hitherto central categories such as 'nation', 'state', 'identity' and 'otherness' without either resorting to the formal-metaphoric level of in-between-ness and hybridity, or the generalized label of postmodernism.
>
> (2005: 78)

Elsaesser looks forward to the emergence of new terms 'that can think cinema and Europe, independent of nation and state while still maintaining a political agenda and an ethical imperative' (ibid.).

It is clear that both Higson and Elsaesser are careful to avoid a grand announcement such as 'the end of national cinema'. They recognize the limits of their analyses, which are largely based on research within the British or the European context, and acknowledge therefore that national cinema may remain a useful or even necessary concept in other circumstances and contexts. In their introduction to *Brazilian National Cinema*, for example, the authors Lisa Shaw and Stephanie Dennison argue that it is almost impossible *not* to speak of Brazilian cinema in terms of a *national* cultural configuration (Shaw and Dennison 2007).

In contrast to the skepticism of Higson and Elsaesser, Susan Hayward remains confident that the concept is still of significant value and emphasizes that the production of a national cinema is 'still extremely important' (Hayward 2000: 88). Apart from publishing extensively on French national cinema, she has over the past two decades presided as general editor over a series of academic books on different national cinemas published by Routledge. She quotes Terry Eagleton's statement that 'To wish class or nation away [...] is to play straight into the hands of the oppressor' (Eagleton 1990: 23, quoted in Hayward 2000: 88). Despite her commitment to developing the concept of national cinema, Hayward does not hesitate in strongly criticizing the processes of inclusion/exclusion and the systematic repression of history/memory in the project of national*ism*. '[M]ost nations practice some form of apartheid or another', she writes adding that 'the role of national culture is (still) to suppress political conflict and disguise it as imagination' (2000: 95–6). Drawing on the work of Judith Butler (1993) she admits that the very concept of national cinema implies that 'there is still a cinema that matters and one that doesn't' (Hayward 2000: 96). However, unlike Willemen and Hill, her arguments in defense of a potentially liberating national cinema are grounded in feminist and postcolonialist theories.

Hayward refers to the symbolic value of the female body in nationalist discourses and the alignment of the nation with the character of a mother. This symbolism, she contends, involves further equations, such as the violation of motherland as the violation of a woman; invasion as rape; and occupation as reproduction of the enemy within the mother-body. Reflecting on the politics of such male-driven narratives, which are based on a denial of female agency and thus never conceive, for example, of the possibility 'that the woman might choose to sleep with the enemy', Hayward brings to the foreground the notion of 'performativity'. By considering nationalism as performance she attempts to show that there is a glimpse of hope and a possibility of deconstructing, if not subverting, the unifying ideology of nationalism. In Hayward's view 'the fact that nations are invented and fictional means that they can be re-defined and re-appropriated by actors' (2000: 99). In this sense excluded groups within a nation have the possibility of re-possessing and re-defining the nation and, for Hayward this is the 'liberating and empowering' aspect within national frameworks.

Drawing also upon the work of Frantz Fanon, Hayward points out that the insertion of a colonizing culture within the maternal body of an indigenous culture involves the reproduction of a new (national) culture, which is distinct from both the colonizer culture and the repressed culture of the colonized. Here, as Fanon has argued, the 'native poet' finds a significant role in mediation and negotiation. This involves denouncing the oppressor in the pre-liberation period, as well as questioning the indigenous past in the postcolonial moment. The 'native poet-filmmaker', writes Hayward, 'must negotiate that pre-history through the colonial past and call everything into question [...] and do so by addressing his/her own people, by making [...] the people the *subject* not the *object* of his/her art' (2000: 100). Echoing Fanon, Hayward emphasizes that it is only from this post-liberation moment that a national culture can be spoken of: 'a culture of combat' that 'calls on the whole people to fight for their existence as a nation' (2000: 101). The fact that cinema is not a pure product but a hybrid of many economic, ethnic, discursive and sexed cultures makes it, in Hayward's view, a multi- or 'pluricultural' entity just as the nation itself. Rather than being the offspring of a sole patriarchal discourse or reproduced within a single maternal body, national cinema's reproducers are varied and scattered. This is, for Hayward, another way in which national cinema can problematize the myth of a unified and homogeneous nation. In doing so it exposes the ideological operations of nationalism and the concealed structures of power and knowledge (ibid.).

Conclusion

The review of some major standpoints in the national cinema debate has made it clear that the relation between cinema and nation is a complex and problematic one. Globalization may have intensified debates about the 'End of the Nation-State' and thus generated further discussions on the meaning of national cinema, yet as Williams (2002b) has noted, cinema and nationalism have *always* had a difficult relationship. There is no simple one-to-one relation between people living in a particular territory and what is assumed to be their shared sense of national culture and identity. To use Rosen's words, the nation is a 'differentiated, local, conjunctural, historical' phenomenon and national cinema is only 'one possible form' of understanding the nation. But we should also bear in mind that cinema or any other art form is not simply a mirror, which merely reflects a nation's culture or identity, in the different and changing meanings that can be attributed to the latter. Any effort made to 'read' national identity or cultural specificity in the films of a particular national cinema should thus take into account the role that cinema itself plays in constructing and reinforcing 'the nation', as well as critiquing and rearticulating the dominant or preferred meaning of this term.

With respect to the question of how to study a national cinema, Hayward's approach in examining what she calls the 'typologies' of a national cinema is useful. The latter, according to her, involves a range of elements such as 'narratives', 'genres', 'codes and conventions', 'gesturality and morphology', 'stars', 'centre/periphery cinema', and 'modes of myth making' that can help in recognizing the differences among national cinemas and within them (Hayward 2005: 8). As Higson has pointed out, however, focusing merely on the production of films, rather than their reception and consumption, would not be sufficient in the study of national cinema (Higson 2002). Taking account of the discourses that constitute the 'intellectual film-culture' and the criteria by which films are praised or denigrated, can provide further insights into how the national is articulated in different geographic contexts and historical moments. Moreover the way audiences make sense of national film productions, whether they identify with and have a sense of pride in them, or ignore and even despise their national cinema for producing unrepresentative or poor quality films in comparison with 'foreign films', are also important matters in this respect.

By analyzing film texts, examining critical film-cultures and researching audiences, however, we should not, to echo Willemen, neglect the 'significant structuring impact' that national institutions, political organizations and economic infrastructures have on different cultural forms, including cinema. As Williams has put it, apart from being mere artifacts, films are also seen – primarily by governments and industry lobbyists – as cultural and economic weapons. The study of national cinemas therefore needs to pay appropriate attention to cultural policy, government decrees, legislations on cinema, statistics and logistics of the film industry, and regional or international frameworks of production and distribution.

On the question of the relevance or usefulness, or otherwise, of national cinema in an age of globalization, it can be argued that there are still strong reasons that justify the continued relevance of this term. Firstly, contrary to the earlier predictions of hyper-globalists, nation states are not yet showing any significant sign of decline. They remain strong institutions and continue to determine many aspects of the political, economic, social and cultural spheres of human life. The 'global financial crisis' of 2008–9 and the unprecedented levels of state intervention in the 'free market' have discredited not only the neo-liberal policies of 'deregulation', but also the utopian claims about the 'End of the Nation-State'. Even when the problem is understood as a *global* crisis and there are moves to intervene across a common transnational front, nation states remain the key players.

We do need to understand, as the above shows, that the national is not fixed or unified other than in ideology, that is it only dangerously confused with nationalism, and that it is constantly in the process of construction by many active participants, from governments to media and ordinary citizens. It seems, therefore, that there are still strong reasons for academics to debate national cinema in a globalizing context, to analyze the transformation of its meaning over time, to inform and influence film policy, and to continue exposing the processes of inclusion and exclusion involved, with the hope of expanding the opportunities for the marginalized and the under-represented.

The second point that can be raised in defense of the continuing relevance of national cinema in the age of globalization is the observation by many cultural analysts and globalization theorists that 'far from destroying it, globalization has been perhaps the most significant force in creating and proliferating cultural identity' (Tomlinson 2003: 16). Cultural and national identities certainly do change and transform, yet their significance, though in differently articulated hybrid and syncretic forms, seems to have generally intensified following the advancement of global communication systems and the rapid increase in the transnational movements of people, capital and commodities. In a world where territorial borders can no longer effectively block inter-cultural communications and interactions, people seem to become more and more aware of their differences from others, as well as realizing their similarities. National cinemas can play a significant role in this respect, enabling nations to recognize 'the other', to acknowledge differences and similarities, and to experience the possibility of mutual understanding and respect.

The third reason why it is still meaningful, even necessary, to speak of national cinema is, to quote Hayward, the 'empowering and liberating' aspects of national cinema. Many nations continue to be engaged in a long and difficult struggle toward self-definition and liberation. The hegemonic forces of global capitalism continue to dominate the world of politics, economics and culture and the fight against the exploitations and excesses of the 'Empire' continues. The neo-colonialist desire to incorporate all nations and cultures and dismantle any site of rebellion and defiance still faces resistance movements in different parts of the world. In many of these instances 'the nation' and 'the national' provide common ground for action, although both local and transnational groups and networks are also becoming increasingly influential. As Fredric Jameson has noted:

> when one positions the threat of identity at a higher lever globally, then [...] it is not national state power that is the enemy of difference, but rather the transnational system itself, Americanization and the standardized products of a henceforth uniform and standardized ideology and practice of consumption. At this point, nation-states and their national cultures are called upon to play a positive role, hitherto assigned – against them – to regions and local practices.
>
> (Jameson 1998a: 74)

Indeed the 'national' can find new meaning in such conditions, by which it is refined and situated, rather than being cancelled. National cinema is in this respect a major standpoint for the colonized, the marginalized and the oppressed to reclaim their agency. It is a means to return the denigrating gaze of 'the civilized world'. It is an opportunity for the subaltern to assert his/her subjectivity in defiance of the humiliating identity ascribed to him/her. It is a site for the representation of those who are unrepresented or misrepresented within the hegemonic discourses and images of the global corporate media.

Of course in recognizing the empowering and liberating aspects of national cinema, we should not overlook the possibility that national film productions may also retreat into reactionary politics, or fall within the framework of the hegemonic discourses of neo-colonialism. The fact that an allegedly high-art progressive film about Afghanistan, produced by an internationally celebrated Iranian director receives public admiration and publicity by the White House just a few weeks after the US bombardment of Afghanistan[4] clearly demonstrates why we should be more cautious in making idealistic generalizations in this respect.

---

[4] This incident relates to the film *Kandahar* (2001) by Mohsen Makhmalbaf, which will be discussed in more detail in Chapter 4.

PART II

IRANIAN CINEMA AND GLOBALIZATION

Chapter 3

Iranian Cinema in the World Cinema Circuit: Politics, Economics and Aesthetics

The foundations of a 'new cinema'

The rise to prominence of Iranian cinema's profile on the world stage in the 1990s was unprecedented in its entire history and unexpected given the post-revolutionary circumstances. During this decade the number of short and feature-length Iranian films present in international film festivals increased sharply from 88 appearances in 1989 to 980 in 2000.[1] The number of awards won by these films also demonstrates a significant rise from 17 to 98 in the respective years.[2] As early as 1992 the director of the New York Film Festival considered Iranian cinema as 'one of the most exciting in the world' and the Toronto International Film Festival declared it as 'one of the pre-eminent national cinemas' (quoted in Naficy 2002: 53). There were, however, a number of different factors involved in facilitating such a significant development that should not be overlooked. First and foremost, as Eric Egan has pointed out, was the establishment of 'an industrial and economic base capable of supporting and sustaining a production capacity [of] around fifty productions per year', which played a major role in this process (Egan 2005: 22). This begs the question of why it was necessary in the 1980s to *establish* a sustainable base for Iranian cinema while the industry had in fact been operating for decades.

The economy of Iranian cinema had gone bankrupt a year before the 1979 revolution due to the influx of cheap foreign films, an increase in taxes on local films and the growing number of films on cinema screens with explicit sexual content that alienated many of the traditional and religious, as well as educated and intellectual audiences. Local production was shattered from around 100 films a year in the 1960s to a record low figure of only 11 films in 1978. Following the consolidation of power under the Islamic Republic and the establishment of a stable government, a number of significant measures were taken by the new government to revitalize Iranian cinema (Naficy 2002: 36–43). Film imports were monopolized and strictly controlled through a newly created Farabi Cinema Foundation, which acted as the Ministry of Culture and Islamic Cultivation's executive branch for cinema. 'The banning of foreign films, of Hollywood in particular', writes Hamid Dabashi, 'will go a long way in explaining how the Islamic censorship had the unanticipated consequence of creating a considerable domestic market for critically acclaimed films' (Dabashi 2008: 12).

---

[1] Figures from a report titled *25 Years of Iranian Cinema* issued by Farabi Cinema Foundation in 2004.
[2] ibid.

The banning of Hollywood might have had *unanticipated* outcomes, but there were also a number of other measures taken by the post-revolutionary authorities that show a clear intention to facilitate the creation of a new cinema. Hamid Naficy has demonstrated, for instance, that many more public-sector institutions, government agencies and semi-government organizations became engaged in the production of films than in the previous regime. To boost the economy of the local film industry the municipal tax on tickets sold for foreign films was increased from 20 per cent to 25 per cent, while for local films it was decreased from 20 per cent to 5 per cent. In the 1987 national budget proposed by the government and approved in the Parliament, a particular clause was added that obliged state banks to offer long-term loans for film producers. A year later a new rating system was introduced that would enable 'high quality' films to have higher ticket prices, be screened in better film theaters and enjoy a longer run in exhibition. Of course new regulations and film production guidelines were also put in place to 'purify' Iranian cinema of its previous 'corrupt' content, as well as assuring the films' compliance with Islamic codes of conduct and revolutionary values.

Acknowledging the above developments and their cultural and political implications, Naficy concludes 'that the Revolution led to the emergence of a new, vital cinema, with its own special industrial and financial structure and unique ideological, thematic and production values' (Naficy 2002: 29). From a different perspective, Dabashi, who considers 'national traumas' as being highly influential in the emergence of national cinemas, states that '[i]t is not *despite* the Islamic Revolution and the republic that succeeded it but in fact *because* of them that we can have a causal insight into the rise to global prominence of Iranian cinema' (Dabashi 2008: 12, emphasis in original).

The emergence of Muslim film-makers

One of the outcomes of the 1979 revolution in terms of cinema was the emergence of a group of committed Muslim and revolutionary film-makers, who sought a radical departure from the cinematic genres, themes and conventions prevailing in the pre-revolution cinema. This group who largely had urban working-class or lower middle-class backgrounds became distinguished from the *pre-revolution* film-makers and artists who, if not banned from artistic and cultural production, were generally viewed with a degree of skepticism by the new cultural authorities. The reasons ranged from their association with the cultural institutions of the Pahlavis to producing 'immoral' and 'corrupt' art and film. Even pro-revolution artists who had Leftist or Nationalist agendas such as Masoud Kimiai and Bahram Beizai were not seen in the same light as the Muslim revolutionary artists and film-makers who, though relatively small in number, received more official support. This may partly explain the continuing tensions between film-makers like Makhmalbaf and Beizai, which will be mentioned below.

One important issue that should be considered, however, is that because of the largely secular orientation of its practitioners and the dominance of a permissive western intellectual culture, the pre-revolution cinema industry excluded a considerable section of Iranian society. Participation in the field of cinema or the arts in general was at the time largely considered incompatible with religious observance, and even those who dared to enter this field were most likely to be marginalized, if not stigmatized as fanatical and reactionary. This point is usually neglected in most accounts of Iranian cinema published in the West. Had it not been for the Islamic Revolution, many post-revolution film-makers would probably never have become involved in film. On the other hand, there was a deep distrust within religious families about the fields of art and film. Post-revolutionary film-makers like Mohsen Makhmalbaf and Ebrahim Hatami-kia – whose work will be discussed in the following chapters – have spoken of how their families even prevented them from going to the movies before the revolution (Dabashi 2002: 129; Mir-ehsan 2006: 43).

After the revolution and with the formation of an Islamic Republic, traditional and religious sections of Iranian society began gradually to trust cinema because they believed it had been 'purified' of its 'immoral' and 'corrupt' pre-revolutionary elements such as nudity and scenes of an explicit sexual nature. Ayatollah Khomeini's famous phrase in his first speech after the revolution was influential in this respect: 'We are not against cinema, we are against decadence'. Yet Muslim artists and film-makers felt an urgent obligation to go further and contribute to the establishment of an 'Islamic' and 'revolutionary' cinema. They soon realized that there was hardly any theoretical framework available that could clarify and define the notion of 'Islamic art', particularly when it came to modern art forms such as film. Some of them like Mohsen Makhmalbaf and Sayyed Morteza Avini sought to articulate such a theoretical foundation. Being merely engaged with the theory of 'Islamic art' or a critique of western art, however, did not totally satisfy them. They were also deeply concerned about the revival of the vulgar pre-revolution cinema in a new revolutionary and Islamic guise (Dabashi 2001: 181). Makhmalbaf, therefore, decided to make a film that would act as an example of an 'Islamic film' and set the standards for other Muslim and revolutionary film-makers. As one critic has put it 'the main motivation behind their involvement in film was not merely an interest in art or cultural production [...] they wanted to express their personal experiences and convey their messages' (Talebi-nejad 2006: 32).[3]

The result was that Makhmalbaf made his first film *Nasooh's Repentance* (1982) while he had no prior experience or training in film production. It therefore clearly contains many cinematic flaws and artistic shortcomings, which film critics were quick to identify. For some critics *Nasooh's Repentance* was so much below the 'professional standards' of film-making that they even refused to accept it as a 'film'. This was very frustrating for Makhmalbaf who comments on the event with anger: 'Some began to say that my work wasn't really

---

[3] All quotes from Farsi sources are my translation. I have used transliteration of the Farsi titles of the references in the bibliography to distinguish Farsi sources from those accounts that were originally in English.

"cinema," – which I have concluded is an idiotic charge – all of my work is cinema. Whose definition of "cinema" do the rest of us have to conform to?' (Dabashi 2001: 185). Most studies of Makhmalbaf's cinema dismiss his early work on the grounds of its poor cinematic structure, and its 'Islamist' and 'ideological' content. Dabashi, for instance, uses terms such as 'disastrous', 'malignant catastrophe' and 'mental malaise' to describe the films of 'the early Makhmalbaf', suggesting that this was a 'valley of dead certainties' that he had to pass in order to reach some 'glorious conclusions'. In Dabashi's view Makhmalbaf

> had to exorcize [his ideological demons] from his creative body and project them onto the screen to see their monumental emptiness for himself. These films thus cure him of his afflictions. They are so therapeutic precisely because they are so poisonous.
>
> (Dabashi 2002: 132–3)

Such dramatic judgments expressed from secular and elitist standpoints pay little attention to how these 'poisonous' or 'catastrophic' films were received by different audiences in Iran at the time. One reason behind the Muslim film-makers' rise to prominence in the post-revolution era was that their films, despite many technical flaws, were rooted in the depth of impoverished sections of the society and therefore captured the hearts of millions of the poor and pious people of Iran, who were largely unrepresented or misrepresented in the pre-revolution cinema. One Iranian critic's words on 'the early Makhmalbaf' are illuminating in this respect:

> We, who are nothing in the world of cinema but audiences, have the right to be enthusiastic about *Marriage of the Blessed* (1988), and to be stimulated to think about our afterlife by *Nasooh's Repentance* (1982). We don't care at all whether what we saw was a 'film', or if it could be named 'cinema' or not. Whatever [merits] the early Makhmalbaf may have lacked, he was appealing and unique [...]. We, as the poor and the repressed, did not have any festival to award him for his films then. We could only pray for him: 'God bless you Mohsen! You have voiced [the pains of] our hearts'.
>
> (Abak 2007)

The results of a survey conducted in 1989 by the Centre for Cinematic Research and Studies in Tehran shows that while most masters of Iranian cinema received only 1 per cent of the participants' approval as 'the best Iranian director', Makhmalbaf topped the list by a staggering 19 per cent (Baharloo 2000).

Another issue ignored in the many accounts on Iranian cinema is how the films of Muslim film-makers contributed to building trust and transforming skeptical views toward an 'alien' medium called cinema. These efforts even resulted in cinema being admitted to sacred spaces and reaching audiences, which it had scarcely done before. In an interview with the Iranian *Cinema Weekly* in 1996, Makhmalbaf credits himself with having practically reconciled religion and cinema in Iran: 'My film *Nasooh's Repentance* (1982) was being screened in mosques.

This was no small incident' (Mansoori 1996: 6). Bearing in mind the serious antagonism of religious authorities to cinema prior to the revolution and the burning down of cinema theaters by angry religious revolutionaries, there is certainly no exaggeration in Makhmalbaf's claim. The local reception and strong impact of Makhmalbaf's early cinema, as we shall see in the following chapter, stands in sharp contrast with his more recent 'transnational' films such as *Sex and Philosophy* (2005) and *Scream of the Ants* (2006) that have disappointed and alienated even the most loyal and sympathetic film critics on the reformist side of the Iranian political spectrum. But the debates and controversies over the international awards of Iranian cinema, as I suggest below, began long before Makhmalbaf's recent controversial films were made.

Debate and controversy over international awards

Different authors and critics have offered varying explanations for the international prominence of Iranian cinema in the 1990s. Egan, for instance, argues that apart from the establishment of a sustainable economy, an equally significant reason was 'the emergence of an atmosphere of increased artistic freedom' after the end of the eight-year war with Iraq in 1989 and the subsequent change of the government (Egan 2005: 22). Egan maintains that the Iranian government's intention to re-establish relations with the western world and its desire to deconstruct the stereotypical images of Iran in western media led to an 'officially sanctioned' promotion of Iranian cinema in international film festivals and art-film circuits (2005: 119). He believes the Iranian government manipulated these films to present a 'false image of the existence of a liberal and vibrant cultural atmosphere' in Iran (2005: 128). This statement, not only contrasts with Egan's above acknowledgment of 'an atmosphere of increased artistic freedom' in the post-war era, it also contradicts the remark from the Iranian religious leader, quoted on the same page of Egan's book as saying, 'It does not impress me if we win foreign awards because these film [festivals] often have dubious agendas' (2005: 128).

While the international promotion of Iranian cinema by the Farabi Foundation and its International Bureau since the 1980s is no secret, we should not neglect the fact that many powerful branches of government in Iran, as well as some official and semi-official media, have always been highly skeptical of western festivals and their 'hidden agendas' in awarding prizes to certain Iranian films. Kiarostami's celebration by French critics in the early 1990s coincided with his facing some extremely harsh criticism about the content of his films by some Muslim Iranian critics (Dabashi 2007b: 286–91; Elena 2005: 103–4). More recently in 2006, Iranian television broadcast a series of programs entitled *Cinemaye Jashnvareh'i* ('Festival Cinema') produced by the veteran film critic Masoud Ferasati who has been one of the most fierce and outspoken critics of Kiarostami and Makhmalbaf over the past two decades.[4] Skeptics like

---

[4] The program comprised a series of interviews and debates involving Iranian film-makers, critics and policy-makers regarding Iranian cinema's presence in international festivals. The transcription of the interviews and debates were recently published in Iran as book titled *Cinema-Jashnvareh* (*Cinema-Festival*): (Moazzezi-nia 2009).

Ferasati maintain that the majority of films that are celebrated and awarded prizes in western festivals are those that represent either a gloomy and dark image of social conditions under the Islamic Republic, or an exotic and primitive image of Iranians in rural settings.

Not all Iranian films critics, however, agree on this point and there are also critics and historians who have written or edited books in praise of internationally successful filmmakers like Kiarostami and Makhmalbaf (Baharloo 2000; Karimi 1987; Qookasian 1996). Hooshang Golmakani, a veteran film critic and editor of the most influential film periodical in Iran (*Film Monthly*), even made a documentary on Makhmalbaf entitled *Gong-e Khabdideh* (*A Dumb Man's Dream*, 1996), which represents the evolution and different stages of Makhmalbaf's career in a very sympathetic tone, largely based on Makhmalbaf's own narration of his life and films.

It is important to note that these contested readings of internationally celebrated Iranian films are also visible within the Iranian diaspora. The success of post-revolutionary Iranian films has been subject to much debate and controversy among artists, critics and ordinary viewers who live outside Iran. Naficy, for example, describes how he faced some strong opposition and protest from a group of pre-revolutionary Iranian film-makers when he was organizing one of the first retrospectives of Iranian cinema in the United States (Naficy 2003b). Artists and film-makers like Parviz Sayad, who left the country after the 1979 revolution, maintained that all post-revolutionary films serve as propaganda for the Islamic state.

The debates on the politics of international festivals will be further discussed below. Meanwhile there are other audiences for Iranian transnational cinema within the diaspora who, far from viewing these films as propaganda, consider them damaging to the image of Iran in the West. Mehrnaz Saeed-Vafa, another Iranian academic based in the US, writes of Iranian audiences abroad who feel 'betrayed' when they watch some of the Iranian films screened in the West that portray images of 'backwardness' and 'underdevelopment'. Saeed-Vafa suggests that many Iranians in North America or Europe have already experienced the negative impact of the western media's stereotypical images of Iran and thus when confronted by some Iranian films 'have expressed shame and anger at the screen images they have seen of Iran' (Saeed-Vafa 2002: 201). As we can see from the above responses, not all audiences of Iranian 'festival films' praise these films for having the aesthetic qualities or progressive themes that 'international critics' identify in them.

The economics and politics of international festivals

Some critics of 'The New Iranian Cinema' have highlighted the politics and economics involved in the operations of international festival and exhibition venues that have celebrated Iranian cinema. Farahmand (2002), for example, points to the investment of European companies in Iranian films and argues that this is inspired by economic rather than merely cultural reasons. She believes that the very low budgets of Iranian films – compared to international standards – and the profitable market that some of these films have found have encouraged such investments (2002: 94). Even the motives of a festival director like Marco Muller, who has played a major role in the international success of Iranian cinema, are, in Farahmand's view, derived from economic interests – through his involvement in private companies that finance and (co)produce 'world cinema' – and not just his fascination with distinct film cultures (2002: 94).

In terms of the active involvement of the Iranian government in the promotion of Iranian films abroad, Farahmand argues that western festivals have in fact been politically selective in showcasing Iranian films. In her view these festivals have excluded many of the more political and critical Iranian films – like those of the veteran Bahram Beizai – and preferred film-makers like Kiarostami, who has been cautious in avoiding the 'circles of perturbation', as defined by the Iranian cultural authorities (Farahmand 2002: 99). Kiarostami's 'political escapism', Farahamand writes, 'caters to the festival taste for high art and restrained politics' (2002: 99). Dabashi has also commented on the 'catalytic effect' that European and North American venues of film festivals and distributions have 'on degenerating the effective politics of the films they thus showcase into a liberal transnationalism that robs them of their revolutionary form and rebellious function' (Dabashi 2008: 32)

The total absence of female characters in many of Kiarostami's films, for instance, is seen by Farahmand as evidence of his compliance with the Islamic authorities' guidelines regarding female actresses and their 'proper' characterization in cinema (2002: 99).[5] As further evidence, Farahamand refers to the intervention of Iran's Foreign Minister in facilitating the last-minute entry of Kiarostami's *Taste of Cherry* (1996) in the Cannes Film Festival.[6] For Farahmand the success of *Taste of Cherry* in achieving the most significant international award in the whole history of Iranian cinema is largely seen as an outcome of the Iranian Foreign Minister's mediation and negotiation: 'Ali Akbar Velayati [the Foreign Minister], came to realize that the film's presence at Cannes would have a good impact outside Iran. He therefore mediated its entry in the festival through negotiation with Gilles Jacob, the festival director' (2002: 95).

Clearly this intervention would not account for the actual judgment of the festival jury. The significant piece missing in Farahmand's illustration of the event is that Iran's Ministry of Culture and Islamic Cultivation, which authorizes the production, exhibition and export of Iranian films, had actually barred *Taste of Cherry*'s entry into Cannes by not issuing a permit for its copy to be sent to the festival. While this was said to be merely for some technical irregularities, most commentators at the time believed that the problem was caused by the film's central theme of suicide. The other point that Farahmand fails to mention is that Kiarostami was at the time already a celebrated figure among French critics and a couple

---

[5] It should be noted that since making the film *Ten* (2002) – which focused on the real life of ten different women in Tehran – Kiarostami has increasingly been attentive to the representation of women in his films.
[6] Kiarostami's film was not officially announced as being included in the festival's competition section at the beginning, but was screened for the jury at a later stage and subsequently won the Palme d'Or.

of months earlier a special issue of *Cahiers du Cinema* with his picture on the cover was dedicated to his films.[7] Clearly this had nothing to do with the Iranian Foreign Minister.

At the time however, Gilles Jacob, who was certainly eager to include Kiarostami's latest film in the festival's program, wrote a letter to Iran's Foreign Ministry requesting him to authorize the submission of the film's copy to the festival through the Iranian embassy in Paris. Of course the Minister did respond to this request and in effect overruled the Ministry of Culture's ban, yet clearly the underlying reasons for the film's success in Cannes were beyond the intentions and actions of the Foreign Minister. Otherwise we should have witnessed at least a few other interventions of this kind that would have involved more Palmes d'Or for Iranian cinema. On the contrary, in the past 15 years that success has not happened again. In 2002 Kiarostami submitted his latest film *Ten* to the Cannes festival, only to be disappointed by the select committee who did not even select it for the competition section. This happened again in 2008 when Kiarostami's *Shirin* was submitted and subsequently rejected by the festival. More recently however, his latest film *Certified Copy* (2010) was selected for the competition section and its actress – Juliette Binoche – won the Best Actress award. It should be noted however that *Certified Copy* was submitted as a European co-production and its narrative and characters were not in any clear sense related to Iran.

Skeptics like Egan and Farahmand are not alone in exaggerating the role played by the Iranian government in facilitating the international achievements of Iranian cinema. Bahram Beizai, widely considered a master in Iranian cinema, has in an interview criticized western festivals for awarding prizes to film-makers like Makhmalbaf who, in Beizai's view, are affiliated with the Islamic government rather than being its opposition:

We have a real opposition but now the opposition of Iran is Mohsen Makhmalbaf. Makhmalbaf is a Muslim. He is not antagonist or intellectual. He is not an Iranian intellectual but Muslim intellectual. He is a pseudo-intellectual who represents them [the government]. Foreigners that award him cannot see the pseudo-intellectual that the Ministry of Information[8] has made. Many Iranian intellectuals are refused these awards. They have no possibilities, no money to make films or theatre and no spectators. I cannot make films because they do not like it. [*sic*]

(Dönmez-Colin 2006: 36)[9]

Beizai, who was disqualified from teaching at Tehran University after the revolution and has had many of his plays and scripts denied a production permit by government

---

[7] *Cahiers du Cinema*, issue no. 493, July–August 1995.
[8] In Iran the Ministry of Information is the authority in charge of secret intelligence and security.
[9] Beizai's quite absurd distinction between 'Iranian intellectuals' and 'Muslim intellectuals' (rather than the more conventional secular intellectuals–Muslim intellectuals), and his clear preference for the former is noteworthy here. This view stems from his well-known passion for 'Persian heritage' as well as his cultural nationalism. For a critique of nationalism in Beizai's film *Bahshu the Little Stranger* (1985), see (Rahimieh 2002).

censorship boards, seems to be implying that international film festivals do or should have a political agenda in supporting artists or intellectuals in other countries, yet in the case of Makhmalbaf, he believes the festivals have mistakenly identified him as an oppositional figure. Ironically, however, while today Makhmalbaf declares himself to be in a state of 'exile' due to the Iranian government's pressure on artists and film-makers, Beizai's most recent film *Vaqti Hame Khabim* (*When We are All Asleep*, 2008) was not only issued a permit by the government, it was also awarded one of the main prizes at the International Fajr Film Festival in Tehran.

Moreover, while Beizai considers Makhmalbaf as a creation of the Iranian intelligence services, during the 2006 Cannes festival Makhmalbaf famously claimed that the Iranian government was conspiring to assassinate him. Following an explosion that took place close to the shooting location of a film by Makhmalbaf's daughter in Afghanistan and led to the killing of one horse, a short documentary of the incident was released by Makhmalbaf at the Cannes festival. He called the incident a 'terrorist attack' against himself and declared that in case of any similar incident in the future that may lead to his death, the Islamic state should be held responsible (Amiri 2007). Another interesting accusation pointed at the Iranian government by Makhmalbaf was that Iranian embassies had lobbied with international film festivals and 'paid them off' in return for the rejection of his films (ibid.).

Regardless of the substance of these charges, they could be seen as evidence of the fact that Iranian cinema's honeymoon with international film festivals may have reached an end. In sharp contrast to the situation a few years earlier in which '[w]hen spotted on the street at Cannes, Locarno, Venice, or Berlin prominent Iranian filmmakers like Makhmalbaf [were] harassed to the point of abuse by directors of film festivals to get their most recent films premiered at one and not at the other' (Dabashi 2007b: 328), today there seems to be little left of that enthusiasm and fierce competition over the acquisition of films that just happen to be 'from Iran' or are made by a limited number of Iranian directors. The problem is that some Iranian film-makers like Makhmalbaf were so enchanted by the delights of international recognition and praise that they took up new careers as 'borderless artists' and became totally detached from the national cinema and local film culture they had emerged from. As it will be argued in the following study of Makhmalbaf, this new 'transnational' status, rather than enhancing the aesthetics and advancing the politics of his work has resulted in self-indulgent styles and parochial, even reactionary, themes. Moreover, the decline of enthusiasm for Makhmalbaf's cinema at the international level is paralleled by an unprecedented degree of scathing criticism from local critics who believe that their national cinema has lost one of its important film-makers.

In sharp contrast to the case of Makhmalbaf and even that of Kiarostami however, we have witnessed in recent years the rise of a new star from Iranian cinema on the world stage. Asghar Farhadi's recent films *About Elli* (2009) and *A Separation* (2011), which both received international recognition and praise, are strikingly 'Iranian' in terms of their themes, characters and primary audience. Unlike many 'festival films', these two films became very successful at the box office inside Iran and were celebrated by local critics.

After many years during which even big names such as Makhmalbaf and Kiarostami failed to win any significant awards at major international festivals, Iranian cinema has now a new face in the world cinema circuit. Farhadi seems to have learned lessons from both classic narrative cinema, and from the realist and documentary-style cinemas of his predecessors in Iran. This appears to be what makes him and his cinema quite different.

Selecting the examples

When it comes to the question of the impact of globalization on Iranian cinema, perhaps most critics and academics will tend to focus on a particular band of internationally renowned Iranian film-makers whose professional career – whether in terms of the funding, production, distribution or exhibition of their films – transcends national territories and geographic borders. One reason for this preference may lie in the fact that in the case of Iranian cinema there is little, if any, evidence of the developments and changes in other national cinemas – such as foreign investment and ownership in the film industry, vertical integration of privately owned media sectors, launch of major multiplex chains, production of 'national blockbusters' – which are usually associated with globalization. It is sometimes ironically assumed, therefore, that the only elements of Iranian *national* cinema that can be examined in terms of the impacts of globalization are *inter*nationally celebrated films and *trans*national film-makers. This strand of Iranian cinema – which we might name as its transnational dimension – clearly deserves particular attention and critical analysis. The examination of Makhmalbaf's cinema presented in Chapter 4 aims to meet this need.

The study of the impact of globalization on Iranian cinema, however, cannot be confined to its transnational dimension, for transnational film-makers and their films constitute a relatively small fraction of Iranian cinema and do not represent it as a whole. Moreover, as discussed in Chapter 1, globalization is not only about the compression of the world through transnational flows and interactions, but also about a new consciousness of the world as a single space (Robertson 1992). From this point of view, the impact of globalization would not be limited to the transnational section of Iranian cinema but could also be traced in its national and local dimensions. We might even go further to suggest that one way of acknowledging the profound and complex consequences of globalization – or 'glocalization' – is by investigating its effects within certain spheres and domains where they are least expected.

With respect to the limits of this research, two other Iranian film-makers who each represent a different dimension of Iranian cinema have been selected as the other case studies. The first is Daryush Mehrjui, one of the pioneers of the 'New Wave' in Iranian cinema, who has been consistently contributing to this cinema for over four decades. In a recent poll published by the leading Iranian film magazine *Film Monthly*, Mehrjui's films were credited by Iranian critics as being exemplarily 'national'. Within Iranian national cinema, therefore, we notice a director whose films are considered *more* national than others. Chapter 5 investigates what this means and explores how globalization has influenced the representation of 'the nation' in Mehrjui's films.

In order to diversify the examples further, particularly with respect to the new condition of Iranian cinema after the 1979 Islamic Revolution, the final case study focuses on the work of Ebrahim Hatami-kia, who is one of the most prominent film-makers of the post-revolution era. Hatami-kia is a founding figure of *cinemaye defa'e moqaddas* (sacred defense cinema): one of the most important components of post-revolution Iranian cinema, which has been hardly acknowledged in the West. Some critics may simply dismiss this cinema as a parochial and ideologically unified – if not propagandist – part of the broader category of Iranian war films. On the contrary, I aim to demonstrate that such dismissive views fail to recognize the diversity and sophistication of some 'sacred defense' films. Moreover, if we are to consider post-revolution Iranian cinema as having an 'Islamic' dimension, then, arguably, sacred defense cinema will be its most significant example. Given the intensification of debates on the relation of Islam and globalization in recent years, particularly after 11th September 2001, I aim to ask how globalization has influenced the work of a highly acclaimed Muslim film-maker in Iranian cinema.

Needless to say, distinguishing the transnational, national and Islamic aspects of Iranian cinema does not mean that these are clear-cut categories. Many Iranian films and film-makers may straddle these groupings, including some of the films discussed in the following chapters. The blurring of the borders between the transnational, the national and the Islamic, as it shall be indicated, can itself be considered as one of the outcomes of globalization.

Chapter 4

Mohsen Makhmalbaf's 'Transnational' Cinema and Globalization

Introduction

In his book *Makhmalbaf at Large: The Making of a Rebel Filmmaker*, Hamid Dabashi rejects the universal validity of Jean Baudrillard's observation that the postmodern world has created a transaesthetic realm of indifference in the field of arts (Dabashi 2008: 199). Dabashi accuses Baudrillard of Eurocentrism and, on the contrary, refers to Makhmalbaf's cinema as an example of emancipatory and liberating art in the age of the postmodern. This is a cinema, Dabashi writes, that 'harbours, and allows for, no *transaesthetics of indifference*', since Makhmalbaf is 'a caring intellect, a vision of the otherwise, the sound and the fury of the im/possible' (Dabashi 2008: 201). With respect to the issue of globalization, Dabashi suggests that Makhmalbaf has applied 'a guerrilla tactic of planting a Trojan Horse in the belly of globalizing capital' (ibid.).

This chapter investigates how globalization has influenced the films, the politics and the cultural status of Makhmalbaf in Iranian cinema. As a film-maker who played a significant role in the (re)construction of a national cinema after the Islamic Revolution, it is important to see where he stands today as a 'transnational artist' and how his 'borderless' work is received within or outside Iran. But I will begin by examining one of the recent theoretical elaborations on 'transnational art'.[1]

Critique of the 'transnational institution of art'

In a recent article titled 'Globalization and Art; Then and Now', Noël Carroll argues that a new 'integrated, interconnected, transnational artworld' has now emerged (Carroll 2007: 139). International art exhibitions and film festivals, in his view, play a major role in this respect since they pave the way for 'foreign language' and independent artists and film-makers to exhibit work that 'challenges the routine product of the mass media'. Such festivals, he writes 'bring *sophisticated work* from everywhere to *serious audiences* in search of something different' (2007: 133, emphasis added).

---

[1] Since the first manuscript of the present book was submitted for review and publication, other literature on transnational cinema have become available, which are not discussed here (Ďurovičová and Newman 2010; Higbee and Lim 2010). A revised and updated version of this chapter is due to appear in a collection of essays titled *De-Westernising Film Studies* (Higbee and Maty Ba forthcoming).

Prior to this stage, Carroll states, art and cultural products did travel across borders yet their 'canons' and 'artworlds' remained discrete. Citing examples such as the impact of Turkish music on Mozart, African art on Picasso, and Japanese Ukiyo-e School on Impressionist painters, he emphasizes that 'while Europeans appreciated [Asian] artifacts and collected them, neither the works nor the masters who produced them were incorporated into European art narratives or artistic canons' (2007: 138). Today, on the contrary, artists and critics from different parts of the world 'share a number of conceptual frameworks and hermeneutical strategies that facilitate understanding transnationally' (2007: 140–1).

For Carroll different aspects of 'progressive politics, such as postcolonialism, feminism, gay liberation, globalization and global inequality, the suppression of free expression and other human rights, identity politics, and the politics of representation, as well as a generic anti-establishmentarianism' can be considered as recurring themes in transnational art (2007: 141). He contends that there are also some common forms and 'sense-making strategies' among these artworks which make them accessible to their audiences. Forms such as pastiche and strategies such as 'radical juxtaposition, de-familiarization, and the de-contextualization of objects and images from their customary milieus' are some examples he provides. These themes, forms and strategies, says Carroll, together create 'a worldwide discursive framework' or a 'toolkit' for accessing and interpreting 'if not all then at least a very great deal of ambitious art from all over' (2007: 141–2). He thus concludes that today we witness a 'unified transnational institution of art': 'a culturescape with its own language games and networks of communication, distribution, and reception' (2007: 141–2).

There is certainly more than a grain of truth in Carroll's description of the developments and changes in the field of arts in the age of globalization. Yet it seems that Carroll's observation stems from a rather elitist standpoint, which largely focuses on 'sophisticated work' and its modernist and postmodernist techniques that amuse 'serious audiences'. His perspective appears to be that of western critics and theorists located at the metropolitan centres of the world, who are enthusiastic about the new opportunities available to them, including the privilege of having access to artworks from other parts of the world, or the possibility of watching 'foreign language' films from other national cinemas, which are discovered by American and European connoisseurs. It seems that in such a theorization of a 'unified' transnational artworld, the histories and national cultural configurations that influenced the vision and the work of 'transnational artists' are by and large transcended.

Glancing at the list of examples Carroll provides as the shared themes and forms – or 'language games' – of the 'transnational institution of art', we notice that most of them in fact originate in European and North American schools of thought and art. It may thus be suggested that what Carroll is really celebrating is the fact that nowadays many artists from all over the world have, thanks to globalization, been elevated to the standards of artistic expression and creation as defined in 'the West'. Rather than signalling a new transnational space of artistic production, which transcends national boundaries and broadens the artists' vision and imagination, this account seems to imply the compliance of artists from marginalized sociocultural formations with the requirements of a dominant intellectual and artistic discourse originating from another local or national formation. This, as the present chapter will demonstrate, seems to be the fate of some 'transnational filmmakers' who seem to have submitted to a rather limited understanding of transnationalism.

In terms of reception Carroll seems to be only concerned about 'transnational audiences', who regularly attend international festivals, galleries and art-houses: those who have the 'cultural capital' necessary for accessing and interpreting transnational art and film. Divergent or contesting readings and interpretations by local audiences and critics, or diasporic audiences who may or may not appreciate the 'transnational cinema' produced by film-makers of their origin, is not taken into account. The celebration and admiration of a number of Iranian film-makers such as Abbas Kiarostami, Mohsen Makhmalbaf and Majid Majidi in European and North American festivals, for instance, remains a matter of debate for many Iranians at home, as well as for those in the diaspora, as demonstrated in the previous chapter.

The reappearance of similar themes in 'transnational art' is for Carroll merely an indication of the fact that artists witness similar problems arising from capitalism and modernization in urban contexts. But it might be added that the politics and economics of international festivals and the preferences of their directors and programmers also play an important role in this respect. Carroll's positive description of the 'transnational institution of art' totally ignores the power relations involved in such institutions and the impact that their choices and awards have on local and national art production.

It would be insufficient for any study of 'transnational cinema' to neglect these concerns and consequences, and to focus merely on the supposed ideal of the emergence of a new 'transnational institution of art'. For the present study it is equally crucial to investigate the changes that may take place in the career of a national film-maker when, as Carroll describes, s/he becomes part of a transnational 'culturescape' with its particular language games and networks of communication, distribution and reception. In what follows I examine Carroll's argument in relation to Iranian cinema and the career of Mohsen Makhmalbaf as a 'transnational film-maker'.

Makhmalbaf: From 'the local' to 'the transnational'

Over the past 15 years Mohsen Makhmalbaf's cinema has arguably become one of the clearest examples of transnational film-making in Iranian cinema. Abbas Kiarostami is without doubt the most distinguished and celebrated among Iranian film-makers in the world of cinema, yet he is quite different from Makhmalbaf in terms of feeling a sense of attachment to his homeland. This is not to say that Kiarostami has not been involved in making transnational productions such as *Certified Copy* (2010): a film with dialogues in English, French and Italian; funded by institutions and companies across Europe; and shot in Italy, featuring a French global star (Juliette Binoche) and a British opera singer (William Shimel). Despite his international reputation and transnational projects, Kiarostami remains deeply attached to what he calls his 'roots' and 'origins'. In an interview he openly expressed these feelings in response to my question on cosmopolitanism:

> I do think global issues and cosmopolitanism are important and the world is, in a sense, our home. But how can we neglect the homeland or forget about it? I don't remember who [rightfully] said that 'being local is the precondition for becoming global'. You have to belong to somewhere; you have to have your roots and origins, but at the same time keep an eye on the global perspective.
>
> (Appendix I).

When asked whether he considered himself as belonging to Iranian 'national cinema', and if he thinks there is, or should be, any such thing at all, Kiarostami replied:

> I really don't know. One thing I'm sure of is that I can't enjoy a nice and relaxed sleep anywhere in the world more than that I do in the closed alley where my house is located. Nowhere else in the world do I feel the peace and comfort which I feel here. When there is no particular reason for me to stay abroad, I can't stand being there even for one day. I belong here [...] I make a film every two years, but I live 365 days a year. This is what I am concerned about. I am a resident here and I can't live anywhere else. I may be able to work in other places, but there is more to life than work.
>
> (Appendix I).

Such an attitude has made Kiarostami an accessible character at the local level.[2] He has remained actively involved in many national and local cultural events, including organizing workshops for young film-makers; exhibiting his photographs; publishing his own poems; and even publishing a series of his selections of classic Persian poetry. As such he also serves to complicate Carroll's notion of transnational artists.

Makhmalbaf, on the contrary, has not spent much time in Iran after directing *Kandahar* (2001).[3] This film which dealt with the fate of Afghan women under the Taliban achieved an unprecedented level of global attention following the events of 11th September 2001. In his own words, Makhmalbaf has preferred 'voluntary vagrancy' as his artistic disposition. Under the 'Frequently Asked Questions' section of the Makhmalbaf Film House website[4] and in response to the question 'Why don't you make films in Iran anymore?' Makhmalbaf says:

---

[2] In my own experience, he personally picked up the phone when I called his house number, and, to my surprise, agreed for an academic interview rather promptly. He invited me to one of his workshops with two dozen enthusiastic film students and responded to my questions during the break.

[3] He did not respond in the present instance to requests for an interview or to questions sent to the Makhmalbaf Film House website.

[4] www.makhmalbaf.com. The question and answers are available in English on the website, although the translation is not always very good. Where necessary I have made changes in square brackets.

We usually live in or around our film locations [...]. This is for better understanding the conditions of our film's subject or in other words to internalise it [...]. This is [also] sort of a voluntary artistic vagrancy in order to avoid the censorship pressures in Iran and also out of keen interest in making films about human issues that happen in places other than Iran. Life is too short and we cannot afford, for example, to wait a decade and waste our time in order for better filmmaking conditions to prevail in our own country.

(Makhmalbaf 2005a).

It is clear that in contrast to Kiarostami who believes 'there's more to life than work', for Makhmalbaf 'better filmmaking conditions' is what determines where he chooses to live. In addition Makhmalbaf has on various occasions proposed the idea of 'filmmakers without frontiers' and argued for the formation of such an alliance or organization. In the following statement, again from the FAQs on his website, he explains the idea in terms of a dual strategy in defiance of both 'the global' and 'the national', which for him respectively stand for 'Hollywood' and 'censorship':

The concept of filmmakers without frontiers is [advanced] because although there are over 200 countries and thousands of languages and cultures on earth [...] the dominant cinema that occupies 90 per cent of movie theatres in the world belongs to Hollywood. Under Hollywood's economic and commercial [dominance] not only the artistic and documentary but also the national cinema of many countries has faded [out] and many nations remain without [images]. There are other filmmakers that have fled their countries because of censorship [...]. These filmmakers can create their work under more adequate conditions and their films will gradually reach their fellow citizens, but if they remain in their countries they will not be able to create any work.

(Makhmalbaf 2005a).

Dabashi further describes this idea with reference to Makhmalbaf's personal experience: 'filmmakers without frontiers' are those who 'shoot their films in Tajikistan, edit them in India, premiere them in Cannes, launch them in the United States, and then sell them around the world on Amazon.com' (Dabashi 2007b: 361). Bearing in mind the significance of Makhmalbaf's earlier position within the post-revolutionary political and cultural context, we can better examine his achievements and influence in the 'transnational' period of his cinematic career.

It is not necessary here to enter into a detailed study of Makhmalbaf's career prior to his emergence as a transnational artist in the age of globalization. There are already a considerable number of published studies and interviews on this period (Dabashi 2001, 2002, 2007b, 2008; Dönmez-Colin 2006; Egan 2005). What can be said in brief is that between 1982, when Makhmalbaf began his cinematic career, and 1996, when he made his last film inside Iran, there lies a period of prolific and high-profile film-making during which he not only mastered the techniques of film-making, but also repeatedly altered and modified the religious, social, political and philosophical views that informed the themes of his films. He also employed a variety of different genres and aesthetic forms and styles to convey his messages. In some of his films like *Boycott* (1986) Makhmalbaf followed conventions of the classic Hollywood style to impress mass audiences; while in others such as *The Peddler* (1987) he claimed to have combined elements from a range of art schools such as Symbolism, Expressionism, Surrealism and Neo-Realism to create what he called a 'Quranic style' (Nabavi 1987). He even made dark comedies such as *The Actor* (1993), which featured a popular actor of television sitcoms and commercial cinema.

Foreign films and film-makers as well as international festivals played a significant role in inspiring Makhmalbaf's outlook and imagination. This is probably one of the earliest manifestations of globalization in his cinema. He has on many occasions referred to his experience of watching Wim Wenders' *Wings of Desire* (1987) during his first trip to a film festival in the West (Dabashi 2001; Golmakani 1995). Makhmalbaf explains how the shock of the encounter changed his predetermined and stereotypical image of the West:

> The shock was so great that I became ill, so much that for fifteen days my head ached [...]. All the religious slogans I used to chant were there in that film, and yet the film represented the west.
>
> (Dabashi 2001: 195)

This inverse culture shock happened at the peak of a period in which Makhmalbaf had gradually distanced himself from his earlier position as a totally devoted proponent of the Islamic Revolution and the great defender of 'Islamic art'. Far from portraying idealistic representations of the newly established state, he was now acknowledging some bitter realities of life under the Islamic Republic in films like *The Peddler* (1987), *Marriage of the Blessed* (1989) and *The Cyclist* (1989). In these films, which Eric Egan has named the 'Mostaz'afin Trilogy',[5] Makhmalbaf deals with issues such as poverty, inequity, exploitation, social stratification, crime and casualties of war. He uses his privileged position as a 'trusted' artist to voice his criticism of the continuing social problems in the post-revolution society. In this period, as Egan notes, Makhmalbaf 'may have turned his back on the dogmatism and religious zealotry of his earlier work but he has not turned his back on God' (Egan 2005: 101). Rather than blaming Islam or the revolution for the plight of the poor, in most of these films Makhmalbaf mounts his attack on the corrupt capitalists and merchants (*bazaries*).

By the time he made *The Nights of Zayanderood* (1991) and *Time of Love* (1991), Makhmalbaf was clearly expressing not only his disillusion with the very idea of revolution, but his suspicion of any claim to absolute 'truth' or overarching ideology. Instead he had moved on to express enthusiasm for relativism, pluralism and humanism, celebrating them

---

[5] Mostaz'afin is a Quranic term that referes to the oppressed and exploited masses who are promised that they will eventually defeat the oppressors and inherit the world. The term was widely used in the revolutionary discourse to refer to the poor and disadvantaged classes who supported and sacrificed for the sake of the revolution.

as 'ideology-free' standpoints (Mansoori 1996). A film like *Nasereddin Shah, Actor-e Cinema (Once upon a Time, Cinema*, 1992), which reflected on the history of censorship and state intervention in cinema, played a big role in re-branding Makhmalbaf as a liberal and anti-establishment director. In addition, he created a rich cinematic collage in this film using footage of many well-known films in the history of Iranian cinema, both from the pre- and post-revolutionary era. In doing so, Makhmalbaf paid homage to many pioneers and masters of Iranian cinema. This was a significant move in his career, since Makhmalbaf had been extremely hostile toward pre-revolutionary film-makers in the early 1980s and not only had called them *Taqooti* (aligned with the oppressor), but even suggested that they should be prosecuted for their cultural crimes (Nabavi 1987). For some critics, therefore, *Once upon a Time, Cinema* was 'Makhmalbaf's repentance'.

In *Noon va Goldoon* (*A Moment of Innocence*, 1996) Makhmalbaf uses his own life story (a revolutionary teenager who attacks a policeman with a knife) to make a film that denounces violence and celebrates tolerance. He emphasizes in this film that unlike his generation in the pre-revolutionary era, the new generation no longer finds violence a solution for social and political problems. In fact he even goes further to imply that instead of attempting to change the world or the society, we must first focus on changing ourselves and learn to live with others who are different from us.

Gabbeh (1996), the last feature film that Makhmalbaf made in Iran, marks yet another transition in his art and thought. In Egan's words, this film heralded 'the emergence of a more tranquil, esoteric and poetic sensibility, rooted in rural idyll' (Egan 2005: 155). It was a colorful and stylish celebration of life, filmed in a rural setting among the community of the nomadic Qashqai tribe. *Gabbeh* is also a significant film in the history of Iranian cinema for its remarkable success in the global film markets. It became the first Iranian film to be distributed and exhibited widely in cinemas across Europe and the United States. This global achievement also revolutionized the production, consumption and export of the Iranian *gabbeh*: a unique hand-knotted rug made by women of the nomadic Qashqai tribe. Some critics have thus accused Makhmalbaf of making a 'packaging of a fabled Iran for tourists' and offering 'an uncritical picturesque work', which serves as 'a fairy-tale substitute for the realities of life in the country', while others have praised it as 'a critique of patriarchial culture and the censor of women rights' (quoted in Egan 2005: 156). While recognizing that in this film Makhmalbaf is '[highlighting] the problems of male chauvinism in Iranian society and [giving] voice to those denied freedom by it', Egan suggests that the film also expresses a 'conservative religious belief in the strength and stability of the family/community' (ibid.). The humanism in *Gabbeh*, argues Egan, is not non-religious or anti-religious:

> Focusing on the human, in an attempt to go beyond the structure of spiritualism and transcendental consciousness, not only questions man's relationship with God, but also draws man closer to God. This is achieved in a more personal and spiritual form of religion than the blind obedience of the Islamic man demanded by the Islamic Republic.
> (Egan 2005: 161)

Whether we agree with Egan's reading of *Gabbeh* or not, it would certainly be very difficult to maintain such an interpretation with respect to Makhmalbaf's more recent films such as *Scream of the Ants*. An analysis of Makhmalbaf's more recent films will be presented below.

As a 'disenchanted' former political prisoner and revolutionary, Makhmalbaf became a major source of attraction to international festivals and western critics. His international reputation enabled him to secure funding for his films from sources outside of his homeland and thus overcome the problem of censorship. Since 1996 he has not made any films inside Iran and has preferred to invest in his internationally recognized brand name and establish a film company called Makhmalbaf Film House with his wife and children. They have all become involved in film productions that are financed, produced and mainly screened outside Iran. The most significant among these films is *Kandahar* (2001), the production of which Dabashi describes as follows:

> A prominent Iranian filmmaker makes a film about the status of women in Afghanistan, finances it by a French producer and distributor, premieres it in Cannes Film Festival in France, and from there it starts circulating the world, with a stopover in Iran, before the events of September the Eleventh and October the Seventh [beginning of the US-led military campaign against Afghanistan] make it a global sensation. The phenomenon is a text book case of globalization, with the corresponding ideas of *cinematic nation, national cinema,* and ultimately *nation* itself completely collapsing and superseded.
>
> (Dabashi 2008: 207, emphasis in original)

Makhmalbaf is perhaps the most obvious case among Iranian film-makers who have largely benefited from the new possibilities brought about by globalization. He has experienced a different kind of professional film-making, which is apparently not attached or confined to any particular territory. Yet in what follows I intend to challenge Dabashi's assertion that Makhmalbaf's experience demonstrates a complete collapse and superseding of 'cinematic nation' and 'national cinema'. Through an analysis of his films, as well as some of his interviews, I argue that Makhmalbaf's perspective is still quite strongly informed by a 'national' framework of analysis, rather than a 'transnational' one. It is also notable that in 1998 Makhmalbaf was awarded one of France's most prestigious 'national' awards, namely the *Chevalier de la Légion d'honneur* medal. In 2004 he officially became a French citizen and had until recently lived in Paris.[6]

---

[6] A recent CNN report on Makhmalbaf indicates that he has moved from France to the United Kinkdom and currently resides in London. ('Exiled Iranian film director's flight to freedom', cnn.com, 22nd September 2011, http://edition.cnn.com/2011/09/22/world/meast/iran-film-director/index.html?hpt=imi_t4, accessed 12th November 2011).

Banal transnationalism

At the time of writing, *Sex and Philosophy* (2005) and *Scream of the Ants* (2006) are the most recent outputs of what we may describe as Makhmalbaf's transnational career in film-making. Both films are financed and distributed by the French company Wild Bunch, which, early in 2001 and only months before 9/11, had been the lucky producer of *Kandahar*. Despite having a small budget by European standards, this film became an absolute bargain for the French company following the US campaign on Afghanistan. The profit generated by *Kandahar* may explain why the company continued to finance Makhmalbaf family's later films. *Sex and Philosophy* was shot in Tajikistan with a Tajik cast, and although the film's diegetic world is in Tajikistan, there is little emphasis on local and national spaces in the film. *Scream of the Ants*, on the other hand, was entirely shot in India with a clear intention on the director's part to highlight certain aspects of local culture and rituals. There are, however, two actors[7] of Iranian origin in the film, who play the role of a couple originally from Iran but apparently resident abroad, on their honeymoon visit to India.

Sex and Philosophy

In *Sex and Philosophy* a male dance instructor invites four women to the location of his dance class on his fortieth birthday. In an act, which he describes as 'revolting against himself', the man apparently wants the four women to meet each other and realize that he has had affairs with all of them in the past. The man himself, however, does not turn up and spends the day driving his car around the city with 40 candles lit on its dashboard. Through a number of flashbacks, which involve endless dialogues about the philosophical, psychological, social and sexual implications of love, we are given vague indications of the four women's characters and their relationships with the dance instructor. These flashbacks are intertwined with musical scenes, which include tightly composed choreography and dance performances by a dozen or more dance students. It is notable that all the students are women and most of them are young. At the end of the film one of the women – who is more mature – is inspired by what she calls the dance master's 'honesty' in revealing his past, and thus invites him to her house, along with three other men, whom neither we nor the dance master have seen before. She informs them that she has been in affairs with all four men and continues to love them all. One of the men slaps her in the face, and another one swears at her and they both leave. The dance master and the only other man remaining stay and continue discussing the philosophy of love.

---

[7] The actress Mahnoor Shadzi and actor Mahmood Shokrollahi were appearing for their first time in a feature film. Shadzi lives in the United States and formerly worked as a presenter in the Voice of America Persian satellite channel (affiliated to the US Department of State). Shokrollahi lives in France and has directed and produced a number of short films and documentaries.

In terms of photography, lighting and set design, *Sex and Philosophy* is a highly stylish – even ostentatious – film, with the colour of red being dominant in most scenes. These scenes quite clearly resemble European art-house films such as Krzysztof Kieslowski's *Red* (1994). There is also a quite long aerial plan-sequence in the film that depicts the lovers' leave. This scene is clearly reminiscent of Kiarostami's famous closing sequence in *Under the Olive Trees* (1994). But the film's problems go beyond the lack of originality. Even in their most ordinary and intimate moments, the characters of *Sex and Philosophy* speak in a formal style like that of a poet or philosopher's discourse. There is no indication of time and sequence in the flashbacks. At one point we have the impression that these affairs have been going on at the same time – and the unchanging appearance of the man in the flashbacks, as well as the quarrel he has with one of the women seems to confirm this – yet there are also other indications that imply that they have happened at different times.

We understand that some of the women had left the man because they discovered his other relationships, yet it is not clear why they all agree to come back on this occasion, or why the man wants them to meet each other (again). While the man emphasizes that every mistress has revealed to him 'a part of love's mystery', it is not entirely clear in the film what each of these four women have meant to him, how different they are, or what they represent. As in the case of some of his earlier films such as *Time of Love* (1990) where Makhmalbaf provided his puzzled audiences with a 'how to read the film' manual, which was distributed among the audience, in this case too he has written a short note on the film with this purpose, which only serves to complicate things further:

> These four women in fact represent one woman to me in four different phases of the evolution of the meaning of love in a feminine life experience: 'Period of romantic innocence', 'Period of love revenges', 'Period of indulging in sex and forgetting love', and 'Period of melancholic maturity and recreation of love'. The man however, does not see the different phases of a woman's maturity in every one of these women. In each woman he seeks love but finds loneliness.
>
> (Makhmalbaf 2005c)

Given all the clear indications of the man's four different affairs in the film, the idea that the four women somehow metaphorically represent one woman's different phases of life seems rather unconvincing. Even more problematic is Makhmalbaf's claim that in this film he is depicting different phases of the 'evolution' and 'maturity' of 'feminine life experience'. How, we might ask, has he discovered this neat periodization and teleology in 'feminine life experience' and what do each of these phases stand for?

It would be more meaningful to argue that the story of this film is first and foremost about different relationships in a 'masculine life experience'. The narrative is largely told from a narcissist and self-indulgent male point of view and, apart from the short final scene, women only become significant when they are subject to the male gaze. If we accept that this male-centered story is about 'the evolution of the meaning of love in different phases of a feminine life experience', what then would the story of that final woman be who reveals that she has had relations with four men? Why has not Makhmalbaf placed the latter character at the center of his film?

Regardless of the femininity or the masculinity of the perspective, the key statement in *Sex and Philosophy* is that there is nothing 'eternal' or 'divine' about love. As Makhmalbaf's main character lectures us, love is 'just a romantic circumstance [which] will only last until the next romantic situation'; it is merely 'a short passion that yields from ordinary incidents' (Makhmalbaf 2005b). One such incident, the amorous dance master informs one of his mistresses, can be 'diarrhea'. This condition, we understand, had brought the man to a hospital where the woman works as a doctor. Makhmalbaf could not have been more explicit in providing a materialist interpretation of love, which departs from any form of idealism and romanticism. Yet the irony lies in the huge contrast between the theme and the form of the film. If love derives from such a mundane 'accident', why has Makhmalbaf applied such an over-aestheticized cinematic form in representing it? While the dance master's philosophy is 'I love, therefore, I am', he makes every effort to convince us that 'love lasts with love, not [with] loyalty'. He stresses that 'the story of Romeo and Juliet belongs to the past' adding a further conclusion that 'we can't rely on these stories [anymore]. We have arrived at liberty, sexual liberty' (Makhmalbaf 2005b).

Leaving aside the problem of how late (with about a half-century delay) Makhmalbaf's main character has realized that a sexual revolution has taken place in the world, it is rather confusing to hear, in the closing scenes of the film, the same *Don Juan* character express fear that 'true love is dying on Earth' and that 'love is endangered in the contemporary world'. If, as the dance master has been lecturing us, love is the result of 'ordinary incidents' as banal as diarrhea, and if it is an ephemeral 'circumstance', which can be repeated many times, why are we in the last sequence of the film suddenly presented with the moral that 'true love' is dying in 'the contemporary world'?

One possible answer to this sudden twist might be that by adding a critical reflection on 'contemporary life', Makhmalbaf is modifying his film in accordance with what Carroll calls 'the discursive framework' of transnational art. Including one of the common themes in transnational art, namely the impact of modernity on relationships and the nostalgia for an uninterrupted past, would perhaps help the film in catering to the tastes of international festivals. This suggestion is supported by the fact that in the synopsis of *Sex and Philosophy* on Makhmalbaf's website, which is used to market the film, we notice an over emphasis on the nostalgic message of the film:

> A 40 year old man who has celebrated his birthday alone by himself invites his four lovers to a dance class that he teaches in order to search for the roots of his own loneliness and by reminiscing the memories of how each of his love affairs were evolved and diminished, he realises that the more the contemporary world has become sexually oriented the [further] it has moved away from love.
>
> (Makhmalbaf 2005c)

For those who have seen the film, this synopsis may seem a misrepresentation. After all, the film does not in any sense denigrate having multiple or simultaneous love affairs or being 'sexually oriented'. On the contrary, the film appears to be criticizing those who do not tolerate their partners' affairs. The dance master clearly considers love as a mundane 'accident' and ridicules the concept of 'loyalty' as being irrelevant to love. We hardly see any evidence in the film that Makhmalbaf disapproves of his main character's view. In addition, the idea that one should tolerate his/her partner's love affairs had also been implied in Makhmalbaf controversial film *Time of Love* (1990).

It seems that in *Sex and Philosophy*, Makhmalbaf attempts to distance himself from the history of Sufism and Mysticism and abandon the tradition of idealized representations of love in Persian poetry, which informed some of his earlier films such as *Gabbeh*. Yet he does not feel comfortable in fully embracing and celebrating what he calls the 'sexual liberties' of modern – or to be more precise – western life either. This ambivalence and anxiety may be an outcome of the displacement, homelessness and 'vagrancy' that Makhmalbaf has been experiencing during his transnational adventures. In fact in the opening and closing scenes of *Sex and Philosophy*, there is an emphasis on the notion of 'solitude', and at one point in the film the central character says 'loneliness is our fate'. It might be noted here that the theme of solitude has appeared in other 'transnational' films of Iranian directors who left Iran and made films in other countries, particularly in the work of Shahid-Sales and Naderi (Naficy 2001).

Scream of the Ants

In comparison with *Sex and Philosophy* the experience of *Scream of the Ants* is far more challenging. This film lacks the visual and formal sophistication of the first, and watching it feels more like attending a very long, incoherent and poorly presented theological lecture. A middle-class couple comprising an atheist man and a believer woman, whose roles are poorly performed by the film's two main actors, travel to India on their honeymoon. The woman is in search of the *Ensan-e Kamel* (literally 'the perfect human'): a spiritually accomplished wise man who could bless and advise her. The two characters squabble throughout the film over the existence of God, the causes of poverty, the meaning of beauty and the importance of sex.

The man, a former communist, claims to be in a state of doubt, yet he is quite confident that the poverty and misery in people's lives is clear evidence that God does not exist. He has a peculiar character all through the film: in one scene we see him admiring his spouse with romantic words; in another he shouts at her and ridicules her views. He leaves his wife during their honeymoon after a quarrel, and spends a night having sexual fantasies with an Indian prostitute. This involves asking her to pose as a table on which he rests his goblet of wine. While drunk, he continues to debate theology and philosophy with the statue of a bull: the 'God of power'. He loathes God for the sufferings of human beings, yet admires him for creating women and wine. In a scene that combines surreal imagination and sexual fantasy, we see the man applying soft clay over a naked woman's body, as if imitating God in his creation. More surprisingly, after these scenes that began with the couple's quarrel, we see them hugging and laughing in a taxi, as if nothing had ever happened. The taxi is taking them to meet the wise man. The driver however, drops them off in the middle of a desert in order to return a fly to its 'home' after it had accidentally entered the taxi on the way.

At some points *Scream of the Ants* appears to be an atheist manifesto, depicting the traditional rituals and religious beliefs of Hindus and other believers from a rather scornful and even humiliating point of view. We learn in the film that 'miracles', like that of an old man who can stop a train with his eyesight, are simply fake stories fabricated by hungry people who earn a living by creating such tourist attractions. In one particularly disturbing scene we see graphically explicit images of naked old men and naked children jumping in the 'sacred' river Ganges, a scene which emphasizes the 'primitivism' of these people. Images of Indian beggars and poor people in the streets are also edited in parallel with images of stray animals. The only 'civilized' Indian we see in the film, apart from the prostitute, is a journalist who also does not believe in miracles and like the tourist couple carries a camera to document the exotic and primitive aspects of his own people.

The fact that there are two main characters in the film, one believer and one atheist, may suggest that the film is impartial with regard to issues such as faith and belief. But the character of the woman, who represents faith, is so weak and passive in comparison to the vocal and active character of the atheist man that such a view would be difficult to defend. The arguments and statements of the atheist man are quite dominant throughout the film and even get amplified by a German adventurer – also in India in search of meaning – who seems to have arrived at the grand conclusion that all faiths are simply the opium of the masses. The following exchange takes place between the atheist man and the German adventurer while they are watching Hindu rituals of burning the dead: [8]

–This universe is full of shit [...]
–No [...] it is not only shit there [...] the shit is constantly raining on you. It is a process, shit is happening, continuously [...]. And then in the different cultures, they have found different answers to that. For example the Catholics are saying: 'you deserve it'. Protestants are saying: 'let it happen to others'. The Muslims are saying: 'it is the will of Allah'. And the Jews, they always say: 'why is it always happening to us?' Buddhist they are saying: 'actually it is not really shit'. In Japan the Zen Buddhists listen to the sound of shit happening. But you know

---

[8] A very poor English transcription of the full dialogues of *Scream of the Ants* is available on the Makhmalbaf Film House website. Matching this script with the dialogues in the film I have edited some grammatical and spelling errors such as 'sheet' instead of 'shit' and 'veal' instead of 'will'.

these are only theoretical views [...]. These are only worn out solutions by some people who try to console the people, who try to help the people survive all that constant shit business.

(Makhmalbaf 2006)

In the scenes where the couple venture on their pilgrimage to meet the wise man the atheist man emphasizes the number of ants they kill with every step that they take. The message is clear: all metaphysical quests inevitably involve some kind of criminal activity at the material level. 'The wise man' is also represented in a rather humorous manner, to the extent that it gives us every reason to suspect he is either a fool or another fraud. As in *Sex and Philosophy*, however, there is a paradoxical twist at the end of *Scream of the Ants*, where the advice that the wise man gives the woman is read out. At this closing scene we find out that the wise man did in fact possess some sort of vision or wisdom. His advice to the woman is a poem with an interesting message:

I crossed the seven seas, I climbed up the seven hills, I walked down all the valleys, I went into the deepness. Through all the seasons, I travelled around the world. And when I came back, I was ashamed to see, that all the world was there, in a tiny drop of dew, on the leaf of the plant, in my home garden.

(Makhmalbaf 2006)

If we drop the philosophical message of this final scene – which seems to be implying: 'don't waste your time in search of "the truth", look for the little truths around you' – and read it as it appears in the poem, we notice another striking contradiction. Here is a self-proclaimed 'borderless artist', who has over many years championed transnationalism and cosmopolitanism, yet is concluding his latest 'transnational film' with a clearly 'localist' message. There is no need to travel all around the world, the ending seems to suggest, assuring us that all is to be found in the local spaces where we are already situated.

In terms of the politics of the film, it can be argued that Makhmalbaf's view toward India and its inhabitants resembles the view of an eighteenth-century European anthropologist who is baffled by the ignorance, barbarism and superstitious beliefs of the people of the Orient, while also shedding tears for their extreme poverty. It could also be suggested that by exploiting the cultural and economic resources of India (such as exotic landscapes, Hindu rituals, colorful traditional clothing, naked bodies of local inhabitants, cheap cast and crew, cheap production and post-production costs) to the advantage of a transnational business, the film's project is also reminiscent of the project of colonialism. Rather than deconstructing the colonialist and Orientalist discourse, as expected in a film by a 'rebel' film-maker, the film seems to be reproducing it.

In his 250-plus-page book on Makhmalbaf, Hamid Dabashi only dedicates four pages to *Sex and Philosophy* and *Scream of the Ants* put together. Since his voice is perhaps the most sympathetic toward Makhmalbaf, we may find the way he describes *Scream of the Ants* revealing:

> [T]wo hopeless, graceless, boring and banal people, stranger to themselves than they are to us, doing as Makhmalbaf's renewed fixation with absolutist terms of belief, conviction, truth, and reality tells them to do. They all fail – Makhmalbaf, his actors, his story [...]. Judged by this film, here in Paris, there in Afghanistan, or else in India, Makhmalbaf did not seem to be at home in his own craft any more [...] his creative courage seemed to have shied away from his worldly whereabouts.
>
> (Dabashi 2008: 216)

For Dabashi even *Sex and Philosophy* – which in his view is 'by far the most sensually throbbing film' in Makhmalbaf's career – suffers from 'over intellectualization of love' (2008: 216-7). Dabashi writes after watching the two films at Makhmalbaf's house in Paris:

> I went to bed tired and exhausted, but oscillating in my mind between hope and despair as to what was happening to Makhmalbaf's cinema. After *Kandahar* (2001) and Makhmalbaf's increasing attention to Afghanistan, his territorial connections to Iran had been radically uprooted. [...] oscillating between politics and aesthetics, it now seemed to me, can be as much reinvigorating and life-affirming as it might degenerate into a mode of escapism, not knowing quite where to call home.
>
> (2008: 218)

So even a close friend and great admirer of Makhmalbaf as a 'rebel' film-maker seems to have arrived at the conclusion that his recent films suffer from 'a mode of escapism', or in Baudrillard's terms a 'transaesthetics of indifference'. It appears that a banal understanding of transnationalism has emptied Makhmalbaf's cinema of serious meaning. It might be useful to note that the dance master in *Sex and Philosophy* clearly admits to having a problem with all 'serious stuff': 'all of the world's serious stuff seem ridiculous to me. All important philosophies are fallacious' (Makhmalbaf 2005b). It is also ironic that Makhmalbaf's recent films seem to fit perfectly into the category of 'personal films', which he himself denigrated in an interview a couple of years earlier:

> [In making films] we are taking humanity's time. The resources of human beings in cinema are limited. There are only two to three thousand films made each year. How can a filmmaker allow him/herself to waste one three thousandth of humanity's time in cinema for expressing a foolish personal distress which does not matter for anyone but him/her? When you have access to mass media you should address human sufferings. You should agitate humanity's senses and raise its awareness towards human anguishes, rather than merely expressing personal complexes and parochial views.
>
> (Malakooti 2003)

The rise and fall of an 'idol'

With the exception of his early films – that in the view of most critics lacked technical and artistic quality – Makhmalbaf had until recently enjoyed a warm reception from the majority of professional film critics in Iran. Because of his association with politics in the 1980s and his powerful position in the Centre for Islamic Thought and Art, Makhmalbaf had the privilege of a higher level of artistic freedom and thus could securely cross the 'red lines' and make critical films in the post-revolution era. His work was generally appreciated by film critics who not only saw them as innovative cases of social criticism, but recognized their potential for opening up the political and cultural space for other film-makers to follow. In 1990, therefore, when the 'hardliner' newspaper *Keyhan* launched a severe attack against Makhmalbaf and his twin films *Time of Love* and *Nights of Zayanderood*, most film critics fell in on Makhmalbaf's side. Throughout the 1990s Makhmalbaf continued his prolific career with films such as *Once Upon a Time Cinema* (1992), *Salam Cinema* (1994), *Gabbeh* (1996) and *A Moment of Innocence* (1996), which generally received wide critical attention and acclaim both inside Iran and abroad.

However, since 1997 when he made *Silence* in Tajikistan and particularly after making *Kandahar* in Afghanistan (2001), there seems to have been a gradual change in Makhmalbaf's status within Iranian cinema. The attitude of film critics toward his work has also steadily shifted from total enthusiasm, first to almost indifference, and later to strong criticism. In a review that was published in 2007 in the 'reformist' Iranian daily *Shargh*, one Iranian critic described this change of attitude in the following terms:

> Twenty years ago, it wasn't like nowadays when nobody cares whether Makhmalbaf makes a film or not; whether he is [in Iran] or not. Those days, having a close encounter with Makhmalbaf, speaking with him and watching his films was for many a longed-for and noteworthy experience.
>
> (Talebi-nejad 2007)

Further revealing in this respect is a special dossier on Makhmalbaf that was published in the leading 'reformist' magazine *Sharhrvand-e Emruz* in 2007. The title of this dossier was: 'Makhmalbaf against Makhmalbaf: The Man who Wrecked Himself'.

Mehrzad Danesh, a film critic who has contributed to this dossier, writes of his long lasting and warm affection for Makhmalbaf's films in the 1980s and the 1990s, and of how Makhmalbaf 'like an idol' had hugely influenced his views, his life and even his appearance. Yet he maintains that 'there is nothing left of that fire in me. Makhmalbaf's films no longer attract me. If they don't make me angry, they are at best dull and tiring' (Danesh 2007). Referring to Makhmalbaf's claim about the Iranian government allegedly seeking to assassinate him, Danesh considers it 'ridiculous' and concludes that 'Makhmalbaf and his films are significant parts of Iranian cinema, although he seems to be out of date now'

(Danesh 2007). This view is shared by Amir Pooria who describes Makhmalbaf's decision to adopt French nationality as 'blind compliance', adding that 'what remains of Makhmalbaf in Iranian cinema and art today is only a pale title of an important and well-known figure who has now joined history' (Pooria 2007).

Arash Khoshkhoo, another former Makhmalbaf devotee, writes of how his generation was shocked and thrilled by the sharp social and political criticism in Makhmalbaf's films of the 1980s. 'That was a time', he writes, 'that no other filmmaker was allowed or – to be fair – dared to touch upon such themes' (Khoshkhoo 2007a). Khoshkhoo refers to a shift in Makhmalbaf's core audiences in Iran since the mid-1990s when the film-maker became an 'international figure'. For Khoshkhoo, instead of the lower-classes who used to constitute Makhmalbaf's main audience in the 1980s, it was the upper-class technocrats and reformists who were primarily addressed in his later films.

Hosein Moazzezi-nia is among the few contributors to this dossier who, even at the peak of Makhmalbaf's popularity among critics and intellectuals in the 1990s, had been critical of his work. One interesting point in Moazzezi-nia's article is that he reveals some of the 'consequences' of criticizing Makhmalbaf at the time of his popularity in the 1990s. Publishing a negative review on Makhmalbaf in the Iranian weekly *Mehr* had apparently put so much pressure on the editors that he was only allowed to write with a pseudonym for some time (Moazzezi-nia 2007). This incident is in contrast with the range of 'evolutionary' narratives of Makhmalbaf's career, which suggest that he was a dogmatic and violent 'Islamist' in the 1980s, but transformed into a humanist preacher of love and tolerance in the 1990s.[9]

An important contextual point that should be emphasized here is that *Sharhvand-e Emruz* was not associated with the 'conservative', 'Islamist' or 'hardliner' factions of Iranian politics who attacked Makhmalbaf in the 1990s for his deviation from the core values of the Islamic Republic. Rather, this periodical and its editorial board are closely affiliated to the 'reformist' and 'liberal' factions that had until lately been strongly supportive of Makhmalbaf and his work. As Mohammad Qoochani, the editor of this periodical emphasizes, prominent reformists had even 'put their political and cultural reputation at stake' by defending Makhmalbaf at various occasions such as the political controversies of the early 1990s (Qoochani 2007). Contrasting *Scream of the Ants* with Makhmalbaf's early 'Islamist' films, Qoochani argues that Makhmalbaf 'once made films to prove that he is a Muslim, and now makes films to prove that he is not', adding that 'no non-Muslim filmmaker has made such an effort as Makhmalbaf's in exposing his or her disbelief in Islam' (Qoochani 2007). The latter view is also echoed in Dabashi's brief review of the film:

---

[9] It is noteworthy that two of the critical articles published in the special dossier of *Sharhvand-e Emruz* on Makhmalbaf do not include the name of their authors (Shahrvand-e Emruz 2007a, 2007b).

Scream of the Ants returns to Makhmalbaf's earliest cinema – full of passionate intensity – but this time it projects an absolutist and flamboyant metaphysical break with Islam, let alone with any Islamic Revolution or an Islamic Republic; and thus as all acts of metaphysical break ups it becomes exceedingly metaphysical itself.

(Dabashi 2008: 215)

Transnational film-makers and territorial attachments

Makhmalbaf's trajectory could be compared with that of two other major Iranian film-makers who left the country long before him and established a cinematic career abroad. Sohrab Shahid-Sales and Amir Naderi are considered by many Iranian critics as key figures of the 'New Wave' of Iranian cinema, the early signs of which emerged before the 1979 revolution. Shahid-Sales left Iran for Germany years before the Islamic Revolution in 1974, following the problems he faced with government officials in making his uncompleted film project *Qarantineh* (*Quarantine*). Between 1974 and 1991 he made 13 films and telefilms in Germany some of which were awarded prizes in festivals. Despite being one of the most prolific 'diasporic film-makers' in this period, Shahid-Sales had to move to Canada in the mid-1990s and later to the United States in search of funding for his film projects. This did not turn out to be a successful quest and therefore following some years of isolation, which involved excessive drinking, he died in Chicago in 1998 at the age of 54 (Naficy 2003a).

Abbas Kiarostami has referred to the influence of Shahid-Sales in inspiring his particular style and form of film-making, which became globally recognized and celebrated two decades later (Elena 2005: 16). The two most influential films of Shahid-Sales in this respect were *Yek Ettefaq-e Sadeh* (*A Simple Event*, 1973) and *Tabi'at-e Bijan* (*Still Life*, 1974), which he made prior to his migration. In making films abroad, Shahid-Sales was no longer addressing Iranian audiences or dealing with issues related to Iran. These films, as Naficy has argued, fall into a particular category of 'accented cinema': a cinema of displacement produced by exilic and diasporic film-makers from various origins in diverse host countries (Naficy 2001). In a more recent chapter titled 'Iranian Émigré Cinema as a Component of Iranian National Cinema' (Naficy 2008), Naficy identifies six thematic categories within Iranian accented films, one of which is 'transnational cinema'. He defines the latter as a cinema 'made by hyphenated Iranians or by Iranians who transcended national belonging, [and do] not necessarily deal with Iranian but with universal issues of love, alienation, and displacement' (2008: 181). Shahid-Sales and Naderi are key examples in this category.

Naderi, unlike Shahid-Sales, continued his career in Iran after the revolution and his film *Davandeh* (*The Runner*, 1985) is considered as a landmark in post-revolutionary cinema for its unprecedented number of appearances in international film festivals. The latter, it is generally held, paved the way for further achievements of other Iranian film-makers on the international stage. Following his last film in Iran *Ab, Bad, Khak* (*Water, Wind, Dust*, 1987) Naderi migrated to the United States and resided in New York. Since 1993 he has made six feature films, most of which do not include any reference to Iran. While Naderi's *The Runner* (1985) and *Water, Wind, Dust* (1987) both won the Golden Montgolfier from the Nantes Three Continents Festival, and were more or less praised by local critics, none of his post-migration films have so far received any remarkable international awards.

It is noteworthy that unlike Makhmalbaf, who has blamed the political conditions in Iran for his migration, neither Shahid-Sales nor Naderi have accepted that they are 'exilic' film-makers, indicating perhaps that they chose to migrate (Naficy 2003a). Naderi's description of how he began a 'new life' in New York is a striking illustration of the operations of 'deterritorialization' and 'reterritorialization':

> First when I came to New York I was broken. In those days of vagrancy I did not yet have my own apartment. I used to live temporarily in the 125th street in Harlem since it was a cheap area. Every night I wandered in the streets of Harlem like a dog and cried out. I couldn't sleep and I barely lived my life. Once I noticed I am no longer what I used to be. I locked myself up in a room and thought about who I am and what I want to do and how I should do it. I realised that without abandoning all the signs of the past I cannot move forward [...]. I started with my wife whom I loved and was really attached to. I closed my eyes and 'cut'. Then I left all my friends and relationships. I quit smoking. I stopped eating meat, and drinking coffee which was my fervour, every thing. Every day I was looking for something to ditch until I became worthy, like a monk, to find my path.
>
> (Naderi 2006: 23)

There are indications in some of Makhmalbaf's statements that explain why he has been less inclined to address local and national issues in his recent films. When asked in an interview why he and his family have focused on Afghanistan and continue to make films about Afghan people instead of Iranians he responds:

> Some times a person is only important in his own family. Sometimes s/he becomes well known in his town or in his country [...]. The reality is, when I make a film, it gets screened in forty to fifty countries. I don't mean just in film festivals, in each country between 10 to 100 thousand people are expecting to see it. In such conditions how can I be apathetic towards the tragic events that are taking place in my neighbouring country? In other words when you have a greater audience, you should have greater pains. I can't imprison myself in the geographical place where I was born. We don't live in a closed world any longer.
>
> (Bani-yaqoob 2002b)

Here Makhmalbaf's argument shows close affinity with progressive notions of cosmopolitanism and humanism. His words bring to mind the idea of 'the intellectual' who – as theorized by Edward Said – should maintain an exilic, marginal and amateur status and resist co-option by patriotism and nationalism (Said 1996). In fact following the making of *Kandahar* in 2000, Makhmalbaf became closely involved in raising international awareness about conditions under the Taliban-ruled Afghanistan. Following the defeat of the Taliban regime, he was engaged in various humanitarian and reconstruction campaigns in Afghanistan ranging from building and equipping schools to educating young Afghan film-makers (Bani-yaqoob 2002a). His efforts in Afghanistan as well as his attempts to improve the conditions of Afghan refugees in Iran are no doubt to his credit as a transnational artist and activist. Yet, as suggested below, it seems that rather than acquiring the position of an intellectual, who in Said's view always maintains a degree of skepticism toward all received wisdoms, Makhmalbaf's approach to Afghanistan – both in his film *Kandahar* and in some of his allied statements – is based on a framework of binary oppositions such as tradition/modernity, superstition/science, darkness/light, blue-eyed liberated women/veiled repressed women, which resembles the mentality of the European Enlightenment and the perceived burden of a global 'civilizing mission'.

While broadening the scope of his work and becoming involved in international humanitarian campaigns may justify Makhmalbaf's temporary departure from dealing with local issues in his films, it seems that even in the post-*Kandahar* period – as films like *Sex and Philosophy* and *Scream of the Ants* demonstrate – he has not managed to reconnect himself with local audiences. We can agree with Dabashi that Makhmalbaf 'emerged from the very depth of his nation', yet there is little evidence to support the claim that 'the further [he] has travelled in the world the closer he gets to the dreams and nightmares of his own people' (Dabashi 2008: 225). In fact it appears that as Makhmalbaf's profile has extended from the local and the regional to the global, his mode of address has been accordingly modified in favor of an imagined 'transnational audience'. Makhmalbaf has himself described this procedure:

> When a film is shown to audiences with different languages and cultures [...] you can notice that there are moments where all audiences laugh regardless of their language and culture. This part of the film for me would be for all humanity. But there are other occasions when a single statement can cause laughter in some audiences, while it makes others cry, and may infuriate a third group. In this case I would assume that such statements are local and not for all humanity. When I watch my films with foreign audiences I think about what can be subtracted, what is humanly and what is local. For me [these screenings are] like attending a lecture and learning.
>
> (Malakooti 2003)

As well as the shift in his audiences from the lower classes to the upper classes mentioned earlier, there seems to be also a noticeable shift of focus here from local audiences to 'foreign' audiences. In adjusting his film's language, Makhmalbaf might in fact be seen as conforming to what Carroll calls the 'discursive frameworks' and 'sense making strategies' of the 'transnational institution of art'. Rather than making his films more accessible to local and global audience, he seems to be curtailing them to suit a privileged class of transnational audiences, and in doing so alienating both global and local audiences who do not have access to the 'toolkits', 'language games' or 'cultural capital' required for understanding and enjoying transnational films.

As mentioned earlier not all Iranian film-makers who achieved international recognition became totally distanced from the local and the national. For Kiarostami being local is the precondition for becoming global. He states that film-makers should primarily think about 'themselves' and 'their societies' when making films, but should keep an eye on the global (Appendix I). Majid Majidi, another internationally celebrated Iranian director, also stresses that 'a film should first and foremost be based on the local roots and beliefs of its nation before it can become influential across borders and impress a global audience' (Appendix II). Majidi acknowledges that his 'particular style' of film-making has evolved over time and has been influenced through his experience of attending international festivals, yet he emphasizes that for him 'the local audience has always been the priority when making films' (Appendix II). He also sharply criticizes 'a new generation of directors' in Iran who, in search of international prizes, make formulaic films *for* festivals and according to festival tastes. Such an approach, Majidi says, 'has alienated their films from local audiences', giving such 'artificial and fake' films only the chance of surviving a short 'greenhouse life' in festival circuits (Appendix II). Winning the Silver Bear for Best Director at the Berlin Film Festival for the film *About Elli* (2009) did not make Asghar Farhadi shift his focus from local audiences to international festivals. In fact in his next film he went deeper into examining the ethical dilemmas and cultural contradictions in Iranian urban life, as well as the bitter consequences of poverty and social stratification. In a recent interview he says:

> After the success of *About Elli* in Berlin, I thought it would be wrong, and perhaps impossible, for me to try and make another film that could repeat that success in international festivals. On the contrary, I though that I should make a more indigenous film which would better illustrate the local spaces which I knew, so that the film would go down better with local audiences [...]. When I gave the script of *A Separation* to some friends, every single one of them warned me that in comparison to my previous films, this would not be successful outside Iran.
>
> (Mehrabi 2011)

Yet Farhadi went on to make the film, and to the surprise of himself and others, and in a rare occasion at the Berlin festival, *A Separation* not only won the Golden Bear for Best Film, it also won two Silver Bears for the whole group of its actors and actresses. As mentioned earlier *A Separation* also became the second top grossing film of the year in Iran, while achieving an extraordinary successful public screening in cinemas in Europe, particularly in France. According to a Paris-based Iranian critic, no other Iranian film had ever received so much attention and publicity in France before (Haqiqat 2011).

De-territorialization and re-territorialization

It is noteworthy that like Kiarostami and Majidi, Makhmalbaf also acknowledges that artists are rooted in the soil of a particular territory. Using the metaphor of 'trees' and 'fruits', he suggests that art carries elements and characteristics of the place the artist is rooted in. Yet he takes this metaphor further and speaks of the desirability of transplanting pistachio, the well-known Iranian agricultural export, to France. This of course may be seen as an early announcement of his intention to adopt French citizenship:

> We can even transplant pistachio to France and produce a pistachio with a French flavour, while the outcome, nonetheless, will still be pistachio. Why not?! Why should such an act be seen as a betrayal of a nation's ideals? Why should someone who changes the geography of his artistic production be considered unfaithful to his/her origins?
>
> (Malakooti 2003)

Makhmalbaf's words here bring to mind the notion of 'cultural hybridization', which, though not necessarily a new advent of the global age, has increasingly become a celebrated process in cultural analysis (Garcia Canclini 1995). One major advantage of transnational hybrid cultures is that they transcend local and national borders and are positioned 'in-between' established cultural formations. They can maintain, therefore, a critical distance from and reflect on the two or more cultures that constitute them. In other words, they allow for a wider perspective, which can acknowledge both the vices and virtues of the self and the other, of the local and the global, of the national and the international. Yet in Makhmalbaf's case it appears that there is little evidence of such advantages of a transnational perspective. His view seems to have merely shifted from one binarist local perspective – in which the Islamic was glorified and the West was demonized – to another equally limited view in which the West is purified while the Islamic and even the national is reduced to its worst traits. In one of the interviews available on his website, for example, Makhmalbaf uses a wide range of scornful generalizations to describe 'the Iranians':

> In comparison to other nations, I feel the reason for our historical misery and depression lies in: first, absolutism; second violence and the sanctification of violence as revolutionary action; third indolence; fourth jealousy; and fifth lying, insincerity and hypocrisy. In my view Iranians are an arrogant, lazy and jealous nation.
>
> (Razi 2002)

In another interview, Makhmalbaf is asked about the 'cultural maladies' of his nation, as well as the positive elements or possible sources of emancipation within Iranian society. In response to the first question he talks quite extensively on a wide range of problems and miseries in Iranian culture and society, yet when he comes to the second question he unconsciously returns to the failures and negative characteristics again. When the interviewer reminds him of this, he simply admits that he cannot think of *any* positive or emancipatory aspects in Iranian culture and society (Dabashi 2001: 202–12).

From a psychoanalytic perspective, we might interpret Makhmalbaf's deeply skeptical and degrading view of his fellow citizens as a consequence of his horrific memories of being jailed for over four years before the revolution. Makhmalbaf, who was only 17 at the time of his imprisonment, admits that 'I, who had gone to jail an enlightened person, was released a much more dogmatic one. There was nothing good there – from prison rapes to the suicides, fascism, lies, hypocrisy. I was completely fed up with it' (Dabashi 2001: 176). The most terrible experience of prison, he says, was not torture by the interrogators or prison guards, but the intimidation and perhaps violent treatment he faced from fellow political prisoners who were affiliated to other ideologies and organizations such as the *Mojahedin Khalgh* (MKO):[10]

> Imagine, living in a cell with thirty other people, and then suddenly all thirty of them are boycotting you. Imagine no one speaking to you for six months straight. And think of going to take a shower and finding when you're done that they've taken all of your clothes so that you're forced to walk around naked, looking for something to wear. [...] even the worst conditions that I've observed under the ruling clerics, I'd still prefer their rule a thousand times to that of *Mojahedin*. They're Stalinists! [They were] a catastrophe waiting to happen.
>
> (Dabashi 2001: 176, 178)

Whether being 'betrayed' by cell-mates in the Shah's prison is really the underlying cause of Makhmalbaf's contempt for 'Iranians' or not we may not know. But this contempt clearly stands in sharp contrast with his passion for three 'other lands' that have fascinated him: India, Afghanistan and France. A closer examination of how he describes the first two, or the way he illustrates them in his films, however, leaves us with some indication of where his 'true love' lies.

Makhmalbaf praises India 'for Gandhi and his non-violence; for Satyajit Ray and his non-sentimentalism; for a nation with a thousand religions and traditions that live together in a high degree of tolerance and peace' (Razi 2002). Apart from the fact that he seems to simply

---

[10] *Sazman-e Mojahedin-e Khalgh* (Organization of the People's Fighters) was one of the largest underground organizations in the Pahlavi era. It was initially formed by a number of Muslim students in the 1960s. The organization later adopted a Marxist-Leninist ideology and carried out a number of bombings and armed attacks, which, in some cases, targeted American citizens in Iran. After the 1979 revolution the organization turned against the Islamic government and, following many bloody clashes, moved its leadership and thousands of its members to Iraq. The MKO collaborated with Saddam's regime during the Iran–Iraq war and was supplied with heavy artillery and financial support. The United States, Canada, Iran and Iraq consider MKO a 'terrorist organization'. The organization was also considered 'terrorist' by the EU until 26th January 2009 when EU foreign ministers decided to remove the organization from their list of terrorist groups. For more on the history of MKO, see Abrahamian (1992). For a recent update on the group from an American perspective, see Fletcher (2008).

reduce a nation of almost a billion people to two individuals, Makhmalbaf's description of tolerance and peace in India fails to mention the violent sectarian bombings and terrorist attacks that have frequently taken place in India over the past decades. The Indian government's brutal repression of Muslims in the Indian-controlled regions of Kashmir – which has been documented by various human rights groups[11] – is also totally neglected in Makhmalbaf's romanticized description. Makhmalbaf's alleged passion for India also seems incongruent with the gloomy – if not humiliating – image of this country we see in *Scream of the Ants*. As pointed out earlier, in this film India is depicted – from the eye of a 'civilized' tourist – as a land of misery, poverty, backwardness and bizarre superstitions. How Indian audiences or critics would react to the film remains a matter for further investigation.

Makhmalbaf's admiration for Afghanistan, however, is much more dubious since he in effect praises the country for its 'primitiveness'. He describes a journey on foot to Afghanistan as 'a trip to humanity's primitive stages; to the first experiences of human beings in creating a basic, intimate and peculiar civilization' (Razi 2002). Such a view of Afghanistan, it might be argued, informs Makhmalbaf's feature film *Kandahar* (2001). The film tells the story of a white, blue-eyed, 'liberated' female Canadian journalist of Afghan origin, who secretly travels to the Taliban-ruled Afghanistan in search of her sister. In the film Afghan women – and Afghan people in general – are depicted as helpless victims under repression. As Cynthia Weber has noted in her in-depth analysis of *Kandahar* eloquently entitled 'Not without My Sister'[12] (Weber 2005), all the local people who attempt to help the journalist in her quest, of course in return for money, fail to do so and disappoint her. While the film exploits Afghan women's colorful burkas to create some visually stunning images in an otherwise dull and grim landscape, the repression of Afghan women is reduced to the burka itself. On some occasions in the film when the lead character Nafas is speaking about the 'imprisonment' of Afghan women, the image depicts the point of view of a woman inside a burka. Liberating the Afghan people is thus simply understood in terms of lifting the veil.

It is quite revealing that only days before the US military campaign on Afghanistan, in a speech after receiving the UNICEF Federico Fellini Award for making *Kandahar*, Makhmalbaf publicly states:

> I wish this award were bread that could be distributed among the hungry Afghanis. I wish that this award were rain that would pour over the arid land of Afghanistan. I wish this award were the breeze of freedom casting away the Afghan women's burka.
> (Dabashi 2008: 188)

---

[11] See for example the report entitled 'Everyone Lives in Fear' issued by *Human Rights Watch* in 2006. Available online at: http://www.hrw.org/en/node/11179/section/1, last accessed 15th January 2009.

[12] This title is of course reminiscent of the 1991 Hollywood movie *Not without My Daughter* (Brian Gilbert) starring Sally Field, which was a catalogue of stereotypical anti-Iranian propaganda.

Perhaps 'breeze of freedom' was too soft a name for the military operation that soon followed, but the idea of 'liberating Afghan women' soon became one of the objectives of the US campaign. In his next film *Afghan Alphabet* (2001) Makhmalbaf goes even further than 'wishing' for the burka to be 'cast away', and practically gets involved in persuading a school girl to lift her veil. This short film was commissioned by UNICEF to advertize the schooling projects for Afghan children in refugee camps inside Iran. Noticing that some girls did not attend school, Makhmalbaf's camera sets out to find them and investigate the reason. He is surprised to find out that even far from the reach of the Taliban, one girl still does not want to lift the veil. He thus tries to persuade her to lift her veil and the happy ending of the film is that he succeeds. For Makhmalbaf 'not going to school' and 'wearing a burka' are conflated in this film as one single problem and both are represented as backwardness and fanaticism.[13] The problem, he explains in a note on the film in his website, is that the girl does not know that she is imprisoned by 'male chauvinism':

> [Bombing] can ruin a political regime but it cannot change a culture. You cannot free a woman who is imprisoned in the burka [by using] rockets. The Afghan girl needs education. She doesn't know that she doesn't know. She is imprisoned but she does not know that she is a prisoner of poverty, ignorance, prejudice, male chauvinism and superstition.
>
> (Makhmalbaf 2001)

It seems that for Makhmalbaf 'male chauvinism' is repressive only when it forces a girl to wear a burka, not when it forces her to lift it. But this double standard was not missed by the UNICEF, who had commissioned the film. According to Dabashi they ultimately rejected the film and refused to distribute it (Dabashi 2008: 191).[14]

Although *Kandahar* had been premiered in Europe before the events of 11th September, soon afterwards it suddenly became – as *The Guardian* wrote at the time – 'the most politically important movie in the world' (Edemariam 2001). Despite the fact that Makhmalbaf has on various occasions criticized the bombing of Afghanistan and blamed US allies such as Saudi

---

[13] This is rather ironic, given the fact that Makhmalbaf himself prevented his own children from attending schools in Iran because he assumed it was a waste of their time. Instead he decided to personally teach them at home with lessons of his choice.

[14] Makhmalbaf not only decides what Afghan women should or should not wear, apparently he also decides what films his wife and daughters should or should not make. While for many years critics have speculated about the authenticity of the films directed by Makhmalbaf's wife and daughters, which in almost all cases were written, edited and produced by Makhmalbaf, Dabashi reveals in his book that on many occasions during their friendship Makhmalbaf read out to him 'a seemingly endless number of scripts and synopses' and asked for comments as recommendations on whether Marzieh, Samira, Hana or Mohsen himself should make the film (Dabashi 2008: 220). It is notable that in the same book Dabashi strongly criticizes Mohammad-reza Shajarian – the most prominent Iranian vocalist – for remaining 'undemocratic and patriarchal' in the improvisation and composition of his art along with his son (Dabashi 2008: 196), but he credits Makhmalbaf for his ability to 'improvise with a full awareness of a democratic spirit' (2008: 197).

Arabia and Pakistan for funding and organizing the Taliban, there are troubling similarities between Makhmalbaf's Orientalist approach to a 'primitive' and 'peculiar' nation in need of 'liberation' by the civilized world and the neo-colonialist logic of the Bush administration's military campaign for 'liberating' the Afghan nation. It is no surprise therefore that only a few weeks after the United States began bombing Afghanistan, the White House made 'an urgent request' for a private screening of *Kandahar* (Edemariam 2001), and according to some reports President Bush even encouraged American citizens to watch the film (Weber 2005).

Dabashi, who was personally involved in this episode, writes extensively on the course of events, yet makes every effort to convince the reader that this was simply a matter of 'sheer serendipity', 'coincidence' and 'abuse' of revolutionary art by global capital. He points out that before the film was released in the United States, he had organized a successful screening of *Kandahar* at Columbia University in October 2001. Following this screening, Dabashi was contacted by an NGO named 'Search for Common Ground' (SFCG)[15] who had asked for a copy of the film in order to consider arranging a possible screening at the White House (Dabashi 2008: 193). Dabashi informed Makhmalbaf and sent the copy to SFCG, but they soon called back to say that they thought the film was 'too intellectual for the White House' (2008: 194). Meanwhile, Makhmalbaf had put the news on his website that 'President Bush has asked to see *Kandahar*'. *The Guardian* picked up the story a few days before the film's release in the United Kingdom in a report titled 'The Film Bush Asked to See'. While Dabashi insists that President Bush never asked to see this film and did not see it either, he does confirm that when an American distributor bought the US rights for *Kandahar* from the French producer, both the office of *Mrs* Bush and the office of Secretary of State Colin Powell had contacted the distributor and requested screenings of *Kandahar*. '[A]t [that] point', Dabashi admits, 'the Bush administration was eager to use the film in order to justify their Afghan campaign' (2008: 194).

Weber has discussed in detail the reasons why the film was considered an asset by the US government (Weber 2005). She demonstrates how *Kandahar* provided the Bush administration with a perfect opportunity to shift its justification of the war from indiscriminate targeting of 'the terrorists and those who harbour them' – which the war had begun with – to the more popular narrative of 'liberating the Afghan people':

> As a disturbing display of Taliban-ruled Afghanistan, it may seem obvious that *Kandahar* supports the position of the Bush administration. But reconsidered through what I call a US moral grammar of war – made up of the tripartite axis of foreign policy, popular (often filmic) imaginaries, and narratives of the family – *Kandahar*'s story of separated sisters in need of reunion and apparent rescue also comports well with the stereotypical

---

[15] This is an NGO founded in 1982 mainly by some high-ranking American politicians including former senators and ambassadors. It runs different cultural and educational programs across the world. Its mission is 'to transform the way the world deals with conflict: away from adversarial approaches, toward cooperative solutions'. For more information, see the SFCG website at: http://www.sfcg.org.

way the feminine functions in US national narratives at times of war, as a figure in need of physical and moral security. This theme, in fact, informed official second-wave justifications of the war on terror in both the US and the UK.

(Weber 2005: 1)

Weber maintains, quite graciously, that 'Bush's *Kandahar*' is not entirely based on the intentions of the director. In her view, 'Read onto the US war on terror, Makhmalbaf's *Kandahar* is a damning critique of US post-9/11 foreign policy' (Weber 2005: 6). She provides an alternative reading of the film that is prejudged as 'Makhmalbaf's *Kandahar*' and thus, in line with Dabashi's defense of Makhmalbaf, she suggests that the film was 'appropriated' by the US government:

In the official US story, the US may have gone to Afghanistan for all the wrong reasons, but its joining of humanitarianism to the rescue of Afghan women enabled it to bring Makhmalbaf's story to its version of a happy ending. It could do this, however, only by going a step beyond Makhmalbaf, reminding him and the world that it is sometimes necessary to use military force to realise humanitarian goals.

(Weber 2005: 6)

Indeed 'appropriation' and 'incorporation' are at the heart of global capital's aggressive project, and this incident may be seen as further evidence in this respect. Yet, even in Weber's description of *Kandahar*, we find elements that resemble the tone of Bush's 'War on Terror' rhetoric:

Kandahar codes humanity according to a simple dualism of light vs. dark. What is light is good; what is dark is evil. What is light and good is humanity; what is dark and evil are social, cultural, political, and religious forces within and beyond Afghanistan like the Taliban, civil wars, and proxy wars.

(Weber 2005: 4)

A key question here is that if *Kandahar* was 'abused' and 'appropriated' by the Bush administration – as Dabashi and Weber seem to suggest – why did Makhmalbaf never protest the 'abuse' and 'appropriation' of his film as US military propaganda? Why was he, on the contrary, so eager to spread the news that President Bush has asked to see his film? This question becomes more significant when we bear in mind how vigilant Makhmalbaf has been over these years in not allowing the Iranian government to use even a single line of news about him. One interesting case in this regard happened in March 2001 when Makhmalbaf and his family members were harshly harassed by JFK airport security forces upon arrival in New York. According to Dabashi the incident made Makhmalbaf vow not to enter the United States again in his entire life. However, he avoided breaking the news to the media 'because he did not want the Islamic Republic of Iran to use it in its own propaganda machinery' (Dabashi 2008: 248). Here Makhmalbaf seems to be self-censoring a personal experience that could have generated negative publicity for the United States. By repressing the incident, he is effectively protecting an idealized image of 'the West', which he wants to uplift against the anti-western propaganda of the Islamic Republic.

Makhmalbaf later went on to demonstrate that he has no problem even forming political alliances with Bush's 'fellows'. In the aftermath of the 2009 Iranian presidential elections, he issued a series of statements co-signed by Mohsen Sazgara: an ex-revolutionary guard, businessman and political activist based in the United States who has close relations with the neo-conservatives and is a 'research fellow' at the George. W. Bush Presidential Centre. In these statements the two projected themselves as leaders of the Green Movement and from their residences in Europe or the United States provided detailed guidance, tactical directions and even slogans for the protestors inside Iran.[16] Given Makhmalbaf's advocacy of 'borderless' film-making and his previous engagement in humanitarian projects in Afghanistan, it is striking to see that one of the slogans he recommends to Iranian protestors in defiance of the Iranian government is *Na Ghazzeh, Na Lobnan. Janam fadaye Iran*: Neither for Gaza, Nor for Lebanon: I will sacrifice my life only for Iran (Makhmalbaf 2009).

Despite keeping the list of his 'Films banned in Iran' as a badge of honour, or perhaps an advertizing strategy on his website (Makhmalbaf 2005c), there is no reference in his numerous interviews about the kind of power relations or dominant ideologies that may influence the promotion of a 'transnational' film-maker's work at international venues of exhibition and channels of distribution. Clearly festival directors, multinational corporations, private film companies, television channels and even the host governments' cultural agencies exercise their power and promote their own agenda in funding, producing, distributing and exhibiting 'transnational' films. It was this power which, for example, forced a 'transnational' film-maker like Shahid-Sales to migrate from Germany – as his first place of settlement as an émigré – to Canada, and then to the United States in search of resources and producers for his films. Even exceptionally successful films like *Kandahar* can be subject to demands for 'adjustments' made by festival directors. Referring to the acceptance of *Kandahar* in the 2001 Cannes festival, Dabashi mentions that Makhmalbaf 'had to deal with the *usual* Cannes predicament of cutting a scene here and dubbing a voice-over there' (Dabashi 2008: 187, emphasis added). Apparently the festival did not approve of the controversial scene where artificial legs are dropped with parachutes by helicopters, while dozens of amputee Afghanis are made to race in a humiliating way to grab a leg for themselves.

Bearing in mind Makhmalbaf's comments about 'the Iranians', and his attitude toward India and Afghanistan, his admiration of 'France' is quite sensational:

---

[16] On 27th November 2009 Makhmalbaf appeared on David Frost's show on Aljazeerah English, where he was introduced as the Green Movement's 'official' and 'key' spokesman (http://www.youtube.com/watch?v=OlKDd5JnJ5Y, accessed 28th June 2010). Mirhosein Moosavi, the leader of the Green Movement, later denied having any spokesmen outside Iran (Moosavi 2009).

> For me France is the cultural capital of the world [...] particularly Paris with its cafés and their little round tables on the pavement where one can order just one cup of tea or coffee or a glass of wine and sit and read a 500 page novel through the whole day without being interrupted. It's a city where in every single day you have the option to choose and watch from among a thousand films that are being screened in cinemas, ranging from those of the early days of cinema to those of present times that may be made by an unknown young Vietnamese, Kazakhstani, Polish or Iranian filmmaker [...] and this is not just about cinema. During the past two centuries, the French have always accommodated unrecognized artists from other nations. The history of painting after the Renaissance is the history of unknown painters and artists from other nations being admitted by the French.
>
> (Razi 2002)

Again we can find here a vision that is totally blind to the global configuration of power and in particular the power relations within the history of colonialism. Makhmalbaf does not at all consider why artists 'from other nations' should be 'admitted', 'accommodated' and 'recognized' by 'the French' or any other nation in the first place, in order to find a place in the world of art. Moreover, he neglects the poor record of 'the French' in accommodating non-elite immigrants and fails to notice the widely discussed marginalization and subordination of large minorities, particularly of African and Arab origin, in French society, which has lead to various riots and violent clashes such as those of 2005. In visiting Paris' cinemas, we wonder if Makhmalbaf has noticed French films like *La Haine* (Kassovitz, 1995), *Caché* (Haneke, 2005) and *Vivre au Paradis* (Goerdjou, 1998) that reveal inequalities in the French society and the repression and even brutal killing of Algerian protestors by the French police. We wonder whether in its search of girls who do not attend school, Makhmalbaf's camera will ever find Muslim girls who are forced to leave school in France, because the law of the land does not allow them to wear headscarves?

Conclusion

It appears that in Mohsen Makhmalbaf's case the impact of globalization – understood in terms of a rather limited and banal form of transnationalism – not only has deprived a national cinema of one of its prolific film-makers, but has also uprooted a progressive film-maker from the grounds on which his films were once meaningfully placed. Rather than widening the film-maker's perspective to allow for a more informed critical appraisal of local, national and transnational cultures and the power relations involved at each level, this ideological reading of transnationalism has resulted in a much more parochial, romanticized and dichotomist vision. The latter simply denigrates the local and the national in favor of an alleged transnational that in fact turns out to have a rather local western European orientation. This process, as we have seen, has the potential pitfall of reproducing the ideology of the colonizer in the colonized, and can result in the work of a former political prisoner and rebel film-maker serving the objectives of the neo-conservative onslaughts of the global age. Rather than becoming *trans*national, this case suggests, the artist/film-maker may be in danger of becoming merely positioned within the framework of another 'national' formation that superficially caters to an idea of independent creativity.

While Makhmalbaf's declared intention of leaving Iran and becoming a 'filmmaker without frontiers' was to make films freely without the pressure of censorship,[17] over the past five years he has not made a single film. *Sex and Philosophy* and *Scream of the Ants* both only had a short and insignificant festival life. Apparently the films' French producer did not even care to distribute them in France's art-house distribution channels. Makhmalbaf, however, has managed to remain in the spotlight thanks to his new career as a self-appointed speaker of the Green Movement. In 2010 he was the recipient of a couple of honorary degrees and doctorates from western academia such as Université Paris Ouest Nanterre La Défense and the University of St. Andrews, Scotland. In Makhmalbaf's acceptance speech in Nanterre, there was a notable difference, which, after all, could be considered as a positive outcome of his post-*Kandahar* adventures. In addition to his usual sharp language and damning critique of film-making conditions in Iran, perhaps for the first time he also spoke of the 'hardships', 'censorship' and 'boycott' that migrant film-makers face in what he called 'the free world':

> [T]hose filmmakers who migrated, although attaining a degree of personal freedom, but suffer other hardships for the creation of their poetical art. […] they are crushed by the money censorship in the free world […]. There is political freedom here, but you as an art filmmaker are boycotted by money [*sic*].
>
> (Makhmalbaf 2010)

---

[17] It must be reminded that Makhmalbaf left Iran during the years when the 'reformists' were in power and the conditions for film-making were more open than they had ever been before.

Chapter 5

Daryush Mehrjui's 'National' Cinema and Globalization

Introduction

One of the pioneers of Iranian cinema's 'new wave' in the 1960s, Daryush Mehrjui has maintained his position in this cinema as an influential film-maker to the present day. With a career that has extended over four decades, he still is capable of making films that are both popular among public audiences and highly acclaimed by the critics. Apart from being considered one of the masters of Iranian cinema, what makes Mehrjui a relevant case study for the present book is that he is by and large seen as a representative of 'the national' in Iranian cinema. In a recent issue of the leading Iranian film magazine *Film Monthly*, which involved a special dossier on the concept of national cinema, Daryush Mehrjui's films received the highest number of votes by Iranian critics in terms of qualifying as 'national' films in post-revolution cinema (*Film Monthly* 2008). Not only was his film *Ejare Neshinha* (*The Lodgers*, 1986) at the top of the critics' list of 20 'national' Iranian films, but he was also notably the only director to have four films in this list, followed only by the late Ali Hatami and Bahram Beizai, who had two each.

Mehman-e Maman (*Mum's Guests*, 2004) is another film by Mehrjui in this list that became highly successful at the box office on its release and was also praised by many film critics. Both *The Lodgers* and *Mum's Guests*, however, have received little critical attention outside Iran. While in international festivals and film circuits, figures like Kiarostami and Makhmalbaf are largely considered representatives of 'Iranian national cinema', the above survey clearly indicates how differently a national cinema is perceived within and outside its territorial borders.[1] Following the previous chapter's examination of Makhmalbaf's 'transnational' cinema, this chapter will focus on the impact of globalization on the work of a director whose work has been understood as representing the national. This approach perhaps defies a more dominant trend in film and media studies that focus on the global, international or transnational aspects of film and media production when discussing the impact of globalization. Since this book is based on a theoretical framework that considers globalization as processes, flows and transformations that, despite transcending national borders, have profound impacts at the local and national level, it would not be adequate to limit its scope to global, international or transnational aspects of Iranian cinema.

---

[1] It should be noted however that the Iranian critics' top 20 *national* films do include Kiarostami's *Khaneye Dust Kojast?* (*Where is the Friends House?*, 1987) and Makhmalbaf's *Naseredin Shah, Actor-e Cinema* (*Once Upon a Time Cinema*, 1992).

As noted in Chapter 1, Robertson argues that globalization involves not only a 'compression of the world' through new technologies of communication and transport, but also an 'intensification of consciousness of the world as a whole' (Robertson 1992: 8). It is not just a development 'out there', but it also involves changes 'inside the head'. For Robertson, globalization contributes to a 'relativization' of positions and perspectives, and the latter is the cause of some perceived instabilities and insecurities. By influencing individual, collective and official perceptions of the self (the national) and the other (the global), globalization has arguably changed the ways in which nations are imagined and represented.

The chapter begins with a brief review of the trajectory and the transformations of the meaning of 'national' in contemporary Iran, particularly in the post-revolution era. I discuss the cultural and political context in which the national was initially suppressed and marginalized in the Islamic revolutionary discourse, and highlight how two decades later it was reinvented and re-appropriated in the official cultural policy. Such developments, it is suggested, have paved the way for the funding of national films such as *Mum's Guests* by state television, which operates under the supervision of the *Valiye Faqih* (Authority of the Jurisprudent).

The complex relation of 'the national' and 'the Islamic'

Despite its nation-wide popularity and appeal, the 1979 revolution in Iran has not usually been considered a *nationalist* revolution by either local or foreign commentators. Clearly this revolution was not formed on the premise of overthrowing a direct colonial rule, but rather aimed at changing the political system within the country. Moreover, the dominance of religious symbols and slogans in the revolution, and the undisputable power of its religious leadership distinguished this revolution from nationalist or communist revolutions. However, the fact that a call for *esteqlal* (independence) formed one of the main slogans of the revolution suggests that national aspirations and motivations also played an important role in the uprising against the Shah, who was by and large seen as a western puppet. There was also strong resentment felt by the revolutionaries against the 1953 CIA-engineered coup, which toppled the popular nationalist Prime Minister Mohammad Mosaddeq. It should be mentioned however, that even the rise of Mosaddeq to power would not have been possible without the support of religious leaders such as Ayatollah Kashani, who was then the Speaker of Iran's Parliament. In fact the success of the coup was, at least in part, due to the disputes between Mosaddeq and Kashani and the divisions among their supporters.

Another reason why nationalism was not a dominant theme in the revolutionary discourse may be the fact that the Pahlavi regime had manipulated and appropriated Persian nationalism as a political ideology to legitimize its power, and in doing so had subordinated Islam. The government used Iran's pre-Islamic heritage and civilization to justify monarchism and represent the Shah as heir of the ancient kings of Iran such as Cyrus the Great (600–529 BC). The anti-Arab and anti-Islamic writings of intellectuals such as

Ahmad Kasravi and Sadeq Hedayat, as well as historical accounts like *Do Qarn Sokut* (*Two Centuries of Muteness*, 1951) by Abdolhosein Zarrinkub – which lamented the decline of Persian literary and cultural production during the rule of Arab caliphs – are only examples of a dominant cultural nationalism which prevailed in the Pahlavi era (1925–79). In response to this cultural composition, leading Muslim philosophers and ideologues such as Morteza Motahhari made various attempts to reconcile Islam and some aspects of nationalism. In an extensive study titled *The Mutual Accomplishments of Islam and Iran* (1970), Motahhari argues that in terms of contributing to the enrichment of Islamic thought and the prosperity of the Islamic civilization, no other nation has matched the efforts made by the Persians. Yet he also highlights the hierarchical political system, social stratification and exclusions in Persia before the arrival of Islam, which allowed only the elite ruling classes the privileges such as education. Had it not been for the corruption and injustices of the Sasanid Empire, and the liberating message of egalitarianism in Islam, Motahhari argues, the Persians would have resisted Islam. In his view, the Arabs of Arabia at the time were in no position to impose a new religion on one of the most powerful empires of the time. The relation between Islam and Iran, he thus concludes, has been fruitful and beneficial for both sides (Motahhari 1983).[2]

These theoretical attempts to reconcile the Islamic and the national were not entirely successful in practice. The memories of clashes between the supporters of Mosaddeq and Kashani were still quite strong. There were some nationalist politicians and groups who opposed the Shah, yet did not want to concede to the religious leadership of the revolution either. Some of them, like Shahpur Bakhtiar, had even contributed to saving the monarchy in its final days through reformist solutions. After the revolution, other clashes between the secular nationalists and the religious leaders of the revolution occurred over the introduction of Islamic laws, which did not end in favor of the nationalists. Even the temporary government made up of moderate Muslim nationalists, which was initially approved by Ayatollah Khomeini, did not last long and resigned after the US embassy in Tehran was seized by Muslim students. These events intensified a political and cultural conflict between Islam and nationalism in the post-revolutionary era, and gradually terms such as 'nation' and 'national' were suppressed in official discourse and substituted respectively by *Ummat* (the Quranic term for 'community of the faithful') and 'Islamic'. Even the name of Iran's legislative body, which was initially mentioned as *Majles-e Shora-ye Melli* (National Assembly) in the Islamic Republic's constitution, was later changed to *Majles-e Shora-ye Eslami* (Islamic Assembly).

It was nearly two decades later that there occurred a moment of reconciliation between Islam and nationalism in official policy and discourse. In 1998, during the elections of *Majles-e Khebregan* (Assembly of Experts) – the influential council of jurisprudents that appoints and oversees Iran's religious leader – the official broadcast media for the first time employed explicit nationalist slogans, themes and symbols to encourage people to participate

---

[2] For a comprehensive account of the theological and political thought of Morteza Motahhari and his impact in the Islamic Republic, see Davari (2005).

in the election. The excessive use of Islamic themes and slogans in state media during the Presidential campaigns of 1997 had caused a backlash and resulted in an embarrassing defeat for the candidate who was seen by many to represent a strict Islamic agenda. Unlike the presidential and parliamentary elections however, neither were there any 'bread and butter' issues at stake in the election of the Assembly of Experts, nor was the contest between white-bearded senior clerics as enthusiastic to encourage a massive turnout. Many commentators, therefore, expected a very poor turnout, which could have compromised the legitimacy of the Assembly. The unprecedented use of national melodies, national symbols and nationalist rhetoric by radio and television during the election campaigns, however, proved highly successful in encouraging 18 million people to vote. This event marked an official reconciliation between 'the national' and 'the Islamic' in the post-revolutionary political and cultural context. The Islamic and the national have been further united in recent years, particularly following the labeling of Iran as part of the 'Axis of Evil' by George Bush, and the increasing pressure by western governments on Iran to abandon its nuclear program, which has strong support among the Iranian public.

Another important catalyst in the reunion of the Islamic and the national in post-revolution Iran was globalization. The emergence of new media facilitated an unprecedented flood of foreign cultural products into the Iranian cultural sphere. In the view of some authorities this signalled the threatening arrival of an 'alien culture', which could only be resisted through the union of the cultural forces and resources of 'the Islamic' and 'the national'. However, the government needed a new definition of 'national identity' that would be more inclusive and could encompass both Iranian and Islamic elements. Cultural authorities were beginning to realize that the national and religious aspects of the people's cultural identities could not be easily separated. These two dimensions, along with many other individual and social identities, had coexisted in the lives of Iranians over centuries and, in a sense, had resulted in hybrid cultures and identities, which could not simply be disintegrated.

New meanings of 'the national'

In August 2006 as part of the research that resulted in the present book, I obtained interviews with Mohammad-reza Jafari-jelveh – former Deputy for Cinematic Affairs at Iran's Ministry of Culture and Islamic Cultivation – and Dr Emad Afroogh – former Member of Parliament and Head of the Parliament's Cultural Committee. In response to my questions about cultural policy, it was noticeable that neither of them referred to Islamic principles and obligations to justify the intervention of government in the field of culture. Contrary to what might have been expected of a senior cultural executive appointed in President Ahmadinejad's administration, or of a senior parliamentary figure affiliated with the 'conservative' *Osulgerayan* (Principalists), nowhere in the interviews did either of them make any claims to the effect that 'we have a divine duty to control the field of culture on God's behalf' and the like. They did refer to Islamic world-views and values when arguing, for example, against global capitalist culture and the impact of 'Americanization', yet in terms of cultural policy, Afroogh spoke of the 'cultural rights of the people', which must be delivered by the government, and Jafari-jelveh emphasized that the government 'as the people's representative' has a dual responsibility to preserve their 'identity and fundamental values', as well as 'guaranteeing their freedom' (Appendix III; Appendix IV).[3]

From a skeptical point of view, we might consider these changes in rhetoric as being superficial and insignificant: merely a verbal change that makes no difference in the reality of how the government acts in Iran. Yet the fact that a film like Daryush Mehrjui's *Mum's Guests* can be funded and produced by the Islamic government's state television indicates that the changes have gone beyond the level of rhetoric. It is also notable that in terms of film policy, the promotion of *national* cinema has in recent years become an official motto of the Ministry of Culture and Islamic Cultivation. Government institutions have organized conferences, dedicated special awards in film festivals, and published books on this theme.[4] While some critics remain skeptical of this approach and its underlying intentions (Danesh 2008), others in the film industry who assume, or hope, that an emphasis on *national* cinema will provide a more inclusive and less-restricted space for artistic production have welcomed the move.

One important point regarding the modern concept of nation in contemporary Iran is the way it has been translated into Farsi. The first generation of Iranian intellectuals who became familiar with modern political ideas had a difficult task in translating the relevant terms and concepts. Some historical accounts suggest that these intellectuals, fearful of the reaction of the monarchy and religious authorities, employed religious terms as substitutes for concepts such as nation (Ajudani 1997). For instance the term *mellat*, which over the last century has been used in Farsi as an equivalent for nation, is actually an Arabic term which appears 17 times in the Quran with a range of meanings such as 'path', 'way of life' and even 'religion'. While secular authors like Ajudani criticize this strategy in translation and blame

---

[3] These new standpoints in cultural policy, it can be argued, are also the outcome of the critique of certain interpretations that represent 'Islam' as a single, unified and all-embracing ideology. Before the revolution, the significant theoretical debates between Muslim and secular theorists had shifted Muslim ideologues toward forming a kind of unity in representing Islam. Religious intellectuals such as Morteza Motahhari and Ali Shariati quite often presented their views and theories about Islam as *the* theory of Islam, juxtaposed to *the* theory of Marxism, or *the* theory of Liberalism. It was not until long after the revolution that differences between Islamic schools of thought, or the different interpretations of Islam, were theoretically discussed. The work of some Iranian intellectuals such as Abdolkarim Soroush in the post-revolution era played a significant role in this respect (Paya 2005). The eight years of a 'reformist' government in office (1997–2005) and the dominance of terms such as 'civil society', 'rule of law' and 'citizenship' in official discourse, did no doubt further institutionalized the use of modern political rhetoric among government officials.

[4] See for example the recently published *Tarhi baraye aknoon: dar masire cinemaye melli (A Proposal for Now: Towards National Cinema)* (Jafari-jelveh 2008). This volume consists of a grand development plan for Iranian cinema, which defines a role for all government institutions and organizations in contributing to the establishment of a viable national film industry.

some first-generation intellectuals for distorting the 'intrinsically secular' concept of nation, for cultural authorities of the Islamic Republic such as Jafari-jelveh the double origins of the term *mellat* indicate the hybrid nature of Iranian nationalism and explain why 'a national view is also a religious view' (Appendix IV).[5]

For Afroogh, human identity is not totally fixed and inherited, nor is it entirely invented and constructed. He believes some elements of our identity are fixed, but maintains that there are also 'flexible' and 'unsettled' aspects, which are determined by the acts of the individual. He suggests that national identity should be seen as one aspect of our identity, which can coexist with other identities: 'we are not presenting a concrete or formalistic guideline of identity to the artist', Afroogh insists, '[this] would prevent the diversity of cultural production' (Appendix III). He does, however, recommend that '[I]f an artist wants to be influential within the environment s/he is living in [...] s/he should neither ignore local and national identity, nor act as a totally hostile rebel towards it' (Appendix III). Rather than transforming or revolutionizing people's identities, he stresses, the latter would alienate people from his/her artistic work (ibid.).

When Jafari-jelveh was reminded of some disastrous consequences of nationalism in Europe such as World War II, he maintained that preserving national identity does not require 'blind and extreme nationalism' or confrontation with others. 'There should never be bloodshed over the borders of difference', he stated, adding that such borders are only 'signals and signifiers that help preserve and protect a heritage' (Appendix IV). In his view, humanity begins from a stage where all humans constituted a single community and shared a belief in a 'single truth', but later in history with the dispersion of humans around the world and the formation of diverse communities and ethnicities, 'truth' was also dispersed. If we take account of difference from such a perspective, Jafari-jelveh maintains, we will be able to recognize our 'shared values' with others, as well as the differences. Afroogh similarly employs the concept of *Vahdat dar Kesrat* (Unity in Diversity) – which has deep roots in Sufism, mysticism and Islamic philosophy – to argue for a cultural policy that, while not giving up belief in a 'single truth', recognizes diversity and difference, both within the nation and beyond (Appendix IV). What I want to conclude here is that the production of films like *Mum's Guests* by government organizations of the Islamic Republic is an outcome of such perspectives toward diversity and difference. But before moving on to analyzing this film, it is useful at this point to track Mehrjui's career back to the early days of Iranian cinema's 'new wave' and to discuss, in brief, a number of issues about his pioneering film, *The Cow*, in the light of globalization theories.

---

[5] This suggestion may not be as surprising if we take account of Iran's demographic characteristics. According to statistics over 98 per cent of the Iranian population is constituted by Muslims. Even when considering the different schools of Islam, Shi'a constitutes a significant 90 per cent majority of the whole population. Clearly not all the Muslim or Shi'a population are practicing Muslims. Yet the beliefs and values of the faithful in such a significant majority would certainly influence the policies of any national government.

Iranian cinema's new wave and the early impact of globalization

In 1971, for the first time in the history of Iranian cinema, an Iranian full-length feature film was screened in a major international film festival. *Gav* (*The Cow*) was not initially included in the Venice festival's program that year and did not have any subtitles, but it received a warm reception and won the Critics' Award. The producer of the film – the Iranian Ministry of Culture and Arts – had refused to officially submit the film to the festival and thus a copy was smuggled to Venice at the last minute. *The Cow* had been produced two years earlier (1969) and was subsequently banned in Iran, but following its international success the ban was lifted and the film was screened for the Iranian public.

The film's director, Daryush Mehrjui, was a young UCLA graduate in philosophy, and its script was written by Qolam-Hosein Sa'edi, a leftist playwright and novelist. On the surface, the film was a simple narration of a rural man's emotional relation with a cow that was his only source of income. Following the death of the cow, the man suffers a mental collapse and begins identifying himself as the cow. Within the framework of Iranian film historiographies, *Gav* has generally been recognized as one of the most significant pioneers of the 'new wave' in Iranian cinema. Some have even gone as far as suggesting that '[h]ad it not been for Mehrjui's *The Cow*, Iranian cinema would not be what it is today' (Dabashi 2001: 250).

Bearing in mind Appadurai's notion of 'ethnoscapes' and the role that the movement of people plays in the processes of globalization, one could see Mehrjui as a young Iranian student who had travelled to the United States, studied at an American institute and returned to his home country to take up a career as a film-maker. Mehrjui and some other fellow film-makers such as Farrokh Qaffari, Fereidun Rahnema, Sohrab Shahid-Sales and Parviz Kimiavi, who were largely – though not exclusively – involved in creating the 'new wave' of Iranian cinema in the 1960s and 1970s, all had been trained in Europe or America. They thus had the advantage of a double view, which was a result of being located both inside and outside the local/national culture.

Moreover, Appadurai's notion of 'ideoscapes' can also be applied to demonstrate what was happening in Iranian cinema at the time. This new generation of artists and film-makers, like many of their predecessors, brought philosophical, political, social and cultural ideas of the Enlightenment and European modernity into the local culture. Clearly in the course of this exchange they did not simply play the role of passive importers of foreign ideas; rather they were engaged in negotiations and appropriations with both the local and the global in achieving their distinctive voice and style. Farrokh Qaffari's *Shabe Qoozi* (*The Night of a Hunchback*, 1964) – perhaps the very first of a series of films that were later labelled as 'the new wave' – was an attempt to employ the narrative form of the oriental *One Thousand and One Nights* to tell a grim contemporary story in a neorealistic style. Such pioneers had of course a quite difficult task and their work was open to dispute and controversy. Many of them, were criticized for imitating European intellectual cinema, particularly

French *Nouvelle Vague* or Italian Neorealism.⁶ The unconventional styles and themes of these films alienated and frustrated local audiences, who, in some cases, even vandalized cinema theaters because the films did not meet their expectations of a 'proper' film.

It is also important to remember that despite being funded by the Ministry of Culture and Arts, *The Cow* only got the chance of being screened inside Iran after its profile was boosted by winning an award at an international film festival. The authorities of the time were facing a difficult dilemma. On the one hand, they could not resist the international reputation of the film and the advantage of being credited as the patron of modern arts. On the other hand, the gloomy and deteriorating image of rural Iran in this film was in sharp contrast with the government's intention to propagate the image of an urban, modernized and industrialized country. Finally, the solution was found by adding a caption to the beginning of the film, which informed the viewers that the events of this film took place before 1962 when 'His Majesty the King of Kings' introduced the Land Reforms Bill. The case of *The Cow* was perhaps the first instance in the history of Iranian cinema where global/international support for a film influenced local/national film-making conditions. For some Iranian filmmakers, the global or the international has ever since involved a sense of empowerment and emancipation, to the extent that – as we have seen in the previous chapter – a few have left their homeland altogether.

After the revolution, *The Cow* was the only film that Ayatollah Khomeini, as the religious leader of the Islamic Republic, ever publicly commented on. He appreciated it as an example of 'a good and instructive film', despite the fact that it was written by a Marxist novelist and directed by a secular graduate of an American school. It appears that for Ayatollah Khomeini, *The Cow* was sufficient evidence, in the ambiguous immediate years following the Islamic Revolution, to prove that cinema is not necessarily about sex and moral decadence, and thus it could be officially recognized as a legitimate art under the Islamic Republic.

Mehrjui and the post-revolution circumstances

Despite being the director of the only film that the leader of the Islamic Revolution had ever praised, Mehrjui faced some problems in making films after the revolution. Following the banning of his film *Madreseh'i ke Miraftim* (*The School We Went To*, 1980), Mehrjui moved to France and lived and worked there for a few years. In these years he made a documentary for French Television entitled *A Travel to the Land of Arthur Rimbaud*. Despite his international reputation, however, he did not pursue the position of an 'exilic' or 'diasporic' film-maker and returned to Iran in the mid-1980s. Ever since he has directed 13 feature films with a variety

---

⁶ For example, new wave films such as *Shabe Qoozi* (*The Night of a Hunchback*, 1964) by Farrokh Qaffari, *Khesht o Ayeneh* (*Mud-Brick and Mirror*, 1965) by Ebrahim Golestan, and *Gav* (*The Cow*) have been seen as inspired by Neorealism while Parviz Kimiavi's *Mogholha* (*The Mongols*, 1973) is considered as being 'heavily influenced by the work of Jean-Luc Godard' (Mirbakhtyar 2006: 44, 55, 92).

of themes, genres and styles, ranging from high-art productions with dense philosophical themes, to social satire and comedies that have attracted wide popular audiences. In general, his films before the revolution were more concerned with social commentary, and the characters were largely from the deprived and marginalized sections of the society. After the revolution, on the contrary, he has largely dealt with the problems and contradictions in the lives of middle- and upper-class sections of the society. 'It did not really make much sense to make such socially-engaged films, at least in the beginning [of the Islamic Republic]', Mehrjui explains, 'because now the poor people were ruling the country and they themselves pretty much knew how to deal with the plight of the poor' (Dönmez-Colin 2006: 78). *Mum's Guests* however, as we shall see, marked a return to the issue of poverty, though in a rather different light than his films made before the revolution.

Mehrjui's 2006 film, *Santoori*, which deals with the devastated life of a young musician and pop singer who faces problems in his career and gets addicted to drugs and alcohol, was screened in Tehran's Fajr Film Festival and won a number of awards including Best Actor. Only a few days before its public release in cinemas, however, the film was banned following a direct intervention by the Minister of Culture and Islamic Cultivation.[7] More recently (June 2010), the film was eventually given a permit for distribution in the VCD and DVD market. Mehrjui's *Banu* (1991) had also been banned when the former 'reformist' President Khatami served as Minister of Culture. But Merhjui's relation with the cultural authorities of the Islamic Republic has not always been so hostile. There are a number of films in his record that have been fully or partly funded by government institutions. While generally being considered an 'intellectual filmmaker', Mehrjui has also faced charges of opportunism and pragmatism (Dönmez-Colin 2006: 74). One of these instances, as it will be discussed below, was in the case of *The Lodgers*.

Unlike many other founding figures of the new wave of Iranian cinema in the 1960s, Mehrjui still plays a significant role in Iranian national cinema. Approaching the age of 70, he is still able to make films that simultaneously receive the praise of critics and are widely popular among public audiences. In contrast to transnational film-makers, such as Shahid-Sales, Naderi and Makhmalbaf, who have – at the price of losing local audiences – relied on international film festivals, multinational sources of funding, and transnational circuits of distribution and exhibition, Mehrjui's cinema remains located within national boundaries in terms of its funding and primary distribution. This does not mean that his films have not been screened in international festivals and other venues of exhibition outside Iran. In 2007, for example, Mehrjui was invited to the Pusan International Film Festival (South Korea) as

---

[7] According to Fars News Agency, the Minister believed that *Santoori* is 'not appropriate for public screening' due to some added scenes in the film that were not mentioned in the approved film script (http://www.farsnews.com/newstext.php?nn=8605120156, accessed 20th October 2007). Yet it was not clear which scenes the Minister was referring to. Some believe it was due to the film's depiction of the gloomy fate of some young artists who suffer because of the different prohibitions imposed on their work. Others referred to some scenes of physical intimacy between the lead actor and actress of the film.

a member of the jury, while a retrospective of his films from 1969 to 2007 were screened as part of the festival's 'Remapping of New Asian Auteur Cinema' program.[8] Moreover, some of the anthologies and monographs published in English about Iranian or Middle Eastern cinema include sections on Mehrjui's films or interviews with him (Dabashi 2001, 2007b; Dönmez-Colin 2006; Naficy 2003a).

The rest of this chapter, however, will deal with two of Mehrjui's films that have not received much critical attention abroad. In the present argument, Mehrjui's *Mum's Guests* is compared with *The Lodgers*, in terms of their representation of the nation, their approach to social and political issues and their reception by Iranian critics in their respective social and political contexts. The fact that the two films share a common cinematic genre and address some similar themes, and also that they were both popular among public audiences, makes them meaningful cases for comparison. The films are also linked intertextually: a scene in the first film inspired a novelist (Hooshang Moradi Kermani) to write a novel that subsequently served as a source of adaptation for the second film. *The Lodgers* is widely regarded as one of Mehrjui's most important films in the 1980s. It was also a record-breaking hit at the box office and remains one of the top ten Iranian films of all time in terms of total admissions. *Mum's Guest* on the other hand was a significant come-back for Mehrjui, both in terms of critical appraisal and public content.

The Lodgers

In a visually humorous and comic style *Ejareh Neshinha* (*The Lodgers*, 1986) tells the story of a number of families and individuals who live together as tenants in a four storey residential building. The building's owner and his family have fled the country and apparently have passed away in a car accident. Abbas, an affluent owner of a meat store, who used to be the landlord's representative and the building's warden, lives in one of the apartments and has many problems with the other tenants. The key characters among the tenants are: a lawyer with 'intellectual' interests, who lives with his family; an opera singer who has created a botanical garden on the roof; an overweight estate agent assistant who does Karate; and a disabled man with a poetic attitude, who has nostalgia for the past. They all complain about the deteriorating conditions of the building and blame Abbas for failing to meet his responsibilities. When the news of the landlord and his family's car crash in Europe and their subsequent death reaches Abbas and the tenants, a new battle begins in the building. Two rival estate agents, who know about the building's ambiguous ownership and want to grab their share of a lucrative deal, step in and inflame the two sides, causing more clashes and further destruction of the building.

---

[8] For more information, see the following links from the official website of Pusan International Film Festival (last accessed 12th November 2007): http://www.piff.org/eng/html/program/pro_special_2.asp http://www.piff.org/eng/html/program/prog_list.asp?c_idx=19&sp_idx=sp2

When Abbas, preached at by his 'traditional' mother, reaches a new settlement with the tenants and agrees to allow them to refurbish the building, the two rival estate agents intervene and incite another conflict: first there is a fight over doing or not doing the refurbishment, next there is a fight over who gets credited with doing the 'reforms' in the building. A group of construction workers are hired to do the refurbishment. At one point they are ordered to do the work; the next moment they are forced to stop. Sometimes they are exploited and mistreated; other times they are respected and gratified. In any case they remain confused and unaware of the underlying causes of the dispute. Eventually, when the relentless clashes exhaust the two sides and bring the whole building to a state of total collapse, municipality officials arrive and confiscate the building. However, they allow the tenants to live in the flats and buy them through mortgages.

Despite its diverse range of characters, *The Lodgers*, by and large, deals with the personal and social concerns of the Iranian middle class. The construction workers do not play a strong role in the narrative. They are represented en masse with little characterization and personal detail. At certain points they are even ridiculed for their simplicity and confusion during the conflicts of the upper classes. As Mehrjui admits in the quote cited earlier, we do not see the misery and anguish of the poor in this film. Rather it is the absurd conflicts and power struggles of the middle and upper classes that engages – and entertains – the viewer.

On the surface, the film appears to be a light comedy about housing problems in a metropolitan city like Tehran. In fact the film's success at the box office is reported to have been more significant in Tehran than in other provinces (Azimi 2008). But because of its entertaining quality some 'intellectual' film critics dismissed the film as escapist and accused the director of betraying his political and ideological commitments (Khoshkhoo 2007b). Even those critics who, in their coded reviews of the time, indicated that they had recognized a significant 'message' in the film's symbolism maintained that the 'fast rhythm' and 'numerous comic scenes' in *The Lodgers* 'prevent the viewer from thinking' and do not allow for the 'main message' to be perceived (Haji-aqa-mohammad 1987). As one critic notes, *The Lodgers* was made at 'a time when talking about "big issues" in films was trendy and thus [most intellectuals] believed this was a vulgar film' (Eslami 2006: 209). Within the intellectual film culture of the time, the type of films that were mostly privileged and credited were those that involved complex themes of a social and philosophical nature and were made in either avant-garde or realist forms and styles. A comedy involving many slapstick scenes, therefore, was not very likely to be praised.

Another reason for the critics' discontent was the ending of the film. *The Lodgers* ends with an unexpected promise of hope for a prosperous future. We see government officials who demonstrate plans and proposals for revitalizing the building and its surrounding area as well as offering mortgages to the tenants. It is not clear whether this ending was added to the initial script at the request of the cultural authorities of the time, or if it had been included by Mehrjui in the first place as a concession in order to get the script approved. Mehrjui has recently hinted that the 'real' ending of the film is when the building reaches a

Figure 1: Vulgar Comedy or Political Symbolism? (Akbar Abdi (Qandi) and Ezzatollah Entezami (Abbas) in *The Lodgers*. Photo by: Mitra Mahaseni. Courtesy of Iranian National Film Archive.)

state of total destruction (Qarehsheikhloo and Vafai 2006: 302). This is a scene toward the end of the film where a white pigeon – perhaps symbolizing 'freedom' – lands on an already shaky water tank on the roof and causes it to collapse. It results in a flood in the building that destroys almost everything, as well as flushing all the tenants down the stairway, through the main door, to the front yard. Not many critics at the time were satisfied with Merhjui's 'alternative ending' and thus despite breaking box office records, the film did not receive a warm reception by critics.

Two decades later, however, many critics have looked back and written on the virtues of the film. Following the screening of *The Lodgers* in a series of seminars on satire and comedy in 2007, Ahmad Talebi-nejad, a veteran film critic, named it as 'the best social comedy of post-revolution Iranian cinema' (Moosavi 2007). Another critic went further by suggesting that the neglect of *The Lodgers* has been 'one of the darkest pages in the history of film criticism in Iran':

In the context of those years of war and idealism, *The Lodgers* signals the intelligence and insight of a filmmaker who has a critical and visionary view towards his society [...].

> The critics failed to recognize the degree of intelligence in *The Lodgers* at the time. Today the film seems like a miracle. The critics' attitude towards this masterpiece reminds us of the person who couldn't see the forest for too many trees.
>
> (Khoshkhoo 2007b)

As already suggested, there are in fact some indications in the film's symbolism that would facilitate a political reading. The building itself could be seen as an allegory of the edifice of the newly established revolutionary government. It is mentioned in the film that this four-storey building was built on an infrastructure initially designed for a one-storey building, and that the foundations were not strong enough to hold the structure. Moreover, we learn that due to insufficient resources, cheap and unreliable material had been used for constructing the building. Abbas's mother keeps reminding him that he is not the 'owner' of the building, but only a warden who has the responsibility of 'taking care' of it. The two rival estate agents quite explicitly represent unrestrained factional politics and its destructive polarizing impact on the society.

One person who did identify a political message in the film was Mohsen Makhmalbaf, who at the time was a radical, revolutionary film-maker. He was so infuriated by the film that he wrote a private letter to the head of Farabi Cinema Foundation (FCF) – the government's executive branch for cinema affairs – and strongly attacked him for allowing such a film to be produced. In this provocative letter Makhmalbaf writes that after watching *The Lodgers*, he had even considered going up to Mehrjui and embracing him with a grenade in a suicide attack. Fortunately Makhmalbaf changed his mind after consulting the Quran, and decided to write a letter to the head of FCF instead.[9]

The experience of watching the film again, nearly two decades after its release, produces some fresh insights into other social and cultural specificities and problems of Iranian society that have increasingly become the subject of public debate in recent years. The lack of respectful dialogue between individuals within and across different sections of Iranian society, and the prevalence of verbal and physical violence in private and public spaces is a crucial aspect of *The Lodgers*, which will perhaps be more noticeable today, than it was when the film was first released. The violent fighting scene between the two rival estate agency owners; the aggressive clashes between Abbas and the tenants; the cruelty of Abbas toward his teenage brother; and the careless attitude of Qandi toward his disabled housemate are key examples we can identify in the film in this regard. There is also a hilarious, yet revealing, scene in the film where the tenants are discussing a plot against Abbas, but fail to agree on the details. First they begin shouting at each other, then they invite each other to calm down,

---

[9] This happened at a time when Makhmalbaf was a high-profile revolutionary film-maker with five feature films to his name. It is said that the letter caused Mehrjui to go into hiding for a while in fear of similar attacks. The letter was revealed nearly two decades later in a book by Jamal Omid, a leading film historian, who had worked with the Farabi Foundation. Makhmalbaf's letter and the diplomatic response of Farabi's director general were also published in the Iranian daily *Shargh* on 1st August 2007: http://www.sharghnewspaper.ir/Released/86-05-10/288.htm (accessed 26th September 2007).

and eventually all of them – including the 'intellectual' lawyer and the opera singer – end up shouting: 'why are you shouting?' at each other.

Despite such images, which mirror the dark side of local and national culture, there is one key scene in *The Lodgers* that depicts a moment of reconciliation, collaboration and joy, and implies a potential for solidarity in spite of all the differences and disputes. As mentioned earlier, the relentless clashes in the building between Abbas and the tenants end in the poor construction workers being expelled without getting paid by either side. Abbas's mother, however, strongly criticizes him and reminds him of the socially respected character of his late father. She warns him against violating other people's rights and shredding the family's reputation. Abbas is moved and in a sudden twist in the narrative, he invites all the tenants to his home for dinner. Through one of the best and most hilarious car racing scenes of Iranian cinema, he and the tenants chase the lorry of the unpaid construction workers, who are heading back home in the outskirts of Tehran. Eventually they manage to stop the lorry and invite the baffled workers to join the party.

Figure 2: The Inspiring Feast of Reconciliation. (Photo by: Mitra Mahaseni. Courtesy of Iranian National Film Archive.)

Everyone gets involved in preparing a big feast and the tenants share their food in contributing to it. All those who minutes ago were fighting fiercely are miraculously reconciled, and they sit next to each other along with the astonished workers, who are still in their dusty work clothes. As they all sit at the same level around the dinner, which, as the custom goes in Iran, is set on the floor, we realize that a non-hierarchical space of peace and joy has been established without discrimination or exploitation. As noted earlier, this short-lived moment of emancipation is soon interrupted by the two powerful estate agencies, who do not favor a resolution among the building's residents. The wonderful scene, however, inspired an Iranian novelist Hushang Moradi-Kermani to write a novel with a similar central scene. The intertextual play became more fascinating when almost two decades later Mehrjui – who is renowned for his interest in literary adaptations – made the film *Mum's Guests* based on Moradi-Kermani's story.

Mum's Guests

A poor family is expecting a visit from a newly married couple, and the mother, Effat, who is the groom's aunt, is very anxious to keep up appearances on their first visit. The financial conditions of the family are critical since the husband (Yadollah), who works at a local cinema, has not been paid his salary for a few months. The family shares an old house in an impoverished area of Tehran, with an old Kurdish woman, a pharmacy student and a young drug addict who lives with his pregnant wife. Around this simple story line a 120-minute film full of action, emotion and comedy is constructed, which magnifies many aspects of the largely ignored and unacknowledged 'ordinary' life and everyday culture within the marginal and under-privileged classes of Iranian society.

Like *The Lodgers* this film also begins with images of the city, which form the background for the initial credits of both films. In particular, there is an emphasis on large modern buildings and skyscrapers that since the 1990s have increasingly become a dominant feature of north Tehran's urban landscape. In contrast to *The Lodgers*, however, the main focus of *Mum's Guests* is on disadvantaged classes and the film's central location is a traditional central-courtyard style house, comprising a yard with small gardens and a small pool in the middle, and rooms all around. Another notable difference is the centrality of a female character, who not only has a powerful influence in her own family as mother and wife, but also plays a significant role in settling disputes in the neighbourhood.[10] The film begins with scenes of extreme poverty, misery and violence: a family that has no resources to feed its guests; a worker whose work place – a cinema theater – is going to

---

[10] While most of Merjui's films in the 1980s were either male dominated or had central male characters, he significantly shifted his focus to women in the 1990s. Not only are the central characters of many of his more recent films women, the films' titles were also women's names, usually the name of the central character. These films include: *Banu* (1991), *Sara* (1992), *Pari* (1994), *Leila* (1996) and *Bemani* (2001).

be demolished; a young pregnant woman who is beaten up by her addict husband; a child who is smacked by his father; an old lonely woman from the Kurdish minority who has lost all her family in the war and has been displaced from her destroyed town near the Iran–Iraq borders; and, finally, a poor pharmacy student with a ridiculously undeveloped science lab, whose aspiration is to invent a pill for happiness. It is clear that Mehrjui has brought to the foreground a diverse collection of characters from the margins of Iranian society.

Early in the film we notice that there is no sense of privacy in the environment these people live in. No clear distinction can be made between 'the private' and 'the public' in such a deprived space, and the people cannot hide, therefore, behind their social masks. In the opening sequences of the film there are many instances of cruelty, jealousy, selfishness and insincerity, which portray negative aspects of the local culture, and by acknowledging them Mehrjui is quick to avoid the charge of romanticizing the local. However, it is under the same local circumstances and through these face-to-face relations that Effat's anxiety about serving her guests suddenly turns into a crucial collective task for all of her neighbors. Following a series of events, almost everyone in the neighborhood gets involved in preparing what turns out to be a miraculously lavish and colorful dinner. The neighbors are invited to join a feast, which, as one critic notes, is more like a carnivalesque dinner party – a place where not only misery and despair is replaced by joy and pleasure, but where social roles are also exchanged and tensions, discriminations and hierarchies disappear (Khoshchehreh 2004).

At the beginning of the film, for example, we have seen the 'criminal' drug addict and a young police officer (the groom, Effat's nephew) at each others' throats. This occurs after the addict physically abuses his wife for hiding his drugs. Over dinner, in contrast, we see them sitting next to each other and even playing and dancing, mocking the roles of police and thief. This ecstatic space, however, is soon interrupted when Effat, physically and mentally exhausted in the preparations for the evening, suddenly collapses and is taken to hospital. The bitter aspects of reality appear again when money is required for her treatment. However, things are not as miserable as expected, since a doctor at the hospital turns out to be a next of kin to the guest bride. Effat recovers soon and is returned home. Since it is too late for the guests to go home, a room is specially prepared for the bride and groom to stay overnight. The film ends when the lights in their room, as well as those in other rooms in the neighborhood, are switched off in sequence.

This oscillation between joy and grief, affluence and poverty, solidarity and conflict may be considered an expression of the general conditions of real life, which are never perfect. Mehrjui, however, seems to be emphasizing that even those small spaces of joy and short-lived moments of liberation are of great significance and must not be ignored. Happiness and emancipation were, in his previous films, usually depicted as being far away, perhaps impossible without greater economic, political and social change. Most of his socially engaged films depicted gloomy and hopeless circumstances, which the characters could hardly escape. Despite its bleak opening, *Mum's Guests* stands in sharp contrast in this respect as an optimistic and positive counter to Mehrjui's earlier social films.

Another feature of *Mum's Guests*, as one critic notes, is that in some ways it resists interpretation (Haqiqi 2006: 206). It is quite difficult to identify in this film the kind of social allegories and political metaphors that Mehrjui elegantly interweaved in films like *The Cow*, *The Cycle*, *The School We Went To* and even *The Lodgers*. Unlike *The Lodgers*, we no longer see in *Mum's Guests* the binary power camps and the conflict of interests, which cause clashes and disputes among 'ordinary' people. There is no particular ideological or political cause behind the clashes we see in *Mum's Guests*; they are just ordinary everyday disputes. While Mehrjui's earlier films usually dealt with particular ideological standpoints and 'grand narratives' such as existentialism, socialism and humanism, and raised big, and mainly irresolvable, questions on ethics, social justice, modernity, tradition, identity and emancipation, in *Mum's Guests* Mehrjui seems to have abandoned his enthusiasm for 'grand narratives'. The notion of 'class conflict', for example, is deconstructed in the film when we notice that Yusef, the poor drug addict, is the single heir of a wealthy upper-class family who live in the affluent areas of north Tehran. When Yusof realizes Effat's desperate situation, he decides to go to his parents' luxurious house and bring some food for the dinner. We find that he has abandoned his family after falling in love with a working-class girl; that is the same woman we saw him beating earlier in the film.

It would be easy to use some of the above aspects of *Mum's Guests* and to accuse Mehrjui of, once again, compromising his intellectual integrity and even giving up his social and political concerns. Some may even explain the allegedly depoliticized nature of the film in terms of its source of funding: for the first time in the post-revolution era Mehrjui's film was funded and produced by a company affiliated to the Iranian state television.[11] Yet if we consider the production of this film and *The Lodgers* in their respective historical contexts, it will become clear that in 2004 regulation guidelines in cinema and television in Iran were much looser than they were in 1986. Clearly in 2004, a skillful master like Mehrjui could not have been prevented from using the political symbolism that he used in 1986. Moreover, at the time when *Mum's Guests* was produced, even some in-house television dramas such as *Doran-e Sarkeshi* (*A Time of Rebellion*)[12] and *Bacheha-ye Khiaban* (*Kids of the Streets*)[13] were

---

[11] Apart from the fact that in Iran – as in some other countries – working for television has generally been considered as inferior to working for cinema, another factor that contributed to many film-makers' reluctance to working with television in the late 1990s was the political disputes and clashes between the 'reformist' government – which was strongly supported by artists and film-makers – and the 'conservatives', who controlled the Islamic Republic of Iran Broadcasting Organization (IRIB). By 2003 when Mehrjui became involved in making *Mum's Guests* however, the IRIB had to some extent recover from the damages to its reputation in the aftermath of the 1997 Presidential election. The IRIB managed to improve its popularity through initiating new developments in television and radio channels and adopting more inclusive and moderate policies in terms of programming.

[12] Directed by Kamal Tabrizi, aired on Iranian television in 2001 and 2002.

[13] Directed by Homayun As'adian, aired on Iranian television in 2003 and 2004.

depicting harsh social realities while others like *Qaribaneh*[14] even critically reflected on the post-revolutionary political circumstances.

It is more plausible, therefore, to suggest that in *Mum's Guests*, Mehrjui has deliberately avoided the kind of symbolic and allegorical representation that appeared in his previous films; rather, he has preferred to keep everything as simple as it appears. He makes no attempt to view social issues through the lens of established political ideologies. It seems that the micro aspects of power within the realm of the *cultural* are now more vital and crucial for him than the macro aspects of power in the *political* realm. The latter does not render his more recent film *apolitical*, but rather indicates an entirely different approach to power and politics, which, as suggested below, could be representative of the shifts in global power relations and other transformations in the age of globalization.

In *Mum's Guests* Mehrjui seems to be viewing society, if we are to theorize its social analysis, from a Foucauldian point of view, which maintains that 'power isn't localised in the State apparatus' and in institutions such as government, the army or judiciary. What is important for Foucault is the 'mechanism of power':

> I don't claim at all that the State apparatus is unimportant, but it seems to me that among all the conditions for avoiding a repetition of the Soviet experience and preventing the revolutionary process from running into the ground, one of the first things that has to be understood is that power isn't localised in the State apparatus and that nothing in society will be changed if the mechanisms of power that function outside, below and alongside the State apparatuses, on a much more minute and everyday level, are not also changed.
> (Gordon 1980: 60)

The fact that Mehrjui does not explicitly or implicitly engage with the 'State apparatus' in *Mum's Guests* indicates that perhaps he too does not reckon that all the ills and pains of a society can be healed by changes or decisions made at the top. He tends to emphasize that the processes of change must also take place within the micro domains of power and the neglected aspects of everyday life. From this point of view, tolerance, solidarity and mutual respect are as important within small institutions like the family, or communities such as a local neighborhood, as they are in the official political sphere. In this sense Mehrjui – unlike some transnational film-makers – is still maintaining a political role with respect to local and national culture in his cinematic practice. Not only is he directing the nation's attention to instances of extreme poverty as a major social concern in contemporary Iran, he is also reflecting on some other cultural problems at the local and national level and seeking to influence public opinion toward progressive changes.

While placing himself at the level of ordinary life and avoiding an anthropological perspective, Mehrjui maintains a critical distance from his characters. In doing so he is able to recognize not only their failures, problems and weaknesses but also their achievements, merits

---

[14] Directed by Qasem Jafari, aired on Iranian television in 2004.

Figure 3: The Carnivalesque Dinner Party. (Hasan Poorshirazi (Yadollah) dancing in *Mum's Guests*. Photo by: Shahrokh Sakhai. Courtesy of Iranian National Film Archive.)

and strengths. The realization of a marvellous feast in an impoverished social environment and the possibility of solidarity among a diverse local community may seem utopian – and perhaps herein lies the film's wide appeal – yet such a non-hierarchical carnivalesque space is liberating. Rather than depicting a 'primitive' Third World nation imprisoned in its traditions and doomed to failure, as in transnational films like *Kandahar* and *Scream of the Ants*, *Mum's Guests* recognizes and respects the active agency of individuals at the local and national level and thus rebels against the colonial mentality, which dictates that any form of change and progress must always come from the outside, from the 'civilized world'.

One way of contextualizing Mehrjui's shift of focus from 'grand narratives' to small stories, and explaining his departure from allegorical and symbolic representations of political messages, is by referring to the failures of the 'reformist' government in Iran (1997–2005). Despite being initially supported by many sections of the Iranian society and creating many aspirations across social divides, the 'reformist' government became predominantly engaged with a political and cultural agenda that was targeted at the urban middle and upper classes. This agenda fuelled intense factional clashes and polarized society, but did not result in meaningful changes and accomplishments for its supporters. Moreover, the 'reformists' almost entirely ignored the economic demands of underprivileged and disadvantaged sections of the society, which caused much alienation and frustration among them. The making of *Mum's Guests* happened in such a social and political context.

Exploring the traces of globalization

In a wider context *Mum's Guests* may also be seen as an indication of the 'post-conflict' era and the arrival of the age of globalization that replaced the old world order of two opposing ideological and political camps. Following events such as the fall of the Berlin Wall and the collapse of the Soviet Union, a shadow of disappointment and disillusionment was cast upon many intellectual circles and progressive movements around the world. The expectations and judgments within the Iranian intellectual film culture were thus far less informed by a desire for, and a bias toward, 'committed art' than they used to be in the past. A comparison of the different ways in which *Mum's Guests* and *The Lodgers* were received by critics at the time of their first screening is illuminating in this respect.

While in 1986, and despite its political symbolism, *The Lodgers* was largely ignored or even dismissed by critics, who saw it as an apolitical entertainment film, *Mum's Guests* was affectionately welcomed by a great number of critics. On its release, *The Lodgers* only received two pages of attention in *Film Monthly*, which was the only Iranian film magazine at the time. The piece is clearly written in a cautious and ambivalent style: it acknowledges that '*The Lodgers* is a good and unprecedented comedy in the history of our cinema', yet maintains that the film 'does not count as an advance in Mehrjui's professional profile' and 'does not offer a way forward' for Iranian cinema (Haji-aga-Mohammad 1987: 58). Two issues later *Film Monthly* published a more negative review by a reader who implicitly criticized Mehrjui for complicity with the authorities with regard to the film's ending (Poormohammad 1987).

Following the first screening of *Mum's Guests* in Tehran's Fajr Film Festival, however, *Film Monthly* published the results of a poll among a large number of Iranian critics, which demonstrated that the film was selected as the critics' 'Film of the Year' (*Film Monthly*, 2004a). What was even more surprising about this choice in the political context of those years was that prior to this point most film critics – who largely supported the 'reformist' government – paid little attention to films and series produced by the state television, which was run by the 'conservatives'. When *Mum's Guests* was released in cinemas, *Film Monthly* dedicated a special dossier of over 30 pages to this film (*Film Monthly*, 2004b). A new generation of young critics, in particular, wrote lengthy articles in admiration and praise of the film. 'We have learnt from *Mum's Guests*', wrote the editor of *Film Monthly*'s special dossier, 'to be compassionate, and that if we want to enjoy a pleasant life beside each other, the rules of the game are what Mehrjui and his film teach us' (Hasani-nasab 2004: 79). Whether an outcome of the blurring of political and ideological boundaries in the era of globalization, or the result of wider acquaintances beyond the local and the national, it is clear that the Iranian intellectual film culture had shifted toward a more inclusive stance.

Another impact of globalization that can be identified in *Mum's Guests* is the blurring of a number of conceptual binary oppositions. First and foremost, in this regard is the film's deconstruction of the high-art/low-art dichotomy. There are a number of direct references in *Mum's Guests* to the popular 'song and dance' melodramas of the Pahlavi era. This group of films, among which *Ganj-e Qaroon* (*Qaroon's Treasure*, 1965) stands as a key example, were usually constituted around a central 'don't worry, be happy' theme targeted at disadvantaged classes and suburban dwellers. Most critics of the time denigrated this kind of cinema – stigmatized as *Film-Farsi*[15] – for being vulgar, lacking any sense of artistic value and deceiving the masses. From the point of view of clerics and some Muslim intellectuals, these were considered immoral films that corrupted the youth and prevented them from engaging with serious matters of social life.

While Mehrjui's *The Cow* (1969) initiated a radical departure from the conventions of *Film-Farsi* and became an exemplar of 'intellectual cinema', his *Mum's Guests* (2004) seems to have abandoned the elite/popular distinction altogether. Not only does this film involve a 'don't worry, be happy' theme, it also reproduces, through the character of Yadollah, the movie enthusiast, some dialogues, songs and dance scenes of classic examples of *Film-Farsi* such as *Ganj-e Qaroon* (*Qaroon's Treasure*) and *Sultan-e Qalbha* (*Emperor of the Hearts*). It is noteworthy however, that Yadollah's memories are not restricted to Iranian films, or even Iranian popular cinema. Contrary to the general assumption about the clear divide between audiences of high-art films and popular cinema, Yadollah also impersonates the narrations of the trailer of Sohrab Shahid-Sales' *Tabiat-e Bijan* (*Still Life*, 1974), which is one of the pioneers of the new wave and an icon of 'intellectual cinema'.

The disappearing boundaries between high and low art in *Mum's Guests* and the self-referential aspects of the film (references to cinema) could be thought of as indicating a globalization of postmodernism in world cinema. As a graduate of philosophy, Mehrjui is conscious of the developments in postmodern thought and the critique of European Enlightenment, and has witnessed, in the 1990s and the 2000s, the failures and flaws of many grand utopian aspirations. In one of his interviews, Mehrjui even makes reference to Jean-Francois Lyotard's seminal work *The Postmodern Condition: A Report on Knowledge*, adding that

> We no longer have Existentialism, Marxism or Communism. It is the death of all ideologies. All the '-isms' are gone [...]. The era of great masters is gone. The great narratives, the great ideas or ideologies are gone. This is the era of multi-culture.
>
> (Dönmez-Colin 2006: 81)

---

[15] This scornful term was introduced by the Iranian film critic Hooshang Kavoosi in the 1960s to describe popular Iranian cinema of the time. These films imitated foreign genre films (mainly Indian cinema and Hollywood) so excessively that – in Kavoosi's view – they did not represent anything about 'Iranian culture' and 'national identity' apart from their language that was Farsi. The term is still used by some critics to pour scorn on any poor quality mainstream film.

Bearing in mind theories that have associated 'globality' and 'postmodernity' (Robertson 1992) or globalization and postmodernism (Featherstone 1995), we could see how Mehrjui's new disposition is informed by the globalization of postmodernism and the critique of Enlightenment ideology. In contrast to Mehrjui's previous films such as *Hamun* (1989) and *Pari* (1994), in *Mum's Guests* we hardly notice any quest for far away horizons of emancipation, nor is there any engagement with big questions about life. Rather, the film celebrates life and highlights the importance of achieving solidarity and creating happiness, even on a small scale and at a local level. In this sense, we might suggest, globalization seems to have scaled things down and relaxed boundaries, resulting in a relativization of the world, which undermines many dogmas. It also encourages a return to the ordinary and everyday, where there is perhaps some modest hope for progress.

We can also notice a blurring of boundaries in *Mum's Guests* between the 'Islamic' and the 'non/anti-Islamic'. The diverse characters of the film are neither devoted Islamists, nor are they entirely secular and detached from religion. Yadollah, for instance, has a religious name (meaning the hand of Allah) and his wife and daughter observe Islamic dress codes (*hejab*), but he loves cinema, knows many dialogues of Hollywood films by heart and sings the songs of *Film-Farsi* cinema. Such colorful and hybrid characterization in a film produced by state television stands in sharp contrast to the homogenized and purified image of the subjects of an Islamic Republic that previously dominated television programs.

The blurring of distinctions between the local and the global is another aspect of *Mum's Guests* that is related to globalization. As noted above, Yadollah has a profound passion for cinema and has been involved with cinema ever since migrating to the peripheries of Tehran from his hometown in the provinces. The rooms of his home are covered with posters of Hollywood films, with images of actors ranging from Humphrey Bogart and Steve McQueen to Robert Redford and Al Pacino. The presence of these iconic images of 'global cinema' in a local and remote setting such as Yadollah's house demonstrates that cinema had facilitated knowledge beyond national borders long before the current global era. The familiarity, even intimacy, of a local working-class character like Yadollah with American films and actors, however, stands in contrast with the confusion and alienation of the construction workers in *The Lodgers* when they faced the 'foreign' and 'elite' art of opera singing performed by one of the residents of the building.

Yadollah's dream of becoming an actor, however, ended in a nightmare after he was severely injured in a crash while acting as a stuntman. He was not paid anything in compensation: 'I devoted my whole life to cinema', he complains, 'but cinema was not loyal to me'. After that incident he has only been able to work in cinema theaters as a ticket controller or manual worker. Now he is even about to lose this job due to the economic downturn of Iranian cinema. Speaking about the miserable memories of his life to the guests, Yadollah falls into tears. The only good memories he has, which help him keep up, are the memories of films. When his wife anxiously reminds him of the problem of feeding the guests, and that they have no food at home, Yadollah's response is reassuring. With a mind full of memories of happy endings, he is hopeful that the problem will somehow be resolved in the end, and the film proves him to be right.

For Yadollah, Hollywood films and actors are not 'alien' or 'foreign' phenomena that have infiltrated a supposed authentic local cultural space. As Andrew Higson has argued, in many countries Hollywood has for long been 'an integral and naturalised part of the national culture or the popular imagination' (Higson 2002: 57). Far from considering it a threat to the local, a viewer like Yadollah finds the global empowering, at least in terms of helping him in overcoming the difficulties of a hopeless and painful life. Mehrjui does not seem to follow here the line of, for example, the Frankfurt School theorists on the 'culture industries' and their role in deceiving the masses, nor does he buy into the theories of 'cultural imperialism', which pay little attention to the meanings that are derived from cultural texts or products at the level of reception. Mehrjui is highlighting, on the contrary, the agency of the readers/consumers of such global texts/products and demonstrating how and why local audiences identify with, and derive pleasure from, such 'foreign' texts.[16] If, for underprivileged people like Yadollah, cinema is such a source of empowerment and self-esteem, it is perhaps because these films have enabled them to imagine an alternative world beyond their 'material limitations'. As Hamid Dabashi notes with regard to 'world literature':

[T]he literature my generation of Iranians read did not allude to a chimerical construct called the Third or the First world. To this day I have no clue if Dostoyevsky is 'western literature' or not, or Steinbeck, or Turgenev, or Melville [...]. In what we read we thought ourselves connected, emancipated, admitted to a world beyond our material limitations, into what we dreamed possible, in the company of humanity at large.

(Dabashi 2007a: 108)

The processes of relativization, which – in the view of theorists like Robertson (1992) – are intertwined with globalization, can also be identified in *Mum's Guests*' rather disenchanted representation of 'Science'. Ever since the encounter of Iranian students in Europe with the foundational texts of the European Enlightenment, the ideology of 'Science' has been one of the dominant themes in Iranian intellectual culture and discourse. 'Science' was represented not only as the only valid form of knowledge about the world, but also as an ideology that would guarantee progress, prosperity and happiness. Although the Islamic Revolution to some extent challenged Science's claim of having exclusive access to 'the truth', the authority of Science did not entirely disintegrate even under the Islamic government. In many Iranian films, both before and after the revolution, characters who have acquired scientific knowledge

---

[16] Clearly we should not neglect the crucial role of translation and dubbing in familiarizing 'the foreign' for local audiences and facilitating such inter-cultural understandings. The 'art' of dubbing in Iran has a rich history and is considered a highly creative procedure that includes not only reading (decoding) the foreign script and translating it into Farsi, but also using local expressions, proverbs, slang and even dialects of Farsi language as substitutes for the original dialogues of the film and the actors' discourse.

Iranian Cinema and Globalization

Figure 4: The 'Scientific' Operation. (Photo by: Shahrokh Sakhai. Courtesy of Iranian National Film Archive.)

were represented as being positive, superior, or capable of resolving local problems.[17] Even in *The Lodgers* we briefly notice such a character in the form of a female architect in a stylish outfit who is invited to inspect the building and consider its reconstruction. She lectures the tenants on the scientific requirements of constructing a building and offers to help in conducting repairs, yet due to the clashes between the tenants, she is not given a chance.

In sharp contrast to this image of a confident apostle of Science, we notice in *Mum's Guests* the character of a pharmacy student whose ultimate ambition is to invent a pill for happiness, but in fact has nothing apart from painkillers and vitamin C tablets to offer to the desperately-in-need Yusef. His humorous persona in the film could be seen as a critical

---

[17] Hamid Naficy provides an insightful account of the impact of the US government sponsored 'education documentaries' in constructing and disseminating such an understanding of Science in Iran in the 1950s. These films, usually about health and hygiene, were screened in different parts of Iran using mobile film projectors. This project was executed by a group of film practitioners from Syracuse University who travelled to Iran as part of Kennedy's Point Four initiative to promote modernization and development. The initiative was aimed at countries that were allies of the US at the time but were potentially fertile grounds for the growth of Communism because of poverty and underdevelopment (Naficy 2003b).

reflection on the ideology of Science and its failed promise to deliver happiness to human life. Again it seems that from a postmodern perspective, Mehrjui places this character neither above nor below the other uneducated or religious characters, but on the same level with them. The most significant accomplishment of the pharmacy student in the film happens in a scene where, through a satirically treated hygiene operation, he successfully manages to stitch the wound of a pet goldfish that was injured by a cat. Even after this significant achievement, the student remains modest and uncertain about its result and says: 'the remedy was with me, but healing is up to God'.

And finally, signs of a globally widespread consumer culture, which transcends national borders and infiltrates even remote and impoverished local environments, are also evident in *Mum's Guests* as a consequence of globalization. There is a scene in the film where we notice that the culture of consumerism is no longer limited to affluent sections of Iranian society. When Yusef brings, among other things, some shrimps from his parents' fridge to be cooked for the dinner, his wife is thrilled to have a chance of preparing a rather high-class dish. But being pregnant, she suddenly faints while doing the cooking. After becoming half-conscious again and while still hardly able to breathe, she calls Yusef as if she wants to deliver an important message.

In a scene that resembles romantic films where the extremely ill or fatally wounded lover struggles to say his or her final words to the beloved, she explains in great detail the full recipe of frying shrimps, of course in the familiar tone of television cookery programs. This scene stands in contrast to a scene in *The Lodgers* where we see one of the construction workers go to the toilet in Abbas's relatively luxurious apartment and, being unfamiliar with cologne, spray it into his face and eyes. This innocence resulted perhaps from the fact that in the 1980s, Iranian television did not broadcast commercial advertisements and consumerism was, by and large, considered a 'western cultural malady'. Along with broader trends in the globalization of capitalism, and given the post-war policies of economic reconstruction in Iran during the 1990s, commercial advertisements gradually found their way back to Iranian television channels and have contributed since to the prevalence of a new post-revolution consumer culture and knowing acquaintance with it.

Conclusion

This chapter examined the meaning(s) of the national in contemporary Iranian cinema and analyzed the impact of globalization in the work of the veteran film-maker Daryush Mehrjui. The discussion shows how, within the context of Iranian culture and politics, the ideology of nationalism and even the use of terms such as nation and national have always been a matter of debate and dispute. This situation has mainly stemmed from the ideological disposition of different governments in power, as well as the problematic relation between 'the national' and 'the Islamic', which intensified following the 1979 revolution.

Despite the hostility toward the ideology of nationalism in the early days of the Islamic Republic, over the past decade terms such as 'nation' and 'national identity' have increasingly been employed in official rhetoric and have become dominant aspects of cultural policy. As suggested above, there are multiple reasons for this shift, ranging from political expediency and the perceived threat of cultural globalization to new theoretical elaborations that have reconstructed terms such as 'nation' and 'national' in a mode compatible with Islam. These changing perceptions of the nation and national have lead to more inclusive approaches in cultural policy even within state-owned media, which are under the authority of Iran's religious leader.

In order to examine the impact of globalization on Mehrjui's cinema, this chapter presented a comparative study of two of his films. Apart from being selected as finest examples of *national* cinema by Iranian critics, these films also shared a similar social theme and comic genre, and were hugely popular among public audiences. The main purpose of the comparison, however, was to identify the differences between the two films, bearing in mind that one was made almost two decades after the other.

It was argued that while *The Lodgers* pours scorn on a dysfunctional middle class who – out of a greed stimulated by deeper political rivalries and a clash of interests – cannot achieve a resolution and save their residential building from destruction, *Mum's Guests* celebrates the fact that a diverse range of characters based in the most impoverished sections of society manage to overcome their disputes and collaborate on a project, be it as simple and mundane as preparing a dinner for a guest. Unlike *The Lodgers*, *Mum's Guests* tends to avoid symbolic or metaphoric representation of society or politics. Mehrjui's more recent film, I suggest, can be seen as evidence of the globalization of postmodernism and its disenchantment with 'grand narratives'. The blurring of boundaries between 'high-art' and 'low-art' and the satirical representation of Science are further evidence of the film's postmodern edge.

This observation, however, does not make *Mum's Guests* liable to the charge of being apolitical, as other postmodern or transnational artworks are sometimes accused of being. In its representation of extreme poverty, unemployment, domestic violence, drug addiction and internal displacements caused by war, *Mum's Guests* neither romanticizes the local or the national, nor is it indifferent toward their plight. It is also 'political' in the sense that it reveals repressed or transgressive aspects of local culture, and values the inspiration, rather than corruption, of a cross-cultural knowledge of, and pleasure in, global cinema. Yet at the same time, the film ends in hope by recognizing the possibility of solidarity among a diversified nation, based on a recognition of difference.

The blurring of distinctions between the global and the local in *Mum's Guests* can be considered evidence of what Robertson calls 'glocalization'. While in *The Lodgers* we notice a clear distinction, even distrust, between 'the foreign' and 'the indigenous', Mehrjui's more recent film portrays the intertwined and hybrid nature of local and global cultures and demonstrates how even ordinary audiences, at the local level, can actively interpret and selectively appropriate elements of global culture and combine it with pre-existing cultural specificities, in order to imagine, and even realize, a utopian reality beyond their material limitations.

Chapter 6

Ebrahim Hatami-kia's 'Sacred Defense' Cinema and Globalization

Introduction

Apart from the long history of orientalism and theories such as Clash of Civilizations (Huntington 1993: 68) and Jihad vs McWorld (Barber 1995), the events of 11th September have perhaps more than any other event in modern history intensified the representation of Islam as 'the other' in western media. The prevalence of a fundamentalist image of Islam, which masks the history and the diversity of Muslim nations, in many ways has obstructed the path toward inter-cultural dialogue and mutual respect. In particular it has concealed the changes and developments within the Islamic world and the steps taken by Muslims to rethink their own conditions and go beyond simplistic notions of self and other. This highlights the need for fine-grained studies that take account of the complex, diverse and even contradictory aspects of 'the Islamic' in the field of culture. In his introduction to a collection of essays titled *Islam Encountering Globalization*, Mike Featherstone emphasizes the importance of recognizing the other in the current phase of global interconnectedness:

> It can be argued that only by the recognition of the other, which itself is a product of the past the other has experienced […] one can attain greater freedom and the capacity to develop one's identity. Recognition of the other points towards respect, and the capacity to rethink the same/other dichotomy in us all. It points to the importance of counter-memories and counter-histories, the need to become aware of the grounds on which the current phase of globalization has been constructed.
> (Featherstone 2002: 10)

In many English accounts of Iranian cinema, the relation between Islam and cinema has been primarily discussed in terms of the Islamic government's attempts to 'Islamicize' cinema. Scholars and commentators have documented and analyzed the new regulations and codes of conduct enacted after the revolution, and have explained how the new government manipulated cinema to propagate its ideological agenda. Apart from introducing new ideological regulations, however, the Islamic Revolution also facilitated the introduction of a new generation of committed Muslim film-makers who were primarily concerned with constructing a new cinema that would represent their Islamic beliefs and values.

Following the invasion of Iran by the Iraqi army in 1980, many members of this generation went to the war front and became involved in producing documentaries, short films and eventually feature films about the war. Their efforts led to the creation of perhaps the most original cinematic genre of the Islamic Republic, namely *cinema-ye defa'e moqaddas* (sacred defense cinema). Some of these directors continued making war films in the post-war era, others moved on to address other social issues in their films. While many of these film-makers have been highly acclaimed by local critics, they have scarcely received any critical attention outside Iran, and their contribution to Iranian national cinema has been largely ignored.

In order to recognize the diverse manifestations of 'the Islamic' in post-revolution Iranian cinema and also to expand narrowly defined conceptions of 'the new Iranian cinema' based on the works of a few internationally celebrated auteurs, this chapter takes the Iranian war genre, or sacred defense cinema, as its point of reference. Given the debates on the relation of Islam, Iran and globalization (Ahmad and Donnan 1994; Mohammadi 2002, 2003; Semati 2008), my aim here is to focus on the ways that globalization has influenced the work of Muslim film-makers in Iranian cinema. The films of Ebrahim Hatami-kia, who is widely recognized as a founding figure of the Iranian sacred defense cinema, form the main corpus of this study. The chapter presents a close analysis of three of Hatami-kia's films: *The Scout* (1988), *From Karkhe to Rhine* (1992) and *Glass Agency* (1997). In addition it highlights the social and political contexts of the films' production and takes account of how they were received by local audiences and critics.

Since Hatami-kia and his work remain largely unknown to English readers, this chapter will begin with a review of his life and cinematic career.

Muslim Film-makers: From Makhmalbaf to Hatami-kia

As demonstrated in Chapter 4, Mohsen Makhmalbaf was the most prolific and prominent figure among the generation of Muslim and revolutionary film-makers who began their careers after the 1979 revolution. The contribution that Makhmalbaf has made to the post-revolution Iranian cinema is globally renowned, and his life and cinematic career have been widely discussed and are well documented in English (Dabashi 2008; Egan 2005). Ironically however, Makhmalbaf's success in international festivals and the amount of critical and scholarly attention paid to his work has, at least partly, been rooted in his disillusionments and disenchantments with Islam and the revolution. Dabashi, who has written extensively on Makhmalbaf, admits that 'One of the principal points of my attraction to his cinema is precisely because he was once a fanatical Islamist' (Dabashi 2008: 184).

The study of the Islamic dimension of Iranian cinema is largely restricted in its evidence to the statements and films of 'the early Makhmalbaf', which are translated as obvious examples of dogmatism and fanaticism. The story of Makhmalbaf resembles the evolutionary and teleological (grand)narratives of European modernity: a journey that begins from a stage of dogmatic commitment to 'the sacred', runs through the valley of doubt and disenchantment, and eventually arrives at Enlightenment and embraces secularism and humanism.[1] No surprise therefore that this story is familiar to, and has been appreciated by, many in the West.

'The early Makhmalbaf', however, is not fully representative of 'the Islamic' in the post-revolution cinema. One reason that his work and views on Islamic cinema became so provocative and controversial is that, apart from seeking to establish a new Islamic cinema, he also openly despised film-makers of the pre-revolution era for being *Taghooti* (aligned with the oppressor) and even called for a 'cultural tribunal' that would investigate their crimes (Baharloo 2000). At some points, as mentioned in the previous chapter, he had even written letters that involved implicit threats to other film-makers. Not all Muslim film-makers of the post-revolutionary era, however, were as militant and rigid as the early Makhmalbaf, and not all of them became disenchanted and disillusioned later, at least in the way he did.

Ebrahim Hatami-kia, Rasool Mollaqoli-poor, Kamal Tabrizi, Mojtaba Ra'ei, Ahmadreza Darvish, Jamal Shoorje and Azizollah Hamid-nejad are some of the Muslim film-makers who began their cinematic career by making films about the Iran–Iraq war. Among them, Hatami-kia is considered as 'the icon of professional religious cinema within the context of the Islamic Republic' (Mir-ehsan 2006: 46). If Makhmalbaf was the first major Muslim film-maker to rise to prominence after the revolution, Ebrahim Hatami-kia would no doubt be considered the second. Not all of Hatami-kia's films, however, have been 'religious' in the strict sense of the term. In terms of popular appeal, there are only a few Iranian directors whose names can attract audiences to cinemas and Hatami-kia is certainly one of them. While many critics consider him a 'trusted' film-maker who has close relations with those in power, the cultural authorities of the Islamic Republic – both 'conservative' and 'reformist' – have always had difficulty in deciding whether to consider him friend or foe. Some of his films have been both funded and banned by government institutions. Most of his films have critically reflected on social and political issues under the Islamic Republic. For Emad Afroogh, a sociologist and former Member of Parliament, Hatami-kia is 'the ground-breaking figure of social critique within the framework of the revolutionary discourse' (Appendix III).

Hatami-kia was born in 1961 in Tehran in a traditional lower middle-class family. Soon after the revolution, he took part in some amateur courses in cinematography and started making 8mm animations and short films. Following the invasion of Iran by Iraqi forces in 1980, he joined the newly established Revolutionary Guards and went to the war front with a camera rather than a rifle. He joined a group of young film-makers who produced a series of documentaries about the war that were regularly broadcast on television under the title *Revayate Fath* (*Narrating the Triumph*). The lead figure in this group who edited the films

---

[1] For an excellent example of these evolutionary narratives of Makhmalbaf's trajectory, see Hooshang Golmakani's article 'From Violence and Dogmatism to Tolerance and Compassion' (Golmakani 1999).

and wrote and narrated them was Sayyed Morteza Avini.[2] Avini's specific theory and style of documentary – which he named *Sabke Eshraqi* (*Illumination Style*)[3] – was influenced by his readings of Islamic philosophy and mysticism (*Erfan*). The prose of his narrations was rich with frequent intertextual references to Islamic texts, and in particular it appropriated many elements of Shi'ite rhetoric and symbolism such as those of the *Karbala* paradigm.[4] It can be argued that in many ways the *Revayate Fath* documentaries contributed to the formation of a sacred defense genre in Iranian cinema.

Hatami-kia made three short films between 1984 and 1985: *Torbat* (*Sacred Soil*), *Serat* (*True Path*) and *Towqe Sorkh* (*Red Collar*). These films were mainly based on his personal experiences in the war and helped mold what later became his particular style in the war genre. In 1987 Hatami-kia wrote and directed his first feature film *Hoviat* (*Identity*). The film was about a motorcyclist who, after a severe motoring incident, is mistakenly taken to the ward of wounded soldiers in a hospital. Since his face is covered with bandages everyone respects and privileges him as a pious veteran of war. Through his relations with other soldiers in the hospital, the uncommitted and indifferent motorcyclist becomes inspired to pursue a different way of life. From this very first film, a concern for identity became a

---

[2] Avini was trained as an architect at Tehran's Faculty of Fine Arts before the revolution and was well acquainted with modern art and western literature and philosophy. Soon after the revolution he joined the newly established institute of *Jahade Sazandegi* (Jihad for Construction). The new institute's mission was to facilitate construction and development of Iran's rural areas providing them with roads, electricity, water and health care. Avini was among the founders of the audio-visual division of this institute and began producing documentaries about these projects, particularly in rural areas such as Bashagard, whose existence had not even been acknowledged before the revolution. When the war began, Avini's group focused on producing quality documentaries of the war, which were later entitled *Revayate Fath* and broadcast on television on a weekly basis. After the war Avini developed his career as a writer, film critic and cultural theorist and became editor of *Sooreh* magazine, an influential monthly periodical on culture and art with an Islamic perspective. In 1993 Avini was shooting the new series of *Revayate Fath* in the former war zones when he was killed by a land mine. This little-known figure suddenly became widely recognized as a martyr and has since become the icon of Islamic and revolutionary art. Over the years Avini's books on film, art and culture have sold tens of thousands of copies, an achievement that few, if any other film critic or cultural analyst, has ever achieved in Iran. As a Muslim theorist and documentary film-maker, therefore, he has played a significant role in further legitimizing the 'western' and 'un-Islamic' mediums of film and television in the skeptical context of traditional and religious communities. His image has inspired many young Muslims, even clerics, to study art and film or pursue a career in the cultural sector, careers that were previously considered 'taboo' or 'inappropriate' within these communities.

[3] This name is derived from the title of a philosophical school known as *Eshraq* (*Illumination*) founded by the twelfth-century Muslim philosopher Shahab al-Din Suhrawardi.

[4] In the battle of *Karbala* (680 AD) Emam Hosein ebne Ali, the grandson and third successor of the Prophet Mohammad according to Shi'ite faith, was slaughtered along with 72 of his companions and family members including children by the army of Yazid, the Umayyad caliph. Emam Hosein had refused to submit to Yazid's rule, which he considered corrupt and illegitimate. The martyrdom of Emam Hosein and his companions has been commemorated for centuries by Shi'a Muslims across the world. As a trauma it has deeply influenced Shi'a culture and identity and due to its huge symbolic power has played a key role in mobilizing masses in Iran, both in the 1979 revolution and during the war.

central theme in Hatami-kia's films. His iconic use of the veterans' metal tag as a symbol of identity is well known by audiences in Iran.

Hatami-kia's main ambition in pursuing a professional film career was to represent 'the true nature' of the war, which, in his view, was a sacred act of defense. Most *Revayate Fath* members who had personally attended the war front were unsatisfied with the clichéd representations of the war in the reports of the state television.[5] They were also critical of some early feature war films produced by the pre-revolution generation of film-makers, which took their cue from European and American mainstream war films rather than real events at Iran's war front. For Hatami-kia such films failed to represent the difference of the sacred defense and the feelings and motivations of the fighters: 'I had read many [western] novels about war. But there were things in our war that were quite exceptional. There was a special kind of affection [in the fighters] inspired by the idealism of the time. This moved me to make my next film *Dideban (The Scout)*' (Ferasati 2001: 247). Hatami-kia's two groundbreaking films *Dideban (The Scout*, 1988) and *Mohajer (The Immigrant*, 1990) are largely credited with setting the standards and defining the terms of the sacred defense genre in Iranian cinema. One critic goes so far as to assert that 'without Hatami-kia the sacred defense cinema would not mean anything' (Mostaqasi 2006: 51). In his early career, Hatami-kia was so fully devoted to portraying the sacred defense that he was famously quoted as saying that he would never make a film that is not about the war.

In spite of this promise, Hatami-kia's post-war films cover a wide range of social, political and even international themes, which have gone beyond direct portrayals of the war front as in *The Scout* and *The Immigrant*. He has refused offers from government institutions to make merely nostalgic films about the spiritual and altruistic aspects of the community of fighters, or epic films about heroic military operations (Hatami-kia 2007). Rather, he has preferred to follow the lives of the warriors after the war, depicting the problems, challenges and contradictions they face in the post-war era. This has enabled him to become familiar with characters beyond the community of fighters, and places beyond the war front. He has travelled to Germany to see his wounded characters receive treatment; he has visited Bosnia to witness and portray a new war front where Muslims faced a violent aggression; he has reflected the pain and passion of those families whose sons or brothers went missing during the war; he has followed his lonely veterans in a rapidly changing city where few acknowledge their sacrifice and suffering; and he has portrayed the predicament of his comrades as they face the challenging questions of their sons and daughters about the war and its aftermath.[6]

---

[5] In an interview in 1986, Avini slams some documentaries and films produced by government departments and official media, accusing the producers of 'not knowing cinema' and 'not knowing the sacred defense'. He also criticizes the official War Propagation Committee for refusing to issue broadcast permits for some of *Revayate Fath* documentaries during the war (Avini 2001: 202–7). The War Propagation Committee was then headed by Mohammad Khatami, who became Iran's President in 1997.
[6] Hatami-kia's most recent film *Gozareshe yek Jashn* (*Report on a Party*, 2011) deals with the problems of the youth and presents a highly critical account of the Iranian police and the use of force in moralizing the young generation. Hatami-kia's previous film *Davat* (*Invitation*, 2008) was an episodic film in the style of Robert Altman's *Short Cuts* (1993), which also dealt with the taboo subject of abortion.

All these events have taken place while the processes of globalization have been increasingly influencing not only the economic, social and cultural dimensions of Iranian society, but the mind and vision of directors like Hatami-kia. However, when it comes to the impact of globalization on film production and distribution, Hatami-kia's cinema has not received much advantage from the new global developments. None of his films have been funded by international film companies, nor have they been promoted or awarded prizes in any film festival. Only one of his films has been distributed in the United Kingdom and the United States, and is available on Amazon.[7] Bearing in mind the range of publications in English on Iranian cinema, there are very few texts that even mention Hatami-kia's name or discuss his films.[8] It is interesting that even a great admirer of Iranian cinema such as Fredric Jameson seems to believe that what is represented of Iranian cinema in the West is 'a fair sample of the really great films'. The rest, he reckons, are 'grade B' films and 'religious stuff'.[9] Hamid Dabashi, who has written extensively on Iranian cinema and challenged what he calls 'the inordinate power that festival directors exercise in defining Iranian or any other national cinema', has also ignored Hatami-kia's work in his books such as *Masters and Masterpieces of Iranian Cinema* (Dabashi 2008).[10]

Perhaps it is premature to expect globalization to be an even set of processes, which benefit everyone in an equal way. In terms of national cinemas – as in many other areas – the processes of globalization generate pattern of exclusion and inclusion. The fact that a particular section of Iranian national cinema has become 'globalized' and received wide recognition in European and North American festivals and critical film cultures does not necessarily mean that they are 'a fair sample' of its best productions. The previous chapter on Mehrjui and this chapter on Hatami-kia, however, are based on the premise that we can also trace the impact of globalization on apparently 'non-globalized' sections of Iranian cinema.

---

[7] *Ertefa'e Past* (*Low Heights/Low Altitude*, 2002).

[8] These are: Roxanne Varzi's analysis of one of Hatami-kia's films in a chapter of *The New Iranian Cinema* (Tapper 2002), and her subsequent book *Warring Souls* (Varzi 2006); and Hamid Naficy's useful information on Hatami-kia in his entry on Iranian Cinema in *Companion Encyclopedia of Middle Eastern and North African Film* (Leaman 2003). In February 2007, for the first time a season of Iranian war films was organized at the Barbican Centre in London, which included talks on Avini's *Revayate Fath* documentaries and some of Hatami-kia's films. More recently there were two articles published on Iranian war cinema and Avini's war documentaries in a special issue of the journal *Iranian Studies* (Abecassis 2011; Karimabadi 2011). A collection of essays edited by Pedram Khosronejad and titled *War in Iranian Cinema* that includes an earlier version of the present chapter is also scheduled for publication by IB Tauris.

[9] In an interview in 2003 Jameson says: 'Today Iranian cinema is far and away the most exciting, and fortunately we *do* get to see that in the US. I'm told that Iranian cinema is much bigger than what we get to see; there's grade 'B' Iranian stuff for the home public and there's religious stuff, but we get a fair sample of the really great films'. (King 2003: 187).

[10] This is more surprising when we notice that Dabashi has generously dedicated a full chapter of his book to introducing Marziyeh Meshkini, the wife of Mohsen Makhmalbaf, who has so far directed two films. At one point in an earlier published book Dabashi briefly refers to Hatami-kia as one of the 'great Iranian filmmakers', yet maintains that his films are 'very parochial and simply do not translate, and thus do not get released abroad' (Dabashi 2001: 143).

An examination of Hatami-kia's films in this respect demonstrates that even the 'Islamic' cinema of the post-revolution era and its important component the sacred defense genre are not monolithic and unified bodies of Islamist propaganda and ideological instruction, which simply defy or resist any sense of globalization.[11] In fact many of these films involve critical reflections on the struggles, conflicts and transformations in post-revolution Iran and represent many challenges that Islamic societies face in the age of globalization.

In what follows I shall investigate Hatami-kia's journey in cinema after the revolution through a closer analysis of three of his significant films. The intention is to look for the points of change and to see whether links can be established between these changes and the processes of globalization.

The Scout: Constructing the image of the *basiji*

Dideban (*The Scout*, 1988) tells the story of a company of soldiers caught up in a critical position at the war front. After a failed operation they end up isolated in an area far from the friendly forces and close to the enemy. While many of them are wounded and they are running out of ammunition, the enemy's siege is imminent. Since there is no quick way of sending troops and artillery, a scout is sent on a mission to help them. After a perilous journey he reaches the group and then sneaks toward the enemy front to monitor their geographic positioning. Through radio communication with the artillery, he provides directions for firing shells at the enemy bases. While doing his job, the scout himself is surrounded by a large group of enemy forces. He contacts the artillery and gives the details of his own position as the new target. Just as the scout is surrendering to the enemy forces, the area comes under shell fire. When the Iranian troops arrive at the scene, among the numerous corpses of the enemy, they find the scout's dead body.

The above plot may at a first glance resemble some classic narratives in Hollywood war films that are centered on heroic acts of sacrifice by larger-than-life individuals. Yet as mentioned earlier, film-makers like Avini and Hatami-kia were clear in their intention to distinguish their work from Hollywood and other mainstream war genres:

> In our documentaries we never considered weapons, instruments or war machines as playing a principal role in the war [...] always it was the faith of the fighters that played the essential role. We avoided depicting false courageous and heroic actions like that of American films. The courage of our fighters stemmed from their spiritual confidence and certainty (*yaqin*), not from militarism and adventurism
>
> (Avini 2001: 193)

---

[11] It should be noted however that not all Iranian war films were made by committed Muslim directors who considered the war as being a 'sacred' defense.

In Hatami-kia's film too, we see no sign of the muscled heroes of the Hollywood action films or even the professional warriors of classical war films. Most of the veterans and even the commanders in *The Scout* look like amateurs. They all represent the key character of the sacred defense genre, namely the *basiji*.[12] This term – literally 'self-mobilized' – at the war time referred to volunteer forces that came to the war front out of spiritual and religious convictions rather that professional obligation. The *basiji* forces formed a large and strategic portion of the Iranian armed forces during the war and have been considered as the key to many of Iran's military achievements. The figure of the *basiji* embodied the ideology of the Islamic Revolution, and it became a fundamental concept in the discourse of sacred defense. Faith in God, altruism, piety, modesty, fighting the enemies of Islam, being prepared for sacrifice and the glorification of martyrdom were key elements in the culture of *Basij*. The character of a *basiji* was not necessarily defined as belonging to a particular class, ethnicity, gender, age or level of education, although during the war the majority of this force comprised young males from the lower classes. They were *ordinary* people who devoted their lives to serving and defending the Islamic Revolution. This may explain why the main roles in *The Scout* are played by non-professional actors. The lead actor does not even have a photogenic face, let alone a hero's body. In an attempt to represent 'the truth' about the war, Hatami-kia has kept all appearances in his film simple and ordinary.

Although the film is based on a linear narrative and involves the individual achievement pattern, the viewer's focus is not merely directed toward the accomplishment of a military objective. In fact the central character, Arefi,[13] refuses to consider his action as a personal achievement. From the beginning it seems as if he sets out on a heavenly voyage rather than a military mission. In the school of *Erfan* (Islamic mysticism) this journey is called *Seir o Solook*: a spiritual quest for truth and self-realization. There are many signs that indicate that Arefi's journey in *The Scout* is not merely a military mission. Early on the way to his destination, his motorbike is hit and destroyed by a rocket. Having lost the machine he relied on for transport, he now has to continue the journey on foot, which resembles a kind of pilgrimage. At first he is constantly frightened by the enemy mortars that pour down and explode along the main road. When he hears the scream of a mortar that is about to land close to him, he jumps into a mud field and holds his head in his hands. When he raises his head we see the tail of an unexploded mortar in a shallow pool of water, only a few feet far from him. He is baffled and breaks into tears.

In another scene we see him looking at his image reflected in the water. Then he begins stirring the water with his hand, eventually destroying his own image. He gets up and starts running, this time much more confidently toward his destination. Gradually the sound of

---

[12] *Basij* is the term used to refer to the organization of the volunteer forces, and *basiji* is used to refer to the individual.

[13] Hatami-kia's central character in this film is only introduced by his surname. The name *Arefi* derives from the noun *Aref*, which in Farsi means mystic and spiritualist. It refers to a pious person who has gained special knowledge through spiritual insight.

mortars and explosions fade out and the sound of his footsteps becomes louder. Along with this sound we hear the rhythmic sound of many other footsteps, as if he was accompanied by a brigade of invisible soldiers. This may be a reference to the verses of the Quran where the Prophet Mohammed is informed that thousands of angels accompanied the small army of Muslim soldiers (in the war of *Badr*) where they succeeded in fighting back a large army of enemies.[14] The scout's mission in this film and the very act of participating in the war, in many other sacred defense films, is a ritual of purification and transcendence. It is a process of elevation from the mundane to the divine, which ultimately ends with a reunion with God through martyrdom. Martyrdom is the finale of most sacred defense films, an ending both glorious and tragic, which seeks to inspire a catharsis in the viewers. As Avini has argued, sacred defense films are 'not made for entertainment'; their goal is to cause 'moral inspiration' (Avini 1999: 17).

Apart from its spiritual content and religious symbolism, *The Scout* also deals with some political and social dimensions. Metaphorically the film depicts an image of a people, caught empty-handed in a deadly war, with no allies to help them and little prospect of a glorious conclusion. The only way one could help save the nation is through self-sacrifice. Hatami-kia does not turn a blind eye to the tragic aspects of human suffering in war, or the devastating impacts of material limitations. In one scene he metaphorically indicates how these material limitations were influencing the idealistic slogans. We see that the besieged group of soldiers do not even have enough first aid to treat the injured. To serve as a bandage, the aid worker begins cutting the edges of a white flag that has a verse from the Quran written on it. The verse reads: *Enna fatahna laka fathan mobina* (Verily we have granted thee a manifest victory),[15] which may seem ironic given the severe conditions the group is in. Eventually when the blank edges of the flag are almost all cut out, the aid worker turns to the group commander and informs him that 'we are almost reaching the verse'. Given the sacredness of any script of the Quran, which according to Islamic laws cannot even be touched without certain preconditions, Hatami-kia is acknowledging the limitations and contradictions of the war. In fact it was these material limitations that eventually compelled the Iranian authorities to give up some of the previous slogans such as *Jang, Jang ta piroozy* (*War, war, until victory*), and accept a ceasefire in 1989.

The Scout does not involve a dramatic plot based on the clash of characters or their interests. The group of soldiers we see in the film are a unified and harmonious community. 'There is no crisis or tension in the film', one critic rightly notes, 'no sign of serious disputes or quarrels between the warriors even about war tactics' (Eshqi 2006: 59). It seems that Hatami-kia has not sought to represent an image of a diversified nation. In fact we may even argue that 'the nation', in the modern sense of the term, is almost absent in this film, just as it was largely absent in the Iranian official discourse and cultural policies of the 1980s. In those

---

[14] Surah 3 (*Ale Emran*), verse 124 (Yusof Ali 1998).
[15] This verse is said to have been revealed to the Prophet following one of victories of the Muslims in battle. Surah 48 (*Al-Fath*), verse 1 (Yusof Ali 1998).

Figure 5: The *Basiji* Prepared for Sacrifice. (Mehrdad Soleimani (Arefi) in *The Scout*. Photo by: Mehryar Mahdavi. Courtesy of Iranian National Film Archive.)

days the Quranic term *Ummat* ('community of the faithful') resonated much more in the local media. In *The Scout*, Hatami-kia focuses on one particular community in the nation, which he himself belonged to and identified with. For him, the character of the *basiji* and the community of these voluntary fighters have made this war different from other wars, and it is thus important to bring them into representation. There is no characterization even of the enemy as the antagonist or 'bad guys' in the film. We only see them as a mass, usually in long shots. The enemy is like a 'ghost or shadow', one critic writes, 'we never see the face or the identity of the enemy' (Solhjoo 2006: 33).

Despite the severely distressing and painful situation, the characters of *The Scout* do not panic and most of them are calm and confident. They even crack jokes and make fun of their difficult conditions. They are concerned about saving the lives of their comrades, but hardly show any fear for their own lives. Even when severely injured and in agony, they restrain from drawing attention to themselves so as not to disturb other fighters. While Hatami-kia insisted this was 'the reality' he saw in the war, for some critics it was too utopian: 'all the characters look the same, act the same, think the same and speak the same', writes another critic, 'none of them show any fear of war, or doubt about their way of life. All of them seek martyrdom and are fearless of death' (Eshqi 2006: 58–9). There is also no female character in this film and the fighters do not even talk about their families. This was not to remain, however, the fixed fate of sacred defense cinema or Hatami-kia's career. As time went by, many developments took place in this genre and Hatami-kia was always one of the pioneers of change. In his following films, not only did he portray moments of doubt, dispute and challenge among his war characters, but also took a more inclusive approach toward the nation.

The Scout was exhibited in Iranian movie theaters in 1989 but it did not succeed at the box office. As noted above, Hatami-kia's film was something rather new and different in its style, with little, if any, of the familiar attractions of pre-revolution Iranian cinema, or the tastes of Hollywood and Bollywood that had for long been familiar to the Iranian audiences. *The Scout* was edited by Mohsen Makhmalbaf, who then was an iconic figure of the Islamic and revolutionary art and film, yet even his name did not help attract many audiences. The film has a rather slow rhythm and largely comprises long and medium shots to capture the landscape of the war front. The main line of the story is at times interrupted by other more marginal events and characters, which only serve to familiarize audiences with the war front, rather than helping to advance the narrative. The personal information we are given about the characters is negligible, which makes it difficult to identify with the veterans. There are long sequences in the film with no dialogue or considerable action. The film does not attempt to grab the attention of the viewer 'by hook or crook', and it does not shout its moral or ideological message in the way Makhmalbaf's early films did. *The Scout* was based on a real story and Hatami-kia's aim, as mentioned earlier, was to reflect with the least intervention possible, what he believed was 'the reality' of war. This was the lesson he had learned from Avini at the school of *Revayate Fath*.

In an article written after the screening of *The Scout* and some other sacred defense films at the seventh Fajr Film Festival, Avini praises Hatami-kia's film for the same aspects that the other critics had considered as shortcomings. In Avini's view, using 'cinematic illusions', 'creating false heroes' and 'arousing instincts' are the 'false attractions' of Hollywood, which exploit 'the weaknesses of the viewer' (Avini 2001: 11–12). If *The Scout* does not involve a classic narrative, dramatic events or heroic characterization, he argues, this is because Hatami-kia has 'simply and honestly' reflected the 'reality of the war' and the 'true characters' of the fighters. For Avini, the very nature of the sacred defense prevents it from being fully represented through the devices of western dramatic arts:

> The fighters on the 'front of truth' seek to become close to their role models which are the *Olia Allah* (God's holy saints). In doing so they avoid disguise and pretence, over-expression, fury, sentimentalism, frenzied habits, panic and fantasy. They also distance themselves from heart illnesses such as egocentrism, hypocrisy, envy and boasting. They are not at all, therefore, suitable personas for theatre, film or even novels [...]. What can

be done, then, with such characters who are not heroes, anti-heroes or non-heroes? How can actors perform the roles of these non-performing characters?

(Avini 1999: 11–12)

Referring to the connotations of the term 'film' in Iranian oral culture, which implies any false, sensational, fabricated or pretended act or practice, Avini suggests that the 'great achievement' of *The Scout* for Iranian cinema lies in its overcoming of such a distrust. If we trust what *The Scout* shows us about the war, says Avini, it is because Hatami-kia has avoided 'fabrication and affectation' in making the film. On the contrary, Avini criticizes some other war films such as *Ofoq* (*Horizon*, 1989) by Rasool Mollaqoli-poor, for using the sacred defense as a pretext to produce an 'entertaining' film, which seeks to satisfy the desires of 'unsophisticated' and 'effortless' audiences. It is noteworthy that *Horizon*, also the second film of a young revolutionary Muslim director, became hugely successful at the box office in the same year that *The Scout* was screened. This contrast triggered a debate in the early 1990s on whether sacred defense films should use conventional narratives and mainstream forms and styles in order to reach wider audiences, or should they remain faithful to a particular documentary-style, which aims to represent the 'realities' of the war. In *Az Karkhe ta Rhine* (*From Karkhe to Rhine*, 1992) Hatami-kia attempts to overcome this dilemma by exploring new grounds in his cinematic career.

From Karkhe to Rhine: Recognition of 'the other'

Saeed, a *basiji* who became blinded in the war, is sent to Germany along with a few other wounded veterans to receive special treatment. Saeed's sister (Leila) who had migrated to Germany many years ago and is now married to a German television producer comes to visit him. Following an operation Saeed recovers his sight and gets prepared to return to Iran, but he is diagnosed with blood cancer (leukaemia), which is said to be a consequence of exposure to chemical gases during the war. Different treatments and medications are used and even Leila's bone marrow is transplanted, but neither proves successful. The film ends with a scene in a plane where Saeed's family members are returning to Iran for his funeral.

Az Karkheh Ta Rhine (*From Karkhe to Rhine*, 1992)[16] marks an outstanding shift, both in Hatami-kia's professional career and within the wider sacred defense genre framework. The film extended the definition of the sacred defense genre beyond the time and the place of war, even beyond a focus on the characters of soldiers. It involves a departure from many clichéd stereotypical images within Iranian cinema and marks a break with conventional assumptions about the sacred defense genre. One of the stereotypical images that Hatami-kia deconstructs in this film is that of 'the West'.

---

[16] *Karkhe* is a river in South-West Iran near the border shared with Iraq where many military operations took place during the years of war.

Demystifying 'the West'

Except for a short flashback to the war in its final sequences, *From Karkheh to Rhine* was entirely shot in Germany.[17] This was Hatami-kia's first experience in making a film abroad, and it was also the first Iranian feature film to be shot in the West after the revolution.[18] In addition, for the first time in the post-revolution era the film involved European professionals within the cast and crew. In this sense it may be considered one of the first 'transnational productions' of Iranian cinema after the revolution.[19] It seems that transcending national borders and making a film in the West with the cooperation of western professionals has influenced the way Hatami-kia represents the West in his film. Prior to this film (and even long after it), official media in Iran usually portrayed a unified and homogeneous image of the West, which introduced the latter in terms of colonialism, imperialism, moral corruption and counter-revolutionary conspiracy. This of course had roots in the history of western invasions and interventions in Iran and the hostile relations after the revolution.

Hatami-kia was the first Muslim film-maker to counter such unified and stereotypical images, which defined the West as 'the other'. Not only did he represent a rather glossy image of a modern urban environment, but he also included in his film a much more humane image of European citizens. There are many scenes in *From Karkheh to Rhine* where German characters – such as nurses, doctors, priests, police officers, journalists and television producers – are depicted as friendly and compassionate people. Hatami-kia's transnational experience enables him to distinguish between ordinary citizens in the West and the acts of western governments or corporations. More significantly the figure of Saeed's German-Iranian nephew is also a sign of the extension of a nationally bound family and openness to hybridization. The boy's name Yunas (Jonah), which is the name of a prophet mentioned in the Old Testament as well as in the Quran, also resembles the shared aspects of the Abrahamic faiths.

---

[17] The reason why Hatami-kia chose Germany as the location of his film is not entirely clear. One explanation may be the allegations against German companies who supplied Saddam Hossein with the means to produce chemical weapons. Another reason may be the nationalist myth of 'the Aryan race', which alleges that the German and Iranian nations originally belonged to the same race. The Aryan myth was initially embraced and promoted by the cultural ideologues of the Pahlavi regime as a way of asserting the supremacy of 'the Iranians' over their Middle-Eastern neighbors. Unfortunately this racist idea has resurfaced in recent years following the rise of nationalist sentiments in Iran.

[18] This is about film-makers who were based in Iran. Of course there were many films produced in America and Europe before this date by 'diasporic' and 'exilic' film-makers of Iranian origin. These have been documented and analyzed by Hamid Naficy, who has labelled them as Iranian émigré cinema (Naficy 2008).

[19] A few other Iranian films after the revolution had also been partly or totally filmed outside Iran, mostly in neighboring countries. Makhmalbaf's *The Cyclist* (1989) was partly shot in Pakistan though with a full Iranian cast and crew. His *Time of Love* (1990) was shot in Turkey, with an Iranian crew and some Turkish actors. According to Makhmalbaf both films were shot outside Iran and their stories were modified as happening in other countries at the request of Iranian cinema officials (Dönmez-Colin 2006: 70).

Despite recognizing the similarities of the two cultures and acknowledging the possibility of mutual respect, Hatami-kia does not neglect the differences between 'them' and 'us'. Early in the film, Saeed's sister, Leila, asks him what happened to his eyes. 'They were stroked by the wings of the angels', he replies, indicating his spiritual view toward the war. 'Well, to be quite sure', Leila responds, 'there are no such angels around here. This is a land of logic, reason and thought. Such angels are not allowed in'.[20] Despite Leila's initial description, Saeed finds himself treated fairly well by the citizens of the 'land of reason and logic', who are sometimes as good as angels. Most significantly his blindness is cured and he recovers vision in one of his eyes. The implicit meaning of this event is difficult to miss, and Hatami-kia even refers to it in the words of Leila's husband who, as a television producer, wants to use Saeed's story to make a program: 'A blind Iranian soldier comes to Germany and returns back home being able to see. Isn't this an amazing story?' he asks Leila. But for Leila, Saeed represents more than this straightforward story. She wants her husband to acknowledge Saeed as part of her past life: 'Saeed is not a story; he is my brother, my roots, my identity'. Of course in his own use of this story, Hatami-kia is implying how Saeed's eyes – or at least one of them (the worldly eye) – have been opened to new worlds and new realities.

Hatami-kia's new perception of the West may also be seen as reflecting the wider economic and social developments that were taking place in Iran in the post-war era. Under President Rafsanjani's administration and his 'reconstruction' policy, Iran began liberalizing the economy and re-establishing relations with the West. The aim was to encourage foreign investment and to reconstruct the devastated economic infrastructures.[21] The changes in economic policy were followed by gradual openings in the social and cultural sphere, which led to more liberal and secular voices being heard inside the country. These shifts eventually culminated in the 1997 Presidential election when Mohammad Khatami came to office with a 'reformist' agenda and a much more lenient attitude toward the West.

The positive representation of the West in *From Karkhe to Rhine* did not mean that Hatami-kia had fundamentally changed his opinion about the revolution or distanced himself from Islam. One clear indication of this is a scene in the film where Leila asks Saeed whether he wants to see images of any important event in the world that occurred after he had been blinded. Saeed's choice is noteworthy: he asks for the footage of Ayatollah Khomeini's funeral in 1989. When Leila runs recordings of the event, which depict millions of people in the streets of Tehran, Saeed suddenly becomes deeply affected and bursts into tears. When images of Ayatollah Khomeini's coffin appear, Saeed stretches his hand toward the screen, as if he was attending the real ceremony.

In addition, Hatami-kia does not fail to mention in his film that western countries largely supported Saddam during his war with Iran. Toward the end of the film, a German television news group comes to the hospital to report about Saeed and other veterans who are suffering

---

[20] All cited dialogues in this text are transcribed from the films and translated by the author.
[21] For more on the post-war developments in Iran, see *Iran Encountering Globalization* (Mohammadi 2003).

from the effects of chemical weapons. The timing is crucial: it is the First Persian Gulf War and western media are keen to gather evidence of Saddam's crimes. As one of the suffering soldiers begins explaining how he was exposed to chemical gases in the war, another soldier protests at what his colleague is doing. When the reporter approaches him, he argues that the main question that western media should be asking is 'who supplied Saddam with the means to produce these chemical weapons'? Even in this scene, however, Hatami-kia avoids presenting a stereotypical image of western media, which, in Iran, are usually depicted as being complicit with their governments. When the television group approaches Saeed – whose face is now unrecognizable due to intense chemical medication – he cannot answer the reporter's question. He just coughs and coughs, relentlessly and agonizingly. The sound assistant asks the reporter: 'he can't say anything, what should we do'? The reporter replies: 'Don't you hear? Can there be a voice of protest clearer and louder than this'?

Reconstructing the image of the basiji

The stereotypical image of the West is not the only image that Hatami-kia deconstructs in *From Karkhe to Rhine*. The appearance and attitudes of Saeed as a *basiji* in this film also stand in sharp contrast with the stereotype of the *basiji*, often depicted in khaki uniforms at the war front, or wearing a white shirt hung outside the trousers and with buttons fastened up to the top. As one critic writes 'it was unprecedented to see a basiji in a long rain coat and casual clothes placed at the heart of Europe. Maybe this was why we were so fond of

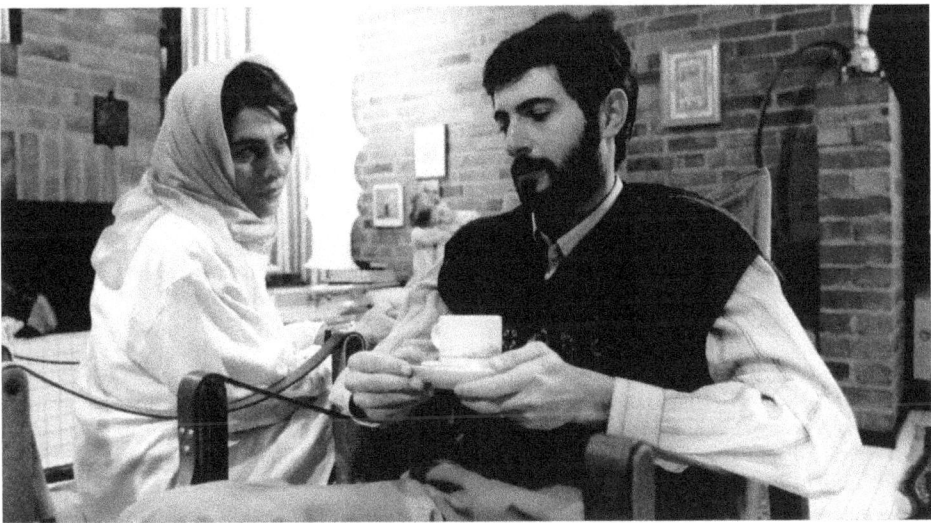

Figure 6: Reconstructing the Image of the *Basiji*. (Homa Roosta (Leila) and Ali Dehkordi (Saeed) in *From Karkhe to Rhine*. Photo by: Peyman Jafari. Courtesy of Iranian National Film Archive.)

Saeed' (Maqami-kia 2006). As mentioned earlier, the change in appearance did not mean the *basiji* had become 'westernised'. In the words of Emad Afroogh, the former Head of Iranian Parliament's Cultural Committee '[w]e may watch American films, wear American jeans and eat American food, but this does not mean our views are American views' (Appendix III).

Apart from the image of the individual *basiji*, the community of veterans in this film is also no longer the same unified and harmonious community it was in *The Scout*. We see many moments of dispute between the former fighters as they quarrel about the war and explain their life experiences after the war. There is a clear range of views from Asghar, who rigorously defends the status quo, to Nozar, who is disillusioned and questions the way authorities handled the war. It was rather audacious of Hatami-kia to depict this range of opinions among the *basiji* community only three years after the end of the war. Official representations of war fighters in general, and the *basijis* in particular, portrayed them as pious, faithful and selfless people who were unreservedly loyal to the Islamic government. The irony of course was that Hatami-kia had himself contributed to the construction of this image.

At this point of time, however, he was taking account of dissident voices among the community of veterans. Thus he included in his film a character like Nozar: a *basiji* affected by exposure to chemical gases whose wife has left him due to his severe illness, and who feels that 'the society' does not respect him as a human, let alone as a war veteran. Eventually in the film we see Nozar going to a German immigration office to apply for asylum. In the context of the history of hostilities between Iran and the West, such an act clearly involved connotations of betrayal inside Iran, particularly in this case where the person involved was a *basiji*. Watching a *basiji* seek asylum in the West was no doubt embarrassing for many authorities, and in portraying this image Hatami-kia was crossing the 'red lines'.[22]

---

[22] Hatami-kia's transgressions have not gone unpunished. When Mostafa Mirsalim held office as Minister of Culture, two of Hatami-kia's films (*The Scent of Joseph's Shirt* and *The Minoo Tower*) were rated 'jim' (or C) by the Ministry's regulatory board in 1995. This rating was attributed to films that 'lacked artistic or cultural value'. It disqualified them from longer screenings in cinemas and imposed a lower ticket price at the box office. Following this rating the producers of the two films went bankrupt and Hatami-kia was not able to fund his next project until the government had changed. He later revealed he had even worked as a taxi driver in those years to earn a living. His film *Mowje Morde* (*Dead Wave*, 2001), which deals with the predicament of a Revolutionary Guard commander who has problems in his family, while being unable to accept the 'reformist' government's lenient approach towards the United States, was also pulled out of Tehran Fajr festival due to the disapproval of the Iranian Revolutionary Guards. Hatami-kia's *Be Range Arghavan* (*In Purple*) was also banned by the 'reformist' government in 2004. It tells the story of an intelligence officer who, while performing his duty in a surveillance project, falls in love with the daughter of a political exile. In 2009, when Javad Shamaqdari – a 'sacred defense' filmmaker and close confidant of President Ahmadinejad – was appointed as Deputy Minister for Cinematic Affairs, some banned films – including Hatami-kia's *Be Range Arghavan* and Tahmineh Milani's feminist film *Tasvie Hesab* (*Payback*, 2007) – were, to the surprise of many, granted permission for public screening. However several months after the completion of Hatami-kia's most recent film *Gozareshe yek Jashn* (*Report on a Party*, 2011), which presents a strong critique of the Iranian police, the Ministry of Culture and Islamic Cultivation has still

Although Saeed acknowledges the physical pain, psychological anguish and social problems that Nozar suffers from, he nevertheless criticizes his decision to seek asylum in the West. Saeed argues that 'it is in these critical and difficult situations when a real basiji becomes distinguished from others'. For Nozar, on the other hand, the label *basiji* is no longer a badge of honor: 'I don't need this crown anymore.' He has given up this 'crown' to pursue a better life in Germany, but Saeed maintains that this exchange is not a bargain: 'you sold it too cheap; you won't even become a good merchant'. Saeed is here indirectly referring to a verse of the Quran that states that the faithful warriors have dealt their lives and their belongings with God.[23] In this view it is only God who can truly and fully reward those who sacrificed for Him. Requesting anything in return from anyone else, Saeed thus believes, would never be as 'profitable' a deal.

Despite his theological view toward sacrifice and martyrdom, Saeed's reaction on being diagnosed with cancer stands in sharp contrast with the way the characters of *The Scout* embraced martyrdom. Unlike Arefi, who seemed to have no attachments to the mundane, Saeed has just begun to reconcile himself to the joys of life in the time of peace: he has married; his wife is expecting a baby; and more significantly, he has recovered his sight. While Arefi was preoccupied with sacrifice at the war front, Saeed is looking forward to life more than ever before. For him, life is no longer like that in the war time when sacrifice was the only option available to those who sought to fulfil their divine obligation. This is another instance where Hatami-kia reveals the human side of his *basiji* characters, even in the case of a faithful and loyal *basiji* like Saeed. After hearing the news of his cancer, Saeed goes out for a walk in the night. Eventually we see him – in a long shot from behind – sitting by the river Rhine and talking with God. His pitch gradually rises; he stands up and cries out at the heavens in these lyrical words:

> *I sought you on the lands, you didn't accept me. I sought you on the seas, you didn't take me. I sought you in the islands, you only took my eyes. But why now? Why here? I have an objection! This wasn't our plan! Why did you give me back my eyes? What did you want me to see? Where is your compassion? Where is your mercy? Why now? Why here?*

In the following scene Hatami-kia goes even further in breaking away from conventional images of the *basiji* and depicts Saeed praying in a church. While the church members are attending the service, the camera slowly focuses on him, sitting on the ground at another

---

not issued a public screening certificate for the film. Despite all this, Hatami-kia has repeatedly insisted in various interviews that he remains faithful to Islamic Revolution and values of the 'sacred defense' and does not consider himself as 'opposition'. He even caused controversy recently by writing a short newspaper article in which he implicitly, but harshly, criticized Asghar Farhadi and his celebrated film *A Separation* (2011). Hatami-kia accused Farhadi of depicting a bitter image of Iranians as liars, showcasing it in western film festivals, and then standing in the queue at western embassies to apply for asylum. See http://isna.ir/isna/NewsView.aspx?ID=News-1873258&Lang=P, accessed 25th October 2011.

[23] Surah 9 (*Al-Tawbah*) Verse 111 reads: 'Allah hath purchased of the believers their persons and their goods; for their's (in return) is the garden (of Paradise): they [who] fight in His cause.' (Yusof Ali 1998).

corner and saying his own prayers. Eventually he attracts the attention of others who gather around him, puzzled at what he is doing. Later the police arrive and say they are looking for a 'foreigner' who has interrupted the church service. The priest denies the charge and replies: 'he is only praying in his own way'. In these scenes we can again identify Hatami-kia's intention in highlighting shared aspects of different faiths and cultures and his recognition of the possibility of mutual respect. In addition, he also reminds us that the diagnosis of a fatal cancer, as distressing and agonizing as it may be, has not persuaded Saeed to abandon his faith altogether.

Recognition of women; reconciliation with the émigré

As mentioned earlier, in *The Scout* Hatami-kia appears to be in a pre-national state of mind. He is almost entirely preoccupied with the representation of the *basiji* and the community of faithful and thus makes no attempt to diversify his characters. In *From Karkhe to Rhine*, however, he not only portrays a more diverse community of veterans, but also takes a step beyond this immediate community and represents a more inclusive image of the nation. The character of Leila in this film is the first major female character in Hatami-kia's films, and she has a very strong and active personality in the film. The role is played by a prominent professional actress Homa Roosta, whose name is in fact the first to appear in the film's credits. Her character is also *different* in a more challenging way with regards to the norms and values of the post-revolution conditions: she is an émigré.

The film does not clearly mention why and when Leila left Iran, but there are indications that she has left after the Islamic Revolution. We also notice that ever since she left, there has been no communication at all between her and the rest of the family, particularly with *the mother*. In one scene Leila calls her mother on the phone and listens to her voice, but she does not speak herself. Clearly at the time she left Iran, the migration of a young girl to the West would have been unacceptable in many traditional and religious families. Leila's decision to migrate, therefore, must have been considered rebellious and transgressive at the time. Her subsequent marriage with a non-Muslim, also a breach of the codes of Shari'a law, may be another reason why she no longer expects a welcome back in Iran. Moreover, the appearance of Leila in her casual outfits is markedly different from that of Saeed's wife, whom we see toward the end of the film wearing a *chador* (long black veil).[24]

---

[24] Although Muslim actresses are not allowed to appear in Iranian films with their hair or body uncovered, Hatami-kia has provided some indications to inform the viewer that although we see Homa Roosta (the actress) wearing a scarf, Leila (the character) actually does not wear one. It should also be noted, as one critic puts it, that 'the very representation of a woman without a proper scarf in a film by a [Muslim] revolutionary filmmaker – who has been brought up in an environment which only privileges veiled women as good women – was itself a delicate crossing of the boundaries defined by the norms of the advocates of the revolution' (Mir-ehsan 2006: 45).

Figure 7: Representing the Émigré. (Homa Roosta (Leila) and Hans Noiman (Andreas, Leila's husband) in *From Karkhe to Rhine*. Photo by: Peyman Jafari. Courtesy of Iranian National Film Archive.)

Despite all these 'deviations', we see in the film that Saeed approaches Leila with respect. He even makes efforts to cross cultural and linguistic barriers and establish a friendship with her husband, Andreas, and their German-Iranian son, Yunas. When Saeed asks Leila why she has never visited Iran in these years, she replies: 'I have thought about it many times, but I fear that *mother* would not welcome me'. When Saeed promises to make sure that she is accepted, Leila indicates that her desire to visit her family does not mean she wants to repent her past choices:

– *You mean you want to arrange a repentance ceremony for me, do you?*
– *No, I want them to see that you are still Leila.*

Saeed is no doubt aware of the changes in Leila's life and her differences from the rest of the family, but he also recognizes continuities and similarities. Leila may not be the same Leila who left Iran, but her name is still Leila, she still speaks Farsi, she cooks Iranian cuisines, and she cares for her family members to the extent that she accepts to have an operation in order to have her bone marrow transplanted to Saeed. Hatami-kia is in this film proposing a kind of national reconciliation between Iranians inside and outside the country: a proposal based on a recognition of difference that goes beyond the narrowly defined ideological criteria of in-group and out-group.

The image of the émigré in *From Karkhe to Rhine* is totally different from the stereotypical images of Iranians in the West that were usually depicted in Iranian films and television programs in the 1980s and early 1990s. The diverse community of the Iranian diaspora were often reduced in local media and film to the following categories: royalists and supporters of the Pahlavi government; affiliates to terrorist opposition groups such as the MKO; the rich and wealthy elite whose financial interests and 'corrupt' lifestyles were at stake after the revolution; and the working-class asylum seekers who, as the cliché went, always ended up having a miserable life washing up in cafés and restaurants.[25] The character of Leila, in contrast, does not match any of these stereotypes: she is married to a television producer and works with him as a colleague. Together with their son they form a happy middle-class family, which is neither royalist, terrorist or Islamist. The character of Leila embodies 'the other' within the nation, which was largely suppressed by a dominant dichotomy that only recognized pro- and anti- government standpoints. It seems that the processes of globalization and transcending national borders have not only inspired Hatami-kia to acknowledge 'the other' outside the nation (i.e. 'the West'), but also to recognize 'the other' within.

Reception and critique of the film

Film critics generally praised *From Karkhe to Rhine* as a significant move in Hatami-kia's career. They credited the film not only for its gripping narrative and sophisticated style and form, but also for its humanist approach and more inclusive representation of the nation. There were, however, a few high-art enthusiasts who considered the film a tearful melodrama with exotic and glossy images of the West. In a recent interview (Azarm et al. 2008) Hatami-kia reveals that Avini, his mentor at *Revayate Fath* also did not like the film. After Avini's death however, his letter to Hatami-kia about this film was published. In this letter, which is tellingly titled *A Letter to a Friend of the War Times*, Avini narrates a dialogue between his reason and his heart. Reason criticizes Hatami-kia for being imprudent, candid and rebellious in this film, while the heart praises him for being truthful, brave and maverick. Both reason and heart, however, agree on the point that *From Karkhe to Rhine* is a bitter film. In conclusion Avini writes that even in its bitter portrayal of the fate of the *basijis*, the film does not humiliate them: 'it is a sweet bitterness, like the bitterness of martyrdom' (Avini 1999: 267–70).

But there were other more strictly committed critics who attacked Hatami-kia for betraying the values of the sacred defense: for depicting a *basiji* who seeks refuge in the West; for showing a *basiji* who has a 'westernised' sister; and for portraying a *basiji* who blasphemously shouts at God instead of welcoming the news of his martyrdom. Given

---

[25] Films like *Hey Joe* (Manuchehr Asgarinasab, 1989) and television series like *Sarab* (1991–2) reproduced such images of Iranians in the West.

the trajectory of Makhmalbaf in post-revolutionary cinema, some skeptics feared that Hatami-kia was following Makhmalbaf's footsteps and distancing himself from the ideals of the Islamic Revolution. The fear of a reaction by radical elements had even led some concerned cultural authorities to arrange a private screening of the film for Ayatollah Khamenei – Iran's religious leader – before the film's public screening. Hatami-kia, who at this time was shooting his next film in Bosnia, has spoken in an interview of how concerned he was about the outcome of this session (Ferasati 1993). The film however was publicly screened as scheduled in 1993 and despite its 'bitter' theme and tragic ending – which some critics had speculated would disappoint viewers – became one of Iranian cinema's top box office hits of the year. *From Karkhe to Rhine* is Hatami-kia's first major success at the box office, which enabled him to communicate with a much greater part of the Iranian nation. The film was awarded the Best Film prize at the eleventh Fajr Film Festival in Tehran where, coincidentally, Avini served as a member of the jury.

Between the making of *The Scout* and *From Karkhe to Rhine*, apart from making two other films, Hatami-kia had attended university and studied cinema in Tehran's School of Cinema and Theatre.[26] He graduated with a specialty in scriptwriting and presented the script of *From Karkhe to Rhine* as his final dissertation. This can explain why in this film we see more evidence of a professionally written script with polished characters and dramatic twists and turns in the narrative. There are far more personal details provided about Saeed in the film than there were about Arefi in *The Scout*. This enables even unfamiliar audiences to engage and sympathize with his character. The actor who plays the role of Saeed (Ali Dehkordy) – though not a professional at the time – was trained in theater and had a photogenic face as well as a gentle voice.

In terms of direction, the film is a big step away from amateurism and toward professionalism: well-designed mise-en-scènes, sophisticated decoupage, stylish camera movements and more dynamic editing. The setting (Cologne, Germany) also provided the director with a colorful range of natural, historical and urban landscapes, which add to the novelty of the film for local audiences. Perhaps the most impressive and memorable feature of *From Karkhe to Rhine* was its heart-rending music composed by Majid Entezami, one of the leading Iranian composers. All in all, Hatami-kia had by this film shifted his style of sacred defense cinema toward more conventional and mainstream forms of cinema, while maintaining some of the key characteristics and symbols of the sacred defense genre. The veteran's metal tag, which in Hatami-kia's iconography stands for the identity of the *basiji*, is clearly visible in this film. In the film's closing scene on the plane, we see Saeed's tag held up by his German-Iranian nephew against the window, as the boy watches the clouds passing outside.

At a time when the intensified processes of globalization were indicating the arrival of a new global age, *From Karkhe to Rhine* was a sign of a new era for Iranian cinema. It took the

---

[26] Here we notice another point of difference between Hatami-kia and Makhmalbaf. The latter has always preferred self-education and refused – even denigrated – formal education.

production of an Iranian film beyond national and regional borders and involved a foreign crew and cast, giving Iranian post-revolution cinema a transnational dimension at the same time as the 'new Iranian cinema' was becoming recognized and celebrated in international film festivals. Unlike the 'festival films', however, *From Karkhe to Rhine* was not distributed or awarded a prize outside Iran. While Hatami-kia recognized the West in his film, not many in the West seemed interested in recognizing him. Perhaps this is the reason why he has always maintained a skeptical attitude toward international festivals.

Regardless of the latter point however, globalization has clearly influenced the way Hatami-kia imagines and represents the world in his film. Far reaching and influential as they may be, the processes of globalization do not however totally determine the fate of local and national cultures, or incorporate them into a single homogenized form of global culture. Resistance and conflict may also be the consequences of the 'compression of the world', which may change the direction or the outcome of globalization processes. Hatami-kia's *Glass Agency* (1997) is a strong statement in this respect and a manifestation of resistance to homogenizing forces in the age of globalization.

Glass Agency: **Return of the rebel**

Kazem, a former *basiji* commander who is now a taxi driver, meets one of his former comrades a couple of days before *Norooz* (the Iranian New Year holidays). Abbas, a farmer who lives in the provinces, has recently been suffering from some physical symptoms and has come to Tehran for treatment. With Kazem's help he is taken to a hospital and receives a medical check-up. Doctors identify a small mortar piece in his neck close to his jugular vein. They suggest he should be transferred to Europe for a special operation. Kazem fails to get urgent support for Abbas from the institutions responsible for the welfare of wounded war veterans. He thus personally gets involved in facilitating this travel. Short of cash, he arranges to sell his taxi and buy the flight tickets. The buyer does not turn up at the right time and the travel agency is about to close for the holidays. They also want to cancel Kazem's booking in favor of two Iranian tourists, who are on the waiting list. Kazem's desperate requests for an extension of payment and even his offer to leave his car as guarantee of payment is not accepted by the agency's chief. After a quarrel, he orders his staff to remove Kazem from the agency shouting: 'This isn't a charity. Go and seek help from those who sent you to war and caused all that bloodshed'.

The already tense Kazem suddenly loses control. In a flash of short shots in slow motion, we see him breaking a huge glass partition, disarming a security guard, shooting a bullet in the air and taking control of the travel agency with all its costumers and staff. The rest of the film deals with Kazem's arguments with the people inside the travel agency, the attempts of two security officers to rescue the hostages, the deterioration of Abbas's health and Kazem's demand to be transferred to London with the next morning flight. The crisis receives

Figure 8: Comrades Marginalised in 'the new times'. (Habib Rezaei (Abbas) and Parviz Parastooei (Kazem) in *Glass Agency* – Photo by: Mitra Mahaseni. Courtesy of Iranian National Film Archive.)

international coverage and becomes 'a matter of *national* security'. While one of the security officers (Salahshoor) is merely concerned with maintaining law and order and punishing Kazem, the other (Ahmad) who has previously been at war and knows Kazem and Abbas, manages to get approval from a higher authority to grant their demand. They eventually get on board for the flight to London, but only minutes after take-off Abbas dies.

For a viewer familiar with Hatami-kia's cinema, there are many recurring themes in *Ajanse Shishehi* (*Glass Agency*, 1997): the isolated *basiji*, social change, crisis of values and identities, the trauma of a fatal illness caused by the war, and martyrdom. In fact the scenes of Abbas's medical check-up at the beginning of this film clearly resemble scenes of Saeed's medical check-up in *From Karkhe to Rhine*. They thus agitate and warn the viewer about the fate which awaits Abbas, who, in some ways, is another Saeed: an honest, humble and faithful *basiji* wounded in the war. Unlike the *urban* Saeed, however, the *rural* Abbas does not enjoy the privilege of being transferred abroad and receiving special treatment. In fact Abbas neither has any relatives living in the West who may help him, nor does he even survive long enough to see the West. Even his travel to Tehran is due to his wife's insistence rather than his own choice. Given the remoteness of both his geographical location and ideological disposition from the global and the universal, Abbas could be considered an embodiment of the local and the particular. In an era when the waves of globalization are rapidly transforming the world, Hatami-kia puts the life of a forgotten local, like Abbas, under the spotlight. He is also demonstrating – and arguably protesting – the fact that even under an *Islamic* Republic, globalization can result in an increasingly dominant culture of capitalism maintained by a strictly rational sense of discipline and order, which marginalizes other values.

By holding people in the travel agency as hostages – or 'witnesses' to use his own term – Kazem is actively resisting the isolation and humiliation of Abbas and the values that he stands for. In an intense exchange of words with Salahshoor, the security officer, who represents the rational and secular concepts of law, order and discipline, Kazem swiftly rejects and undermines the 'universally respected' meanings of these terms. From Salahshoor's perspective, because the BBC and CNN have put this crisis on air, it has become a matter of *national* security, and thus must be dealt with promptly and firmly. He informs Kazem that the Foreign Affairs Ministry has *denied* reports about this incident. Salahshoor translates this diplomatic statement bluntly: 'It means that Kazem and Abbas do not even exist':

Your decade has passed. If that gun wasn't in your hand no one would even listen to what you say. You spoke for a decade; you did whatever you wanted in the war while we didn't say a word. Now let us speak for God's sake! Is this country ever going to enjoy stability and peace?[27]

The tone implies that the generation of Kazem and Abbas is now considered almost akin to dinosaurs, whose time has passed, and what remains of them should be moved to strictly controlled spaces like museums.[28] As Appadurai has suggested, globalization marks a 'rupture' or 'break with all sorts of pasts' (Appadurai 1996: 3). The disjunctures between culture, economy and politics, which in his view mark the complexity of the new global conditions (Appadurai 1996: 32), can be identified as the source of the clashes we see in *Glass Agency*. The '*basiji* culture' of people like Kazem and Abbas that was in accord with the revolutionary politics and socialist economics of the 1980s, no longer suits the new liberal economic and political formations of the 1990s, which Salahshoor wants to keep secure. While Kazem's defiance may be seen here as an act of resistance to globalization, from a point of view such as Robertson's, it might be considered as part of the processes of globalization. As discussed in Chapter 1, Robertson contends that 'anti-global gestures are encapsulated within the discourse of globality' (Robertson 1992: 10). 'Fundamentalism'

---

[27] 'Your decade' refers to the 1979–89 period which is defined by characteristics such as the leadership of Ayatollah Khomeini, the war with Iraq, and leftist economic policies.

[28] In fact roughly at the same time a museum was inaugurated in Tehran, named 'Museum of the Martyrs', where images, objects, personal belongings and testaments relating to some of the martyrs of the revolution and the war are put on display.

or 'the search for fundamentals', he argues, is an aspect, even a creation, of globalization rather than merely being a reaction or resistance to it. In his view 'the expectation of identity declaration is built into the general process of globalization' (Robertson 1992: 175).

From a leftist perspective toward globalization such as Arif Dirlik's, however, we might see the confrontation in *Glass Agency* as the result of global capitalism's attempt to manipulate 'the local'. The global forces of capitalism, he suggests, attempt to 'liberate' the inhabitants of the local from themselves: they strip them of their identity in order to homogenize them into the global culture of capital (Dirlik 1996: 35). As the events of the film demonstrate, such attempts do not go unchallenged. The film may in fact be seen as an early warning sign alerting the forces of global capital to the consequences of repressing and marginalizing the local and the particular. For, instead of maintaining security and stability, it could prove to have further disastrous consequences.

Kazem and Abbas, who were at the time of war privileged for their sacrifice, are now being systematically marginalized in the name of stability and peace. When Salahshoor announces the findings of his 'investigations' on Kazem, the only important facts are: his low ranking job, his debt to the bank for a mortgage, and his son struggling to be admitted at university. For Salahshoor these material facts alone explain why Kazem has committed this 'crime'. Kazem, on the other hand, feels insulted by this kind of 'rational' and 'scientific' investigation, which reduces him, as the object of the study, to a 'guinea pig'. The confrontation between Kazem and Salahshoor turns the whole event into a clash of world-views and identities, as well as a matter of life and death for Kazem and his 'endangered generation'. Kazem makes it clear to Salahshoor that, as in the time of war, the country's *national* security is still determined and maintained by people like Abbas, regardless of what the BBC or CNN may say.

Even without the words of Salahshoor that declare the end of Kazem's era, however, we can notice in the film how the times have changed and people like Kazem and Abbas have been moved to the margins of the society for which they once sacrificed themselves. The film's story takes place at a time of year when most Iranians are in a rush preparing for *Norooz*. Everyone is thinking about arranging holidays, cleaning and refurbishing houses, and buying food, clothes and gifts for their families and friends. Even government offices are half-vacant, refurbishing and redecorating rather than functioning properly. Hatami-kia uses this background to highlight a *national* atmosphere in which no one is concerned about the fate of Abbas. Reza Kianian – a prominent Iranian actor who played the role of Salahshoor and also supervised the cast – suggests that *Glass Agency*'s script is full of monologues: 'every one is speaking, but no one is listening. There is no dialogue between the characters and this truly represents a big problem in our society' (Kianian 2006: 41).

By using the term 'witnesses' to refer to the hostages in the travel agency, Kazem wants the people to witness the suffering of Abbas and to remember this forgotten generation. He is conscious of the negative impressions created by his action and the antipathy that the hostages have toward him. He tries to communicate with the hostages and explain who he is and why he has done this, but he fails and is usually misunderstood. In the age of global interconnectedness and transnational communication, Kazem eventually sits down face-to-face with his 'witnesses' and resorts to the ancient medium of parables to deliver his message:

> *Once upon a time, there were a people who were celebrating their liberation. Suddenly a monster came around and attacked their land. No one knew what to do. But an old wise man among them said: the young and strong should go and fight the monster. So they went. But it was a deadly and horrific monster. You cut off his hand and he grew two more, you cut off his head and he grew three more. The young men, however, eventually fought the monster out of their land. But when they came back home, the people looked at them in a strange way, as if they were strangers. Fighting with the monster had changed these men. They no longer felt comfortable and welcome in town.*

When Kazem finishes narrating this story one of the hostages comes to see him in private and offers money in exchange for his freedom. This deeply disappoints Kazem who replies: 'where in my story did you feel I was begging'? Another hostage, a woman who lives abroad, also approaches Kazem and expresses her confusion about the situation. Kazem, who clearly

Figure 9: Lack of Communication. (Kazem freeing one of the hostages who 'lives abroad' and cannot understand him. Photo by: Mitra Mahaseni. Courtesy of Iranian National Film Archive.)

understands how this woman may have misunderstood his intentions, gives her the door key and allows her to leave the agency. Kazem's problems in communication are not limited to social and public spaces. For the first time in Hatami-kia's films we even see the offspring of the former fighters who, as one critic writes, 'cannot understand their fathers' ambitions and ideals' (Mostaghasi 2006: 55). Kazem's son quarrels with him about the decision to sell their taxi, which is the family's only source of income. From the son's point of view, Kazem should give priority to his own family, who are also in need, rather than being altruistic toward Abbas.

There is only one person who can truly understand Kazem and remains beside him in all situations: his wife Fatemeh. In fact the film opens with a scene where Kazem is writing a letter – or a testament – addressed to Fatemeh. It is after a long flashback that we return to this scene in the end. Kazem is writing as the crisis is reaching its peak and he is not sure whether he will survive to see his wife again. We notice that initially he begins the letter by addressing the public: 'Ladies and Gentlemen', but he can not continue and draws a line through it. He uses 'Brothers and Sisters', as it was the convention in the first decade of revolution, but again he draws a line through it. Finally he addresses the letter to his wife Fatemeh and continues narrating what has happened. Kazem's wife does not speak or intervene very much in the film, but by one significant move she demonstrates why Kazem can only write to her.

When Kazem is deeply stressed by the circumstances in the travel agency, and almost every one is criticizing, if not loathing him, Fatemeh sends him a small pack that comes as a great relief. The pack contains Kazem's *chafyeh*[29] and his metal tag of the war times. By sending these symbolic items, Fatemeh has acknowledged, contra many others, that Kazem is fighting for a right cause as he used to do in the war. Unlike the time of war when the community of fighters seemed totally detached from, and independent of, their families, it seems that in the post-war era women have a much greater role to play in the lives of the veterans.

In terms of representing the nation, although Hatami-kia has repeatedly denied allegations that the characters caught inside the travel agency stand for the nation as a whole, we nonetheless notice a diverse and colorful range of characters that have been carefully hand-picked: young and old, male and female, rich and poor, pious and corrupt, religious and secular, pro- and counter-revolution, resident and immigrant. There is even a figure in a raincoat wearing dark glasses – a familiar habit of Abbas Kiarostami – who introduces himself as a 'cultural person' travelling abroad to attend a festival. While all these people are arranging tickets for their travels within or across national borders, Abbas's illness is deteriorating, gradually making him paralyzed. The contrast between the affluent and highly mobile cosmopolitans, who have the privilege of using fast-moving and far-reaching means of transport, and the marginalized and deprived locals like Abbas, who are losing even their

---

[29] A multi-purpose black and white scarf usually tied loosely around the neck by soldiers – particularly *basijis* – in the war. It has since become an icon of the sacred defense.

basic ability for movement, could be seen as a critical reflection on the highly stratified and profoundly uneven nature of the processes of globalization.

It is notable however, that from the beginning of the crisis Abbas is critical of Kazem's rebellious actions. He believes that, as *basijis*, they should not even expect an expression of gratitude for their acts of sacrifice in the war, let alone asking for their 'share' of life. Speaking from the same theological viewpoint as that of Arefi in *The Scout* and Saeed in *From Karkhe to Rhine*, Abbas reminds Kazem that 'we made a deal with God' and thus should not ask anything in return from anyone else, be it the nation or the state. The only reason Abbas remains in the travel agency beside his former comrade is to not let him down in such a difficult situation where he is so isolated and despised. Kazem, on the contrary, believes the nation has an obligation to remember the sacrifice of Abbas, regardless of the modesty and piety that prevent him from asking for help.

Despite Kazem's efforts however, none of the diverse characters in the travel agency show any sign of sympathy toward their situation: some think they are doing this for money; others believe it is a political blackmail on behalf of pressure groups. This depiction of a disrespectful and inconsiderate group of people in the travel agency led some critics to accuse Hatami-kia of 'humiliating the nation', 'distrusting the people' and representing an 'inhuman image' of Iranians (Mir-ehsan 2006: 47; Solhjoo 1998: 10; Talebi-nejad 1997: 13; Zahedi 1998: 13). The irony was that when the film was released the nation responded to the film in an overwhelmingly positive way. *Glass Agency* reached the second place in the top box office sales of the year and became Hatami-kia's most successful film ever in terms of total ticket sales. It seems that unlike the critics, who had identified with the people taken hostage by Kazem, the nation had largely identified with Kazem and Abbas.

While emphasizing the piety of a *basiji* like Abbas, Hatami-kia also takes into account that former veterans were offered some bonuses, rewards and positive discriminations after the war. This point is raised by some of the people in the travel agency, who find it difficult to believe that a person like Abbas, far from gaining any rewards for his participation in the war, has even lost the tractor he used to have on his farm. In addition, Hatami-kia also points a finger at some former fighters who got involved in pressure groups after the war and used violence for political purposes. He considers them partly responsible for the isolation and despair of Abbas and Kazem. When 'the motorcyclists' – a code name for these pressure groups in Iran – come around the travel agency to help, Kazem refuses their offer and asks them to leave, emphasizing that people like Abbas also suffer from 'the smoke of those motorcycles'.

Kazem and Abbas are however not entirely left alone. While Salahshoor is pressing ahead with his 'iron fist' plan and takes control of the travel agency using 'special forces', his junior colleague Ahmad, who has served in the war and knows Kazem and Abbas, manages to contact a higher authority and receives permission for transferring them to the airport and on board to the London flight. In the released film it is not entirely clear who that authority is, but in the published script when Salahshoor – having Kazem and Abbas in his control – refuses to accept a faxed memo to release them, Ahmad furiously shouts: 'It is handwritten by *Aaqa*'.

Aaqa – literally mister, honourable, master – is an informal term that supporters use to refer to Ayatollah Khamenei, Iran's religious leader. This is a substitute for the term *Emam* (leader), which was used for Ayatollah Khomeini. Although the position of *Velayate Faqih* (Authority of the Jurisprudent) is legally recognized under the Iranian constitution, the source of this power and authority, it is believed, does not merely rest in a man-made constitution. Only a *faqih* (Islamic jurisprudent) approved by an assembly of high-rank clerics can be appointed to this post. Hatami-kia's recourse to the religious source of power for a last minute rescue in *Glass Agency* is noteworthy. It could be seen as a kind of resistance to a secular and liberal world order, which has the West at its center.

For some critics and political activists who are opposed to, or critical of, the current religious leader however, this ending gave the film a 'fundamentalist' moral. Abbas Abdi, one of the masterminds of the student take-over of the US embassy in 1979 who, in the mid-1990s, re-branded himself as 'reformist' along with many other 'ex-hardliners', criticized Hatami-kia and expressed his disappointment with the film in a review published in *Film Monthly*:

> If an authority can provide a private airline for Kazem and Abbas, why didn't he resolve their financial problems or buy them some tickets in the first place?[30] [...] Why should the people be held hostage for a problem that is ultimately going to be resolved by [those in] power.
>
> (Abdi 1998: 105)

We should however avoid overemphasizing the implications of the film's ending, particularly since, after all, there is no 'solution' or 'happy ending' in the film. Hatami-kia is without doubt glorifying faithful and pious *basijis* like Abbas and Kazem, but he is not romanticizing any authority. If we consider Abbas's fatal illness as the main crisis in the plot, even the last minute rescue is not good enough to change his tragic fate. He does get on the plane, but dies before reaching the destination.

In terms of cinematic sophistication, *Glass Agency* has generally been considered as Hatami-kia's masterpiece. It has added such a significant mark to his legacy that some critics believe he was preoccupied with its characters and themes even a decade after its production.[31] Although 80 per cent of the story happens in a relatively small indoor space, Hatami-kia's work as director was, by and large, credited for the tight and accurate mise-en-scène. The constant and harmonious movements of the camera and actors, as well as the breathtaking rhythm of the film, guaranteed Hatami-kia a place among the distinguished

---

[30] Of course Abdi is exaggerating a bit here, since there is no indication of a 'private airline' being provided for Abbas and Kazem in the film. Moreover, Kazem has already mentioned the problem of not having access to the 'busy' officials.

[31] See reviews on *Be Name Pedar* (*In the Name of the Father*, 2006) and interview with the director Ebrahim Hatami-kia: *Film Monthly*, Issue 350, Shahrivar 1385 (September 2006).

Figure 10: Asserting Agency and Refusing to Conform. (Parviz Parastooei (Kazem) in *Glass Agency*. Photo by: Mitra Mahaseni. Courtesy of Iranian National Film Archive.)

masters of Iranian cinema. In some instances the film appears to be staged, as in a theater, and according to Kianian (actor and cast supervisor) this was what Hatami-kia wanted: 'the hostages were the audience and Kazem and the rest were the actors of a play' (Kianian 1998: 24). Again it seems Hatami-kia wants Kazem and Abbas to be seen as delivering a message and narrating a story rather than merely breaking the law and taking hostages.

Despite its radical and rebellious theme, *Glass Agency* is, in terms of form and narrative style, quite in accord with many Hollywood conventions. Some critics have referred to the similarities between this film and *Dog Day Afternoon* (Sydney Lumet, 1975), even drawing one-to-one comparisons of the two films' scripts (Saffarian 1998). As in the case of *From Karkhe to Rhine*, there is no sign of the amateurism or documentary style of *The Scout* in this state-of-the-art professional film. *Glass Agency* won several prizes at Tehran's Fajr Festival including Best Film, Best Script and Best Director. Also, as mentioned earlier, on its release in 1998 the film achieved a greater success at the box office than any other of Hatami-kia's films. Unlike Kazem, therefore, who failed in his desperate attempts to communicate with the people in the travel agency, Hatami-kia was highly successful in getting his message across to mass audiences. He did not shy away from using a globally dominant style in cinema to give voice to the local. And this may clearly raise further questions: should Hatami-kia be criticized for conforming to Hollywood conventions and betraying the earlier 'indigenous' forms of sacred defense cinema, or should he be credited with getting the voice and image of his marginalized characters across to a much greater audience?

Glass Agency is one of the most explicitly political films ever made in the history of Iranian cinema. Coincidentally, its release came after a year of tense political contests during the seventh presidential election campaigns in Iran. In May 1997, President Khatami surprisingly won a landslide victory and subsequently his political team – the majority of whom were called 'hardliners' and 'radicals' by western media in the 1980s – established a new platform putting the 'reformists' on Iran's political map.[32] Hatami-kia, who had been put under pressure by the 'conservative' authorities at the Ministry of Culture prior to this election, supported President Khatami during the campaigns. Ironically however, *Glass Agency* came as a great surprise to both political camps.

On the one hand, the 'conservatives', who always spoke of preserving the virtues and values of Islam and the revolution, welcomed the film without mentioning that they had in previous years accused Hatami-kia of losing his faith and becoming 'westernised'. On the other hand, for the 'reformists', who considered Hatami-kia an ally, the unlawful acts of Kazem were in sharp contrast with President Khatami's famous maxims such as 'rule of law' and 'civil society'. Moreover, many intellectuals and critics who had witnessed some violent actions of pressure groups – such as attacking cinemas and setting fire on bookshops in the name of resisting 'western cultural invasion' – considered *Glass Agency* as a film that legitimated and even 'glorified' the use of violence at a time when the society was 'moving towards civilization' (Nazer 1999; Talebi-nejad 1997).

This all happened at a time of intense, complex and unstable social and political conditions, as some political elements in the Islamic Republic were more clearly than ever incorporating European ideas of Enlightenment – or 'ideoscapes' as Appadurai (1996) has called them – and trying to establish closer ties with the 'international community'. On the one hand, it seems that at this crucial turning point *Glass Agency* had captured a state of personal and social crises arising from the processes of globalization. It portrayed the moral panics and paradoxes of life in a rapidly globalizing world marked by the instability of ideals and values. On the other hand, it appears that through the same processes of globalization, Muslim film-makers like Hatami-kia, who were largely excluded from film and media industries prior to the revolution, have been empowered with the means to voice their concerns and represent their identities that had for long been denied, subjugated or misrepresented. As Stuart Hall (1991) has argued, globalization involves the potential for the marginalised, 'hitherto excluded from major forms of cultural representation', to acquire through struggle the means to speak for themselves. '[N]ew subjects, new genders, new ethnicities, new regions, new communities', he writes, 'come into representation' by

---

[32] It is because of these periodical shifts in the meaning and referent of terms such as hardliner, moderate, conservative, reformist, radical etc. in the post-revolution political context that I have put these terms in inverted commas throughout this book.

'recovering their own hidden histories': 'They have to try to retell the story from the bottom up, instead of from the top down' (Hall 1991: 34–5).

Conclusion

This chapter examined the work of Ebrahim Hatami-kia: a prominent post-revolution film-maker whose work, despite making an important contribution to Iranian national cinema, has been largely ignored in international festivals as well as in most critical accounts on Iranian cinema published in the West. It was argued that the 1979 revolution in Iran facilitated the rise of a new generation of Muslim film-makers like Hatami-kia who became involved in adding a new Islamic dimension to Iranian national cinema. Since many of these film-makers began their careers during the Iran–Iraq war and sought to represent what they believed was 'the reality' of war, their efforts culminated in the creation of a particular war genre, which has been named sacred defense cinema.

The chapter presented an analysis of three of Hatami-kia's most significant films and investigated the changes and developments in their styles and themes. It was argued that despite addressing local audiences and being funded and distributed at a local level, Hatami-kia's films demonstrate both an open acknowledgment of and a critical response to globalization. In other words even the Islamic sacred defense genre, which is by and large a 'non-globalized' section of Iranian cinema, has not merely turned its back on globalization and the developments of the contemporary world and retreated into a fundamentalist standpoint. Hatami-kia's vision, as we have seen, has been influenced and broadened through transnational encounters and international experiences in the age of globalization.

Through these experiences Hatami-kia has moved from a position where he was merely preoccupied with representing 'the faithful' to new standpoints that would allow him to recognize 'the other', both within and outside national borders. He came to acknowledge the diversity within the nation – even within the community of the faithful – and has thus given voice to dissidents and non-conforming emigrants. Moreover, he has also challenged stereotypical representations of the West in Iranian media by including a respectful image of a western society and its citizens. It might thus be suggested that the compression of the world through globalization and the intensification of transnational encounters have inspired Hatami-kia to acknowledge that one of the essential requirements of the global age is be tolerant of others who, once far away, are now very close, and to learn to live with them in peace despite the differences.

Hatami-kia's recognition of 'the other' and his call for mutual respect between cultures and identities, particularly those which have for long been separated by hostility, distrust or misrepresentation, does not mean that he has lost his faith in Islam or become disloyal to the Islamic Revolution. Nor does it mean that he has failed to notice the uneven and stratified structure of the globalization processes and the patterns of inclusion and exclusion that they generate. Hatami-kia has strongly reacted, where necessary, to the marginalization of certain religious cultures and revolutionary identities. He rebels when he notices that even under an Islamic Republic, a globally dominant culture of capitalism is growing that recognizes no value apart from the value of capital. He protests against a global configuration of power in which the nation state is merely preoccupied with maintaining 'stability and security' to facilitate the free flow of capital, goods and affluent citizens, while neglecting the welfare and dignity of its marginalized and disadvantaged people, who are excluded from the luxuries of globalization.

In their resistance to such circumstances Hatami-kia's characters assert their agency as active subjects in the present, and refuse to be categorized as passive and submissive objects belonging to an ancient past. By doing so they demonstrate that far from simply destroying diversity and difference, and creating a homogenized form of 'global culture', globalization has intensified the declaration and representation of alternative cultures and identities. Hatami-kia's films provide further evidence that the global distribution of the capacity to produce images and information – or 'mediascapes' – has increasingly enabled the marginalized to acquire the means of speaking for themselves, retelling their repressed or misrepresented histories, and resisting the hegemony that denies them a dignified place in the contemporary world.

Conclusion

On 27th February 2009, for the first time after the 1979 Islamic Revolution, a high-ranking delegation from the Academy of Motion Picture Arts and Sciences (AMPAS) arrived in Tehran for a seven-day visit hosted by *Khaneye Cinema* (House of Cinema), the body representing Iranian film industry's trade unions. The group included prominent figures such as Sid Ganis, President of the Academy; the actress Annette Bening (*American Beauty*, 1999; *Being Julia*, 2004); former President of the Academy and scriptwriter Frank Pierson (*Dog Day Afternoon*, 1975); and former chairman of Universal Pictures Tom Pollock. Although the news of this surprise visit was not announced until the day before their arrival in order to avoid potential controversies, it had been in the process of planning and coordination months earlier. According to Mohammad-Mehdi Asgarpur, the executive director of *Khaneye Cinema*, this visit was part of this institution's programs for 'scientific and educational development' and 'improving professional skills of its members'.[1] The American delegation participated in a number of seminars and workshops on scriptwriting, direction, acting, production and distribution, in which many Iranian film industry professionals also took part. In one of these sessions, Ebrahim Hatami-kia, whose film *Glass Agency* was considered by some critics as a free adaptation of *Dog Day Afternoon*, was among those who attended a workshop on scriptwriting run by Frank Pierson. The delegation also held meetings with the governing board of *Khaneye Cinema*. Some parts of the visit's schedule, however, such as panels in Iranian film schools and a press conference, were later cancelled due to the increasing pressure by some Iranian media and political figures.

Despite its delayed announcement, the news of the delegation's presence in Tehran received major attention in the Iranian media and sparked a huge controversy. One day after the visit, Javad Shamaqdari, who was then a cultural advisor to President Ahmadinejad, condemned Hollywood in an interview for its 'insults and accusations against the Iranian people, civilization and culture'. He insisted that no government official should attend any meeting with the visitors unless they – as representatives of Hollywood – 'officially apologise' for producing films like *Not Without My Daughter* (1991), *300* (2006) and *The Wrestler* (2008), which he believed had 'insulted' and 'humiliated' the Iranian nation and the Islamic Revolution.[2]

---

[1] Report by Farsnews, available at: http://www.farsnews.net/newstext.php?nn=8712090230, accessed 10th April 2009.

[2] Report by Farsnews, available at: http://www.farsnews.net/newstext.php?nn=8712100828, accessed 10th April 2009. Despite his position as an advisor in the government, Shamaqdari was then critical of the authorities in charge of cinema at the Ministry of Culture, and accused them of being 'liberal' and 'permissive'. Some commentators, however,

Hosein Shari'atmadari, the editor-in-chief of the highly influential daily *Keyhan*, also published a scathing editorial against this visit. He slammed those who had invited, issued visas for, and hosted this group and asked: 'Isn't it disgraceful that in the Islamic Republic of Iran some people have invited the creators and producers of anti-Islamic and anti-Iranian films to convey their experiences and educate Iranian filmmakers'? (Shari'atmadari 2009). The irony was that the Minister of Culture, who was the target of some of these criticisms, had previously served as Shari'atmadari's deputy and was editor of *Keyhan* newspaper.

Ayatollah Mesbah-Yazdi, a senior cleric in the religious city of Qum, also expressed concern about this visit and demanded that the authorities explain why the American delegation had been invited. He said 'the Americans are trying to pursue their agenda in Iran using NGO's, sport personalities and filmmakers, and the recent visit should be seen in line with this project'.[3] A member of the Iranian Parliament's Cultural Committee also announced that three ministers have been summoned to the next meeting of the committee to explain the details of this visit.[4] Government authorities in both the Ministries of Culture and Islamic Cultivation and Foreign Affairs, whose brief comments made clear that they had either authorized this visit or knew about it in advance, however, avoided either openly endorsing or criticizing it.

Alireza Davoodnejad, a mainstream Iranian film-maker, who is not particularly known for being a hardliner, also took the opportunity of this visit to publish an open letter to President Obama. In his letter, apart from a humble request to the United States to 'relinquish the Veto right voluntarily and dismantle all nuclear weapons unilaterally', he recommended that Obama should not follow 'previous [US] cultural policies':

> [Forbid] your Hollywood friends from playing any tricks to dominate the cinemas of Iran. The United States once removed Iranian cinema from [...] Iranian life with the help of the former dictatorship, and ruined our industry with the import of foreign films. The fallen cinema of Iran has once again regained its footing with the Islamic Revolution and has been fighting to survive for thirty years.
>
> (Davoodnejad 2009)

---

believe the reasons behind his attitude are more personal than ideological. Given the role he played in Ahmadinejad's election campaign, many expected that he would be given a high post in the Ministry of Culture under the new government. Surprisingly however, Mohammad-reza Jafari-jelveh, who was a more moderate figure with a long career as radio and television executive, was appointed as the Ministry's Deputy for Cinematic Affairs. Yet in President Ahmadinejad's second term in office, Shamaqdari replaced Jafari-jelveh, and as noted earlier, he quickly began lifting bans from some of the films that were not granted screening permits in the previous governments. Now it was other people's turn to call his policies 'liberal' and 'permissive'.

[3] Report by *Rajanews* website, 14 Esfand 1387 (4th April 2009), available at: http://rajanews.com/detail.asp?id=25385, accessed 15th April 2009.
[4] ibid.

In Davoodnejad's words, we can sense an implicit anxiety about the potential consequences of the return of Hollywood to Iranian cinema theaters. After 30 years, he still seems haunted by the memory of the bankruptcy of Iranian film industry in 1978, which was in part the outcome of massive imports of foreign film.

The Academy visit to Iran also received coverage in a range of international media. Most of them highlighted the reaction of President Ahmadinejad's advisor to the event. In a report titled 'Despite Hopes of Hollywood Visit, Iran's Leaders Stick to the Same Script', *The New York Times* examined the significance of this visit and analyzed the reactions to it (Fathi 2009). *The Guardian* also reported this story in a dramatized style, as reflected in the report title: 'Hollywood Goes to Tehran – and Is Ordered to Apologise for Its Sins' (Tait 2009). In parallel with the harsh reactions to the visit in Tehran, there were also some strong criticisms of the visit in the United States. The online magazine *Digital Journal* published a series of scornful articles by the blogger Johnny Simpson, who expressed his anger at the Academy visit in the following terms:

> [W]hen I caught the news that a gold-plated AMPAS delegation was setting off for the repressive women-stoning, gay-hanging, Jew-murdering, student- and private citizen-butchering religious thugocracy of Iran on a so-called cultural mission, I was so outraged I could have smashed my computer and never written another goddamn word for film again.
>
> (Simpson 2009)

In his articles, Simpson was keen to know whether the delegation had actually apologized during this trip. Perhaps for this reason *The Hollywood Reporter* published an interview with Sid Ganis and Annette Bening while they were still in Tehran. They stated that they had only heard about the call for an apology in the press, and an apology was neither requested by the host, nor given by them (Kilday 2009). On their return to the United States, the delegation members spoke of their experience very positively. Sid Ganis told the CNN: 'It was thrilling to be in Iran, just plain old thrilling [...] We talked [...] We spoke the same language, the language of movies' (Khatami 2009).

An important aspect of this visit, which relates to the theme of global, is that on their first visit to Iran after 30 years of no official relation between, either Hollywood and the Iranian cinema, or the governments of the United States and the Islamic Republic of Iran, the delegation members felt that they were already there before they had arrived. In response to the question 'How familiar were the people you met with each of you and your work'? Sid Ganis says:

> They were surprisingly up on not just our films. They tend to see American cinema whether it's underground or above ground. They knew all of us who were there. They knew *Kite Runner* from Bill Horberg. They knew Annette's body of work, Alfre [Woodard]'s body of work. Sure enough, on the street, in an open-air market, there was a rack of DVDs and I

found a bootleg version of *Mr. Deeds*, a movie I did. Movies are very accessible to them, even though the government frowns on them and we don't send our movies there.

(Kilday 2009)

This indicates that the presence and integration of Hollywood in the local culture, as discussed in the case of *Mum's Guests*, is not confined to the memories of classic Hollywood films of the 1950s and 1960s, which were screened in Iranian cinemas before the revolution. Hollywood has continued to have a presence in Iran over the past three decades despite the discontinuation of official relations. The processes of globalization have no doubt played a major role in this respect by intensifying the flows of images, texts and other cultural commodities. Ganis' observation also reminds us of John Tomlinson's distinction between long distance travels in the pre-modern world and those in the current age of globalization: 'What separates the pilgrims of pre-modernity from those of today [...] is the fact that twentieth-century pilgrims in some senses "know" each other before they arrive' (Tomlinson 1999: 43).

The restrictions on imports from Hollywood in post-revolutionary Iran and the measures taken by the government to revitalize the film industry, as mentioned in Chapter 3, did provide fertile grounds for the development of the 'New Iranian Cinema' in the 1980s and 1990s. This new cinema was celebrated around the world and it brought Iran many international awards from prestigious film festivals, but its economy was highly dependent on government subsidies and the protectionist measures. The government could restrict the screening of foreign films in cinema theaters, but controlling the growing market for video – and later VCDs and DVDs – was a much more difficult task. The processes of globalization meant it was almost impossible to control the borders and prevent foreign films from entering the country, and then being rapidly disseminated across the country. In order to fight the black market, the government decided to lift the ban on video cassette players in the early 1990s. Video shops were licensed, but only to sell and rent Iranian and foreign films that had been issued permits.[5] Another development was the arrival of satellite television, which, despite its subsequent ban by the parliament, posed another challenge to the national film industry with its growing underground market.

As in many other countries, the development of video, VCD and DVD markets in Iran and the access to multiple satellite channels resulted in a sharp fall in cinema attendance during the 1990s. The annual admission figures of Iranian cinema theaters, which stood between 75 and 81 million during the 1985–90 period, significantly declined to 30 million in 1998.[6] In contrast to some other national cinemas, there was no significant private or foreign investment in the film industry, particularly in the exhibition sector, due to restrictions on the imports of foreign films. This meant that while older theaters with deteriorating conditions were closing down, no new cinemas – or multiplexes – were

---

[5] For more on the Iranian governments policies regarding video, see Shahabi (2008).
[6] Figures from a report titled *25 Years of Iranian Cinema* issued by Farabi Cinema Foundation in 2004.

built in their place. 'The multiplex effect', which helped revitalize many national film industries in the mid- to late-1990s, was not felt at all in Iran in the same period. Faced by the challenge of large flat screens at homes and high quality DVDs of the latest Hollywood blockbusters, the Iranian film industry became even more dependent on government subsidies and guaranteed loans in order to survive. By 2002, the annual admissions had dropped to a record low of 17 million; that is approximately 20 per cent of the figure in 1990.[7]

Today while new prospects for Iranian–American relations remain bleak, questions on whether, and how, Hollywood will return to Iranian screens become vital. Will the return of Hollywood contribute to further investments and the reconstruction of a viable industrial base for Iranian national cinema? Given the strict regulations in Iran, particularly in terms of physical appearances and sexual content, will Hollywood distributors agree with their films being further 'edited' before public screening? Will an increased presence of foreign films result in the relaxation of government regulations and control over the content of films? If the liberalization of the economy of Iranian cinema goes ahead, will there be any space or support for the kind of art-films with social and critical perspectives? Could we expect further international awards such as those in the 1990s for a national cinema that moves toward the mainstream? And will Iranian cultural authorities allow foreign imports and investment in Iranian cinema at all?

When I raised this question with Emad Afroogh, who then (2006) was the Head of Iranian Parliament's Cultural Committee, he welcomed the idea in principle, but had some reservations:

> I have no objection to foreign investment [...]. My only concern is about policy-making and supervision. We should not allow our cultural production field to be dominated by a global economy of culture that only cares about profits [...]. If foreign investment respects national regulations, we shouldn't mind whatever profit it makes. But this is different from the liberal ideas of cultural globalization.
>
> (Appendix III)

Afroogh was thus not against foreign investment *per se*, but he disagreed with handing over the full control of the cultural field to the forces of the market. He actually went further to criticize some Iranian films for their poor quality and suggested that foreign investment may help in improving the quality of Iranian cinema:

> Actually global investment and involvement in national cinema production can sometimes have better outcomes than what is routinely produced by local investments. Some of the [mainstream] Iranian films I have recently seen on television are really banal

---

[7] ibid.

and disgraceful. I don't think such films will be respected anywhere in the world [...]. Maybe foreign investment could encourage more quality films to be produced.

(Appendix III)

In response to the same question, Mohammad-reza Jafari-jelveh, then Deputy for Cinematic Affairs at the Ministry of Culture, took a more cautious approach. He began by stating: 'I think whoever is interested in Iranian cinema should be able to invest in it', but went on to describe a step-by-step, or region-by region, approach to inviting foreign investment based on cultural proximity:

First of all we have the neighbouring nations which belong to the great family of Iranian or Persian culture, and have shared histories, myths and languages [...]. The investment of our relatives in the great Islamic family is also definitely desirable [...]. We also belong to a greater Asian family whose members are most welcome to invest in Iranian cinema. In a broader view, the South-South cooperation can be mentioned, nations that have similar sufferings and pains and are taking the same path towards justice and freedom. And finally, even the nations of the west or the north can also invest in Iranian cinema.

(Appendix IV)

In this approach, it seems that Hollywood will be the last to be granted permission to enter Iran, while it certainly has the most significant resources at its disposal. Clearly Hollywood films are most likely to attract audiences to cinemas and generate money at the Iranian box office. In this sense they could help advance Iranian cinema's weak exhibition sector by encouraging new investment, and through paying tariffs, can raise funds to develop the film industry.

It is not only the Islamic government authorities, however, who are skeptical of Hollywood's return to Iranian screens. When I raised the issue with the internationally renowned Iranian director Majid Majidi, he too firmly rejected the idea that Hollywood can play a role in reconstructing the economic infrastructures of Iranian cinema. He emphasized that the return of Hollywood in large scale would be '*The End* of Iranian national cinema, not its reconstruction' (Appendix II). While admitting that 'It is our people's right to watch new films produced around the world on local screens', Majidi insisted that 'we should remain concerned and be selective about the quality of the films which are being distributed and the influences they have on the general tastes of people' (ibid.).

The observation that Iranian people would feel more culturally proximate to, say Egyptian, Chinese or Brazilian cinema rather than Hollywood, may not be accurate, given the long history of the presence of Hollywood in local culture, as we have seen in the analysis of *Mum's Guests*. Even in terms of sexual content and 'family values', Hollywood movies have usually been more conservative than many Asian and Latin American, not to mention European, cinemas. This does not deny the need to diversify the distribution of foreign films in Iran, but the question is, while Hollywood movies are regularly being broadcast on Iranian television and are watched by millions of audiences, why is their screening in cinemas considered a cultural threat? In any case, it is clear from Jafari-jelveh's words that even if Hollywood is granted a permit to officially enter the Iranian film industry, there will be conditions placed upon this:

> [W]e should not forget that such investments must not lead to the investor having absolute control in this cinema. The control of this cinema should remain in national hands [...]. If we want the investment for the sake of national cinema, then our cinema should remain national with those investments.
>
> (ibid.)

While we may speculate about the future, the facts on the ground, as seen above in the reactions to the Academy visit, indicate that even if political relations between Iran and the United States are reinstalled in the future, much more time will still be needed for the normalization of relations between Hollywood and Iranian cinema. This is why the Iranian government, rather than relaxing the imports of foreign films and inviting foreign investment, has in recent years launched new initiatives for the reconstruction, refurbishment and modernization of old cinema theaters.

According to the director of *Cinema-Shahr Institute*, the government body responsible for the reconstruction of cinema theaters, a third of the most popular cinema theaters in Iran – which account for 60–70 per cent of total annual admissions – were reconstructed and refurbished between 2005 and 2008 with funds and loans provided by this institute.[8] In addition, the Ministry of Culture and Islamic Cultivation has also cooperated closely with local councils and provincial municipalities to build new multi-screen cinemas in different cities. One of the first modern multiplexes to be built in Tehran was *Cinema Azadi* (Freedom Cinema), which has five screens with a total of 1400 seats.[9] It was opened on 17th March 2007 by Mohammad-Baqer Qalibaf, the Mayor of Tehran, who had funded the project. Tehran Municipality also funded another five-screen multiplex in Tehran named *Cinema Mellat* (Nation Cinema), which was opened in November 2008. With the support of *Cinema-Shahr Institute* a number of larger and older cinema theaters in Tehran and the provinces have also recently been reconstructed into cinemas with two or three screens.

---

[8] Press conference, 9th March 2009, available at Cinema-Shahr Institute website: http://www.cinemashahr.ir/news_view.asp?nid=151, accessed 15th April 2009.
[9] *Cinema Azadi* was initially built in the late 1960s – then under the name *Cinema Shahre Farang* (literally *Western City Cinema*) – and was one of Tehran's modern cinema theaters. Its owners fled the country after the 1979 revolution, and the cinema was confiscated by the government. Under public control, the cinema continued its operation in the post-revolution era and was one the most popular cinemas in Tehran. In 1998 the cinema caught fire and was burned down to ashes, causing deep distress for many cine-philes, who had decades of memories in this cinema. Almost 10 years later a new multiplex was inaugurated in the same place, keeping the name *Cinema Azadi*. Interestingly, one of the screening salons in the multiplex was named *Shahre Farang*, keeping alive the pre-revolution name too.

Despite all the above efforts, there are currently only 320 cinema screens in Iran, which, for a country with a population size of above 70 million, is far below international standards. In 2007, for example, France, Germany and the United Kingdom respectively had 5333, 4832 and 3514 cinema screens.[10] In South Korea, with a population of approximately 50 million, the number of cinema screens in 2007 was 1975, six times more than the number in Iran.[11] It is clear that even if foreign imports and private investment were to be encouraged by the government, Iranian cinema would still have to go a long way toward maintaining a sustainable economy with a modern infrastructure.

The presence of Hollywood, however, would not necessarily mark the end of national cinema, or the destruction of local/national culture. Even in countries such as South Korea and Argentina, where neo-liberal economic policies were implemented in the 1990s, there were new measures and initiatives by governments in support of national cinema, such as quotas and tariffs on imports, new funds and subsidies for national film production, and the establishment of publicly funded film festivals (Falicov 2007; Paquet 2005; Park 2007; Shin 2005). In terms of national cinema, therefore, it seems that globalization has in fact encouraged a more active nation state that, by maintaining the balance between foreign imports and local production, has in some cases facilitated the (re)construction of a vibrant and modernized film industry that can even beat Hollywood at its own game. In South Korea, for instance, we clearly notice a shift in the ratio of foreign and local films' share of Korean box office sales between 1995 and 2007. While in 1995 the ratio was 80 to 20 in favor of foreign (mainly Hollywood) films, in 2007 Korean films and foreign films drew out an almost equal share of the box office sales.[12] Korean cinema's exports to regional and global markets have also significantly increased over the years.

We should however avoid taking the above comparison too far and suggesting that the policies implemented in South Korean cinema, for example, can be simply adapted and applied in the case of Iranian cinema. There are without doubt many profound cultural, political and economic differences between the Korean and Iranian societies, which should be taken into account in any comparison.[13] One conclusion we can draw, however, is that no nation will succeed in maintaining a sustainable film industry and a flourishing film culture either by retreating into total protectionism and shutting all gates

---

[10] *European Cinema Yearbook 2008*, available at:
http://www.mediasalles.it/ybk08_berlin/index.htm, accessed 17th April 2009.
[11] *Korean Cinema 2008*, published by Korean Film Council (KOFIC). Available at KOFIC website: http://www.koreanfilm.or.kr/KOFIC/Channel?task=kofic.user.eng.d_publication.command.PublicationRetrieve1Cmd&Gesipan_SCD=000000000000000001, accessed 16th April 2009.
[12] ibid.
[13] For example there are currently almost 30,000 US military personnel based in South Korea (Caryl 2007), while the United States does not even have an embassy in Tehran. In terms of the Iranian economy there are no privately owned giant industrial corporations such as the Korean *chaebol*, which could invest in national cinema. Moreover, while almost half of South Korean people do not follow any specific religious faith (KOIS 2009), religion continues to play an extremely influential role in social, cultural and political aspects of the Iranian society.

to the outside world or through relinquishing all government powers to the presumed magic hand of the 'global free market'.

At the heart of the nation state's growing concerns for film and media industries in the age of globalization, there may well be some economic justifications based on profits and jobs. Yet throughout this book it has also been indicated that by intensifying 'the expectation of identity declaration' – to use Robertson's terms – globalization has proliferated the expression of cultural identities and national specificities. The crisis of national identity has created a stronger desire to uphold an image of the nation that would differentiate it from others and (re-)legitimize the nation state. At times when transnational flows and global interactions are increasingly undermining the significance of national borders, national cinemas become significant markers of difference. This is why, even in the age of globalization, the concept of national cinema has not lost its relevance. As demonstrated in the previous chapters, government intervention in national cinema does not necessarily result in the homogenization of national cinemas' output. On the contrary, it could enable local, marginalized or repressed cultures and identities to come into representation and further diversify, if not problematize, the notion of national culture.

The concern for identity and representation in the age of globalization, it can thus be suggested, is not restricted to the national level but can also be witnessed in smaller groups and communities. The new state-funded initiatives as well as the developments in digital video production and electronic communication have further empowered local identities and communities to represent themselves and to create new networks of interaction, which can easily transcend national borders. In the age of globalization, therefore, many national cinemas have become more inclusive and diverse, giving some parts of the public more choice and further access to alternative films and independent cinemas through specialized venues of exhibition and channels of distribution.

While there has been much discussion about the positive aspects and progressive dimensions of 'the transnational' in the fields of culture, art and film (Carroll 2007; Ďurovičová and Newman 2010; Ezra and Rowden 2006; Higbee and Lim 2010; Szeman 2006), the study of Mohsen Makhmalbaf's cinema in Chapter 4 suggests a more cautious appraisal in this respect. In contrast to the assumption that a transnational disposition necessarily widens the artist or film-maker's perspective and allows for a more sophisticated critical reflection on local, national and global cultures, the example of Makhmalbaf illustrates that it could also result in a banal transnationalism with its own parochial and dogmatic attitudes.

A very interesting example that further complicates the national–transnational debate in Iranian cinema emerged in the 2009 Tribeca Film Festival (New York), where two films by Iranian directors were admitted in the competition. Amir Naderi's latest 'transnational' film titled *Vegas: Based on a True Story* (2008) was screened along with Asghar Farhadi's *About Elli* (2009): a film made inside Iran by a film-maker whose focus has been on the local and the national. While Naderi's film failed to win any awards at the festival, Farhadi's film won the top prize for Best Narrative Feature. As mentioned earlier *About Elli* also went on to win the Silver Bear for Best Director at the 2009 Berlin Film Festival. The film was a mystery drama with a very intelligent narrative form, which did not merely target festival audiences. It profoundly engages the ordinary viewer with ethical questions on the difficulty of defining what or who is right and wrong in complex human conditions. Ironically, the Tribeca jury – which included Uma Thurman – ignored Amir Naderi's 'transnational' film, yet they praised *About Elli* for 'the universality of the characters and themes', and the film-maker's 'riveting grasp of [the] story', which, in their view, renders it 'a film that collapses barriers and deepens our understanding of the world we share'.[14]

As mentioned earlier Farhadi's 2011 film, *A Separation*, went further than *About Elli* in terms of sweeping international awards and having successful screenings across the world, despite going deeper, in terms of its theme and characters, in the local and the national. These films are quite different, in terms of theme and form, from the typical Iranian films that previously won awards at international festivals. It appears that they have not been awarded prizes as a result of the fascination or shock involved in the encounter with the unknown, distant or exotic other, rather these films seem to win prizes simply because they are 'good films'. This may explain why they have managed to win awards in Tehran and in Berlin, and have been popular with audiences in Tehran and in Paris. In this sense their success could be seen as a new beginning for Iranian cinema.

To conclude, the analysis of different films presented throughout this book highlights the ambivalence at the heart of globalization processes. The intertwined and dialectical forces of identity and difference, unity and diversity, homogenization and heterogenization, exploitation and empowerment, and localization and globalization make it extremely difficult to determine or predict the precise consequences, whether in politics, economics or culture, of the complex and contradictory processes we may, following Robertson, call 'glocalization'. And perhaps it is in this uncertainty that there lies some hope.

---

[14] '2009 Tribeca Film Festival Award Winners', *Tribeca Film Festival Website*, 1 May 2009, available at: http://www.tribecafilm.com/festival/features/film-coverage/Tribeca_Winners_Announced_About_Elly_Takes_Top_Prize.html, accessed 12th May 2009.

APPENDICES

Appendix I

Interview with Abbas Kiarostami

14th August 2006, Tehran.

Mr Kiarostami! Many believe that Iranian cinema achieved its international recognition and appraisal, first and foremost, through your films. You are now a globally reknowned film-maker. Do you think *being Iranian* and *being global* are contradictory? What is your view on cosmopolitanism?

Well, I do think global issues are important and the world is, in a sense, our home. But how can we neglect homeland or forget about it? I don't remember who [rightfully] said that 'being local is the prerequisite for becoming global'. You have to belong to somewhere; you have to have your roots and origins, but at the same time keep an eye on the global. I must say however, we can't just decide to become a globally renowned film-maker. If it was just with our own decision we probably would by now have thousands of them! Yes, we should have a global view, but I think if we deeply concentrate on our [local] issues we will realize that in fact we are thinking about global issues too. I can't think about the world when I am making my films. I should profoundly think about my self, regardless of the temptations to become an internationally celebrated film-maker. If we do it this way, we may have the chance of becoming so, although I deliberately used the word 'chance' because I think 'luck' is an important parameter too.

So you don't think dealing with local issues in films will run the risk of losing international audiences? In fact you seem to argue the other way: being local is a prerequisite of becoming global…

That's right. We should speak about issues of our own society or issues of our inner selves. Obviously there is only one kind of *human being*. We have different languages, cultures and religions. But we are profoundly the same. My photograph may seem different to a European citizens' photo, but if we take X-ray images or have laboratory tests of our blood, much of the results would be the same. We share in common the serious and fundamental matters in life that we all deal with. So if you contemplate about yourself and be truthful and honest with yourself, what you will say will not be just about yourself. Even a person from Guatemala, with a different culture, or a person from Sweden will understand and engage with your film.

The cultural and economic impact of globalization on national cinemas is also a matter of debate. Some suggest Hollywood as the dominant global cinema will, in this new situation, eventually demolish national cinemas. Others maintain that Hollywood generates money into the exhibition sector of national cinemas and helps them to survive. Otherwise there would be no cinema theaters left to screen local films. It may also be claimed that national cinemas have benefited from globalization in the sense that now some global distributors are marketing for example Iranian films around the world. What do you make of these debates?

Obviously, cinema is an industry. It is the industrial side that has kept cinema alive. Mainstream cinema, what ever we think of it, plays a crucial role and makes the people go watch films in cinemas. This also provides a space for us to make the films we personally like to make. We cannot overlook people's habitual practices. Commercial cinema has influenced tastes and preferences to such an enormous extent that we can not escape from it. American films have shaped people's tastes, and whether we like it or not, they have become references and benchmarks for evaluation of our work. But the other point is: what about the issue of originality and authenticity of our work? We cannot neglect the matter of uniqueness. We can't just copy Hollywood, particularly with the poor production resources that we have.

I must admit however that if I were to have a chance to make a multi-million dollar big production film, I sure won't reject it! But since that option is not available, we should make the most of what we have. We can't just sit and wait for somebody to come and invest a huge sum of money in our film. So I think we should consider both sides of the debate. On the one hand, certainly cinema needs investment and it is commercial cinema that absorbs money into the industry and keeps the wheels running. On the other hand, the beauty of the world is in its differences. The reason why people spend money on tourism is because they want to see different things, different cultures, different costumes, different spaces and different geographies. We shouldn't underestimate the spectacular and exciting country we have. Of course there are currently some exceptional and peculiar conditions of film production in our cinema: we have to show female characters with head scarves even when they are in bed! But under such restrictions we have learned to think of other ways of resolving our problems. This has itself made our films different from other films. Before the revolution Iranian mainstream cinema wasn't very different from, for example, Indian mainstream cinema. But now Iranian cinema is something different. So it's not the end of the world if we don't have the resources to make films just the same as Hollywood films. This isn't our failure. A real failure is when we can't carefully look and see the things around us, when we are ignorant of the wonderful and amazing things that we already have.

You mentioned the regulations and state interventions. Again here some cultural theorists have stressed the vital role of the state in promoting and supporting national cinemas and maintain that without such support the film industries wouldn't survive. But in contrast, others have highlighted the consequences of protectionism and interventionism in the form of direct or indirect censorship or the states' ideological or political demands in return for the funding.

I don't think anyone would support censorship or suggest that it is a good thing. We should first be intellectuals and then film-makers. To be an intellectual means to be informed and conscious of what's going on in the world and around you. But the reality is that we can never make our ideal government. This isn't just about Iran, it is about everywhere on the world. Our conditions here are clearly a bit more complex and complicated. So, as intellectuals who also make films, we can't ignore what's going on around us, or remove the current relations and conditions in the world. We can't assume that all the world, or all the governments are here just for us to make films. This is a fantasy that a film-maker may have, but in my view people with fantasies never meet their objectives.

Considering the realities which we may or may not be pleased about, and I am among those who aren't, we should do what we can. Should we just sit down and wait until the regulations change according to what we think is the best, and then make films? Or must we say: well these are the conditions, what can we do now, and work our way out. I must add however, we don't really have censorship here to the extent that we imagine we do. We have restrictions and limitations, but we shouldn't erroneously consider restrictions and censorship as the same thing. What we have is more self-censorship. We are brought up in conditions that we even go beyond what the censors may do. We are so anxious about our financial investments, even as small as they are, or concerned about our professional career that we self-censor our work. It's these restrictions that disturb and frustrate us the most.

But at the same time, as every living human being, who, in extraordinary circumstances, eventually discovers his or her special powers to survive, we also have found ways to survive our professional lives. Over the years we have found our ways to continue making our films. The regulations which are currently implemented in Iran, if it happened that they became universal, in places such as the United States or India, which produce thousands of films each year, I don't think a handful of those films would be possibly produced. But this is to our credit that with all those complex conditions and problems we have been able to continue producing our films, and even create a new form of cinema.

A friend of mine who is an architect believes that the most innovative buildings he has designed are the ones that had lands with irregular shapes. So, we may just continue moaning about censorship, and I moan about it myself as from about 12 years ago none of my films have been screened; but I think it is because of the power of life that anyone who has wanted to watch my films has been able to do so.

Actually I saw your film *Ten* (2002) recently on BBC2...

Yes, they are everywhere now. Censorship does not work any longer. The restrictions do still work. So if we are to moan, we better moan of the restrictions and disorder, not of censorship. Even the restrictions themselves are not even and equal; there are some who are privileged and are allowed to make films beyond the restrictions, while others can't make any films at all. Someone like me doesn't get the permission to screen any of the films he makes, without any explanation. It's tragic that my film *The Wind Will Take Us* (2002) was banned because of a scene which happens in a dark room where someone is reciting a poem by Foroogh Farrokhzad. The irony is that her poems are regularly republished and are available in all bookshops. Or for another scene which includes a poem by Khayam.

Considering these conditions and how you have been treated, do you have any sense of belonging to something called national cinema? Do you think there is, or should be, any such thing as a national cinema?

Well, I don't really think about *cinema* that much, at least to the extent that I think about myself. I really don't know. One thing I am sure of is that I can't enjoy a nice and relaxed sleep anywhere in the world more than in the closed alley where my house is located. Nowhere else in the world do I feel the peace and comfort that I do feel here. When there is no particular reason for me to stay abroad, I can't stand being there even for one day. I belong here and, as a citizen, have the right to express my opinion. I make a film every two years, but I live 365 days a year. This is what I am concerned about. I am a resident here and I can't live anywhere else. I may be able to work in other places, but there is more to life than work. I originally belong here and even if I was granted freedom to make whatever film I like, I will still make films quite similar to the ones I have already made. I personally don't prefer other kinds of films. I will never make a film with sexually explicit scenes. I will never show actors making love in my films, even if I was making the film in Sweden or the most liberal country in the world. Those films wouldn't be mine. I can't even think of a scene where for instance a naked woman is chatting about politics with somebody else. This is not what I'm familiar with. These rules are for me essential and deep-rooted. I don't need government censors to tell me what not to show. Even if they grant me all the liberties that some may be excited about, I won't be willing or even capable of taking advantage of those liberties. Actually they are now relaxing the regulations but I just can't make other types of films.

The reason for this is that I am more deeply and genuinely committed to my principles than the government officials are to theirs. My moral principles are not based on my political interests. I don't practice such principles in order to keep my job or my post. While for the state, all that matters is maintaining power and it is according to this principle that they provide freedom or restrict it or take sides. My opinions are my personal ideas. My character is too deep seated to be changed according to the day-to-day waves of life. Even if you watch my films made before the revolution, they are very different from other films of the time.

As the last question, what would be your recommendation to those involved in the Iranian cinema industry in order to advance Iranian cinema and its international prominence?

If I were to reply to this question it would imply that I consider myself in such an international or global position to give recommendations to others.

Thank you for your time.

Thank you.

Appendix II

Interview with Majid Majidi

20th August 2006, Tehran.

I would like to start by asking about your first global experiences as a film-maker when you attended international festivals. How did you feel being in such an environment and what influences did it have on you?

I think it's better to distinguish *festival experience* from *global experience* since they are not the same. I believe Iranian cinema still has a long way to go before it becomes a *global cinema*, although it is already a widely celebrated cinema in film festivals. Anyway, my first international festival experience was for my first film *Badook* (1992), which was accepted in the *Directors' Fortnight Section* of Cannes film festival. I had never even thought of this film getting through to a festival like Cannes. I even faced some trouble in returning to Iran after the festival. The film had a tragic narrative, which had the potential of political interpretations, and there is always skepticism and suspicion about the political intentions behind big festivals such as Cannes, which made my situation worse. Suddenly I was in the middle of a game that I had not chosen to start. That was my first and last experience in Cannes. I do believe that there are particular views and taste preferences dominant in

Cannes that do not match my personal views and tastes very much. So my other films have been mostly presented and awarded prizes in other European, North American and Asian film festivals.

You mentioned how you didn't have any idea about *Badook* being screened in an international film festival. What about your films after this first experience? Did it make you consciously think about this when you were making your next films? I don't just mean thinking about festivals and awards, but rather having a global audience in mind?

I must say that my particular style in film-making was formed and evolved over time and through all these experiences. But I have always sought to make films about my concerns. I think that unlike journalists, who are more concerned about what is more fashionable and up-to-the-minute, artists usually have a view toward the world beyond these limits. For me the main concern has always been to make films on subjects and issues that I truly identify with or believe in, whether they are fashionable or not. In this case the viewer can also feel the director's faith in his film and get engaged with it. This brings me to another point regarding your question. I assume a film should first and foremost be based on the local roots and beliefs of its nation before it can be influential across borders and impress a global audience. For me therefore, the local audience has always been the priority when making films.

So you don't see local identity as an obstacle or problem for films that seek global audiences, while others may suggest that having a global audience requires a transnational film language, which is not bound to local or national culture?

No this is nonsense! On the contrary I insist that the more a film is close to its indigenous and local culture, the more it has the chance of finding a global audience, even in the festivals. The problem here is that some festivals, with their particular preferences, are themselves blocking some local films from becoming global. For some festivals all that matters is new forms and styles. In Cannes, I believe there are some unwritten rules and guidelines, for instance, they seem to be more interested in non-narrative or even anti-narrative films, so usually films that involve classic narratives are not privileged. May be this is a kind of opposition to Hollywood, but it excludes many films from their program and also leads some people to make films based on the festival's preference. I understand the importance of experimental cinema for exploring new horizons and expanding the medium, but I personally prefer films that are more inclusive regarding their audiences. Cinema has essentially and historically been formed in relation to mass audiences. It is an art, but an industry at the same time. Films are not paintings that you may just work for yourself and put them on the walls of your home.

Festivals have generally attempted to provide a space for diverse national or indigenous cinemas and to resist the forces of Hollywood. But even the coordinators of such festivals, who are doing a great job, should think of ways to encourage wider audiences for such films and attempt to truly globalize them. They shouldn't just be satisfied with the typical elite audiences of the festivals. If we are really thinking of resisting Hollywood this is far from enough. A comparative analysis of the Oscar awards and the Cannes or other European festivals would highlight the difference of these two approaches to cinema. In Oscars, artistic credit and economic success of a film are more or less associated, while in Cannes even the *Palme d'Or* would not necessarily lead to a film's economic success.

In recent years we are witnessing a new generation of directors in Iran who just make films according to the festival formulas. This process not only has alienated their films from local audiences, but has even disconnected them from their roots and identities. Their films seem artificial and fake and only may survive a short 'greenhouse life' in festival circuits. No one will remember them after a year or two. On the other hand we have many films in the history of cinema that may never have been awarded prizes in festivals but, nevertheless, remain as highly acclaimed and widely remembered films. Hitchcock, for instance, never got an award for his films in festivals but he certainly is a globally renowned director. I think Iranian cinema must go beyond its obsession with festivals and think more about wider audiences. And the problems and challenges of Iranian cinema are not just about the festivals; we have some problems inside the country: narrow-minded views for instance, which can only recognize cinema as an apparatus for short-term political purposes.

You distinguished between the state of *global successes* and *festival success* of a national cinema. When do you think a national cinema can be truly considered a 'global cinema'?

I believe if a national cinema reaches a level of aesthetic and technical innovation and remains faithful to its cultural origins and roots, it will have the potential of becoming global. I think John Ford is a globally celebrated film-maker because he is deeply American. Akira Kurosawa's films are widely respected because he is really committed to Japanese culture. Satyajit Ray is globally admired because his films reflect Indian social and cultural life. This is not just about films. In literature and poetry where, as Iranians, we have a long history, big names such as Hafiz, Sa'adi and Rumi's global reputation is because their poems speak of their culture in styles which are aesthetically unique to themselves. These are the figures who bridge and link nations and facilitate inter-cultural relations.

I also have further ideas on this subject which derive from my religious views. According to the Quran God has created all human beings and granted them *Fetrat* (intuition), which consists of some fundamental internal tendencies and faculties. They are the foundations for common and universal human values and ethics, which can be narrated in diverse social and cultural settings. Love, compassion and sacrifice, for instance, are not local human characteristics. Even if they are formed and represented in local settings, they will no doubt be recognized and respected everywhere. The dust of everyday life may gradually cover up such pure internal faculties, but I believe one important role of art is to remind us of those original values and to motivate people to retrieve them. I think one way of reaching and communicating with a global audience is an approach which aims at the fundamental values that all humans share.

Regarding the current dominance of Hollywood and its powerful global distribution circuit and the struggle that national cinemas face, even in competing with Hollywood in their own country, to what extent do you think national cinemas have the potential of becoming 'globally successful' in your sense of the term? Don't you think 'local success' should be a priority?

It is a very difficult task, and I assume today in the 2000s it is much more difficult than it was in the 1990s, at least for Iranian cinema, which was somehow the newly discovered cinema of the 1990s. It was the first time that Iran was being known for something other than its pistachio, rugs or caviar. Iranian films provided an image of Iran that was totally different from the stereotype image disseminated by western media, which usually associate Iran with war, bombs and terrorism. We have already lost the good opportunity we had in the 1990s. However the first step, as you say, would be to have a locally successful cinema. Even for Hollywood a local audience is a priority since it provides two-thirds of its box office sales. Indian cinema is another case that indicates the importance of a local market for a cinema that seeks global recognition. Without improving the infrastructures of the film industry; without a significant rise in the number and quality of the movie theaters; and without sufficient technological equipment, we would never reach that ideal position. One of the reasons that Iranian cinema has survived to this day with all its poor conditions is that after the revolution it has luckily been prevented from competing with foreign rivals. Had this opportunity coincided with progress and development in the 'hardware' of cinema, we would have by now achieved a better status.

Unfortunately cinema in Iran is not yet fully integrated in the local and popular culture. Some people still remain suspicious of cinema. I think about 30 per cent of the Iranian population never go to the cinema. Among the different administrations and politicians there is no consensus about the significance of cinema and its necessity. Some politicians have at times been concerned about the future of cinema, but this has not led to a big change in reality. There isn't a long-term perspective for the future; most policies are aimed at short-term targets.

Speaking of the role of the state, there is a debate on government interventions in cinema production. Some think 'protectionism' is vital for the survival of diverse national cinemas, others suggest state intervention involves certain limitations and ideological preferences. Even on the economic side of culture, some maintain that government regulations such as fixed ticket prices or restrictions on foreign films inhibits the growth and progress of local cultural industries. How would you comment on these debates?

Appendix II

With all such debates protectionism is still playing a crucial and vital role for national cinemas in many countries, particularly in Europe. The French government significantly supports its national cinema through different modes of direct subsidies or through channels such as *Canal Plus*. Although injecting money into the industry may help a cinema survive for short-term, I reckon if our intention is to help cinema stand on its own feet, we must seek other solutions. In this case what matters is people's tastes. Tastes are not essentially fixed and should not be taken for granted; they are created over time through practice and habit. It is not just McDonalds that changes people's tastes all over the world; Hollywood does just the same. National cinemas, I suggest, should also take this approach. I don't mean they should enforce a single taste; actually they must provide diverse types of films for their diverse viewers. It may take a 20-year period to change people's tastes. In Poland I was fascinated by a school curriculum that included regular screenings of great films from the history of cinema. This helps to improve the pupil's sense of cinema and develop their understanding of the aesthetics of the image and the quality of a film. I believe this is a fundamental long-term approach.

Another approach could be collective action in the form of regional cooperation between countries that share linguistic or cultural grounds. Integrating markets, establishing regional institutions or monetary funds and trusts could be some options to consider. But first the countries involved should agree on a mutual perspective and strategy. For instance, Iranian cinema can have a position both within the Islamic countries and the Farsi-speaking nations. Going back to globalization, I think co-productions can play a role in the globalization of film cultures. But all such hopes and wishes would not come true without the existence of far-sighted authorities who are deeply committed to the promotion and development of their cinema industries. I am not so optimistic; not just about Iran, everywhere national cinemas are shrinking and one reason is that their talented directors are constantly being absorbed by Hollywood. I think it is Hollywood's strategy to track successful film-makers around the world and buy them into the system, while national cinemas generally underestimate the value of such human resources or cannot afford to keep them.

On the issue of foreign investment in national cinema industries, what do you think of foreign investment and ownership of movie theaters? Some people suggest that Iranian cinema is not even capable of producing enough films for the current number of cinema screens in Iran, which is very low in comparison to other countries. There is no interest therefore in such investments, even by local investors and unless foreign films, Hollywood in particular, are allowed to be distributed and exhibited widely in Iran, nothing will happen. Do you agree with such arguments?

I can't totally agree with such arguments. The problem with a large number of our current cinema theaters is that they are not standard and comfortable places. In Tehran many of them are very old buildings with awful environments and the worst possible sound and screen qualities. Geographically, they are all located in the city center, far from the main residential areas, and thus the problem of traffic and parking discourages people to go and watch films in cinemas. Otherwise, you see in the case of standard and well-equipped cinemas that no matter what film they are screening, they always have a considerable number of spectators. My recent film *Bide Majnoon* (2005) was on screen in 15 cinemas in Tehran, but the box office sales in the two standard and first-class cinemas equated with the total sum of the other 13 cinemas. Many families, who constitute the main body of the Iranian moviegoers, never go to watch a film in the terrible and distressing environment of the old cinema theaters.

Well, these facts seem to provide more material for those who argue that Hollywood films are essential to the reconstruction of the infrastructures of national cinema industries.

No, I actually think that would be *the end* of Iranian national cinema, not its reconstruction. I agree that there should be a healthy balance of foreign film screenings, but the numbers should be under control. It is our people's right to watch the new films produced around the world on local screens, and not just on television or through CDs and DVDs. But again I think we should be concerned and selective about the quality of the films that are being distributed and the influences they have on the general tastes of people. We should have the best films screened, not the useless ones that are just being dumped here.

My final question is about 'cultural and national identity'. Although in Iran there seems to be a convention that cultural or national identity is something valuable that ought to be preserved, nevertheless there is not much said about what exactly this national identity comprises? Sometimes disputes are seen between the government and the artists, or the critics and the artists, about whether a work of art or a film is in accord with national identity, or if it they are in contrast with, or even against national identity. The discourse of identity may thus be seen as incongruent with the freedom of an artist, who could possibly believe that whatever s/he creates contributes to the overall shape of national identity.

I think it depends on how we define identity. When we speak of the importance of identity, it should not be understood in the narrow sense of *political* or *ideological* identity, although it could be argued that cultural identities in the form of traditions, beliefs and rituals also have ideological origins. But these are widely dispersed identities, which belong to the whole nation; they are not unified and centralized ideologies under certain authorities. Another problem is that identity is mostly identified through superficial signs and stereotyped customs; in the form of clothing for instance, which may change in different times. These are not the important aspects of identity. What does matter when we speak of identity is the deep roots and origins, which have shaped the history of a nation and lasted for so many years. This is why archaeologists and historians refer to artifacts when they want to study the history of a nation. Art reflects the identities of the people in each historical period. So we should have a broader definition of identity, which goes beyond ideological and journalistic definitions of the term. Artists and film-makers can be free to create anything they want, but they can't escape from the nation, the culture and the language they belong to. When we see a piece of art, we should be able to recognize the geographical, historical and cultural origin of the work. I think the work of an artist, who claims to be completely free of the context which he is located in, would not flourish or even survive in the history of art. Such works usually have short greenhouse-lives and then quickly fade away. Vittorio De Sica's *The Bicycle Thief* (1948) and my film *Children of Heaven* (1997) both engage with the issue of poverty. I personally like *The Bicycle Thief* but what makes my film different from De Sica's is the different world-views and identities we have. For De Sica, social and economic conditions such as poverty determine and justify human action, even in the form of theft. For me the human will is far more prestigious and invaluable to be determined by external conditions. The fact that human life is not totally determined by social conditions, but that, on the contrary, humans can resist and even change the external circumstances is one of the most precious merits that God has granted human beings. This, I believe, is the truth about humanity that sometimes gets neglected when we focus only on the surface of the reality. It is about how humans can remain truthful and maintain their honor and virtue even in terrible conditions such as extreme poverty. This is the view I have learned from the Quran, and I don't think the Quran is just a book for Muslims. They are the words of God to all human beings. The words have inevitably been said in a particular human language, but the messages of the words can be transferred to the entire human world. I think film-makers can play a significant role in translating and transferring this message.

Thank you very much for your time.

Thank you.

Appendix III

Interview with Emad Afroogh

16th August 2006, Tehran.

Dr. Afroogh! As a sociologist you have published articles and books in which you discuss globalization. Do you think there is a particular Iranian perspective on, or theory of, globalization?

When we speak of globalization we should make clear what we mean, since there are many definitions for this term. I personally use two different terms to explain two different understandings of globalization. I think we have a 'conventional globalization', which refers to the globalization of capitalism, and a 'true globalization'. Conventional globalization has some obvious ramifications and definite dimensions that we cannot deny, such as the new communication and information technologies that allow us to learn about distant events and interact from remote places. This is what Giddens has named 'time-space distanciation'; others have called it the creation of 'virtual space' or the triumph of time over space. But globalization as a social phenomenon is much more that such narrow explanations. All social phenomena are multifaceted and complex, and so is globalization. It has political, economic and cultural aspects and even each of these aspects themselves can

Member of Parliament for Tehran and Chair of Iranian Parliament's Cultural Committee (2003–7).

be studied through different approaches. One outcome of globalization is the emergence of 'post-society', which again has political, economic and cultural implications.

Therefore in discussing globalization we should bear in mind all these aspects. I personally think that these days what is meant by globalization is actually globalism. Globalism is certainly a project, not a process or a natural reality. Some prefer to introduce their projects as processes so it would be perceived as an inevitable reality. They try to avoid using '-ism' and never confess about their projects because they know it will cause resistance. So they use '-tion' instead of '-ism'. The conventional globalization should better be termed 'globalizationism'. They say globalization is just an event or consequence. But the human will and actions cannot be neglected. [...]

I think even the conventional globalization has provided us with some conceptual opportunities to think about true globalization. 'Post-society' is one such concept. Today political, economic and cultural relations among humans are constantly crossing the geographical borders and this is a pre-condition to what I call true globalization. If we scrutinize the philosophical foundations of conventional or capitalist globalization, my sense is that they include rationally inconsistent and contradictory assumptions [...] In short capitalist globalization is inherently contradictory because it is theoretically based on humanism and self-sufficient reason. In my view self-sufficient reason is essentially self-destructive, both for the individual and the society.

Conventional globalization in the cultural realm involves the Americanization of life: the Americanization of ontologies and world-views; the Americanization of values; the Americanization of norms; and the dominance of American symbols. In order to proceed, this project must abolish national cultures. In order to construct a cultural 'post-society', conventional globalization must ignore national cultures. The weakening of national cultures in turn results in the strength of local and ethnic cultures. This is one of the contradictions within globalization: it simultaneously provokes globalism and localism while weakening national integration. The ethnic conflicts around the world are partly the inevitable result of this project, even if you don't suspect that they are intentional and deliberate outcomes and not just incidents. Some may seek certain interests when they attempt to thin out nationality and national cultures in favor of a [cultural] anarchism.

The fact that you see the forces of globalism and localism hand-in-hand while nationalism or nationality is being threatened is interesting. Don't you think local and ethnic cultures should flourish in order to strengthen national cultures and enrich them with their diverse resources?

In order to answer this question let me first turn to what I call true globalization and explain what its imperatives and requirements are. Then I shall examine how true globalization will impact upon national and local cultures. In my view the first pre-condition to true globalization is a universalism in the deepest layer of our culture, which is our ontological views. In my view culture is constituted of four levels or layers: the most profound and underlying is ontology or the world-view level; the second level belongs to our values; the third level includes the social norms; and the surface level is the level of symbols. The weight and importance of these levels are not the same. When I say universalism is a prerequisite for globalization I mean the universalism of ontological views, it shouldn't be mistaken with the unification of symbols. True globalization does not require all the symbols to be uniform; neither does the unification of symbols necessarily mean that true globalization has occurred. People may wear the same clothes but this does not mean they think the same.

This could also be meaningful the other way round; contrary to what some worried cultural officials think in Iran, the changes in lifestyles and clothing of the youth does not necessarily mean they have totally deserted their local or traditional culture or have forgotten about their national identity.

That's right. We may watch American films, wear American jeans and eat American food; but this would not mean our view is the same as the American world-view. In social research we shouldn't just look for the visible realities; we should also analyze concepts. Contrary to positivism that suggests we should only be an observer, I think everything we may observe in the society is socially constructed and is concept-centered. My main point is that true globalization is possible because it is based on common universal views in the deepest level of human culture, the ontological level. These views include our general sense of the human, the world, the society and also God. If we have common world-views then we may have common values in the second level and that could lead to shared norms and even similar symbolic representations. In reality these levels are not organically linked and there can always be ruptures and breaks among them. Despite this the relation between people who only have different cultural symbols is not the same as the relation between people who have different ontological views. The ontological views are much more important and play a much more significant role in human life.

The question I have for the theorists of conventional globalization is: how can they define universal common foundations for globalization? Can self-sufficient reason provide a valid and stable ontological view for all human beings? Can humanism undertake such a task after removing God or killing God and replacing the human in its place? I don't think so. One who denies the authentic origins of humanity and proclaims the death of God will also end up declaring the death of the human. To use the words of some postmodern thinkers, modernism killed the God and postmodernism killed the Man. [...]

Now the question is whether true globalization will have clashes or conflicts with national or local cultures. In my view this is not necessarily the case. There is a possibility of 'unity in diversity'.[1] Both on the national and global stage it is possible to have universal ontological content in particular differentiated symbolic forms. In the national case, for instance, you can view this in the diversity of clothing styles among different Iranian ethnic groups. Here you can recognize a certain unity and harmony despite all the differences [...].

---

[1] A theory introduced by the famous Iranian philosopher Molla Sadra (1571–1640 AD).

This 'unity in diversity' can also happen on the global scale, but it requires a universally shared understanding of human life. This is why I suggest that the dialogue of religions has a key role in true globalization. I don't understand 'dialogue of civilizations'.[2] What I understand is the unity and alliance of religions. True globalization will not happen without true monotheism [...].

On the other hand there are some who claim we should move on from universalism in the ontological level to a kind of universal jurisprudence. That is to say everyone in the world should practically follow, for instance, Islamic *Shari'a* if we are to have true globalization. This is the point which I cannot agree with. In this case there wouldn't be any space for 'unity in diversity', instead there will be uniformity. We aren't advocates of formalism and neither do we promote diversity per se, that is to say diversity without any sense of unity and harmony. Uniformity is not a necessary precondition for globalization. In true globalization the local and national cultures are the elements of diversity, while the authentic origin of humanity is the element of unity. Only through 'unity in diversity' is globalization truly possible and philosophically and theoretically consistent. But in capitalist globalization the only thing that matters is the symbol, the consumer styles, the clothing etc. Capitalism has mistakenly considered the universalization of its symbols as the evidence of the universal triumph and global validation of its fundamental basis and values [...].

There are questions about authoritarian forms of national or cultural identity, that they stand at odds with artistic freedom. Why should artistic and cultural productions be subject to evaluation based on national identity? Wouldn't this impede innovation and prevent national cultures from developing and flourishing?

Let us begin by asking a primary question about the link between identity and freedom: Is it at all possible to define freedom in an abstract sense that does not involve any influence or weight of identity? I don't think it is, since the first step would be to make clear whose freedom we are talking about. We already have in mind the identity of a subject whose freedom is going to be defined. So we can't even think of human freedom before we have a presupposition of what we think the human essence or identity is. Theoretically therefore, freedom and identity can not be totally separated.

Returning to the central part of your question, I must say we do not claim that identity is totally fixed. All we say is that some of the aspects of human identity are fixed. There are also flexible and unsettled aspects. In our view identity is neither totally fixed and intrinsic, nor is it completely contingent and constructed. The term identity originates from the [Latin] term *idem*, which means 'same' and implies a sense of continuity. There are constant elements in identity beside the variable elements which change [...]. We can not totally escape from our identities, whether it is individual or collective identity. Many of our different identities

---

[2] Initiative proposed by former Iranian president Mohammad Khatami, which was endorsed by the UN in 1998, and resulted in the naming of the year 2001 as the year of Dialogue Among Civilizations.

can coexist, horizontally or vertically, without conflict. We are not presenting a concrete or formalistic guideline of identity to the artist, which would prevent the diversity of cultural production. Moreover, no artist can claim that s/he was born in abyss. No human can claim that s/he was born outside the net of social relations. Everyone is born into a network of relations, groups and affiliations. We can not escape this just as we can not escape being born with certain racial, sexual and physical identities. Like it or not these identities limit your freedom and choice.

Now [...] the question is why should we consider some aspects of our identity as authentic and valuable, and why should they be privileged? Well, first of all it should be clear that we don't want to prescribe a specific form of artistic production. All we recommend is that if an artist wants to be influential within the environment s/he is living in, or intends to be a groundbreaking figure, s/he should neither ignore local and national identity, nor act as a totally hostile rebel toward it. Even if you want to revolutionize people's identities you have to be able to speak with them and to be understood. You would not succeed if you alienate them from yourself, that is from your artistic work. If you declare war against the whole of people's culture, they will resist and fight you back. Remember when you are trying to reform local identity you are not taking them away from identity to 'non-identity'; you are proposing to replace it with another identity. You are introducing and privileging a new set of symbols, norms or values and thus need to have a sufficient rationale. And let me add that if an artist wants to take on such an emancipatory mission, s/he is gaining the role of an intellectual. An intellectual must have objectives and obligations. To be an intellectual means to believe in a truth and a destiny. [...]

But some may suggest that if an artist is tied to his or her local attachments and cultural identity, this would prevent his or her work from being able to address and reach global audiences.

I am totally in favor of producing films or works of art for global audiences. In my view the precondition to produce art with global reception is universalism, teleologism and essentialism. I would support an artist with an aspiration to think about global issues. But we must be careful about *who* exactly we imagine as 'the global audience'. Sometimes we speak of a global audience and we have in mind an American audience, which is itself a local audience. The problem is that today American lifestyles are packed and distributed as global lifestyles and our Eastern artists are obliged to accept this as a rule. As an advocate of true globalization I insist that our film-makers should make films that would suit all human beings – films that engage with the pains and sufferings of all humans. This does not mean adapting American symbols. In fact, this approach is much closer to our Eastern and particularly Iranian identity, which has a long history – even before Islam – of monotheism, universalism and essentialism. So if I speak of national cinema or recommend to the Iranian film-makers not to neglect local and national identity, I nevertheless do not mean to deny global perspectives. Not to mention that the majority of the films that have achieved global appraisal were indeed very Iranian.

This is an interesting point because there are some officials and critics who think western festivals are politically motivated and that they only embrace certain Iranian films by 'westernized' directors, who advocate western cultural values or represent a dark and humiliating image of Iran, favored by western states.

I cannot deny that there are such cases and that political motivations are systematically involved in western cultural policies, which in turn influence institutions like film festivals. But not all what happens in the West is determined by the system. So I am not ignoring their systematic and politically motivated preferences, but neither do I view everything through the lens of conspiracy theory.

My next question is on the role of government in the cultural field, particularly in supporting cinema, as an industry and as an art. To what extent do you think the government should intervene in the field of culture or cinema?

The relation between the state and culture is defined by the principles of the ruling theories and philosophies of each government. It depends, for instance, on whether society is considered as a collection of individuals – as in liberal social theories – or an organic body, which determines conditions for the individual. It also depends on the views we have on the issue of rights: whether we recognize social rights as well as individual rights or not. And finally if we do recognize social rights or citizenship rights, whether they involve cultural rights or not?

I don't want to discuss these theoretical debates here so I will go on straight to describe my own view as a person living in the Islamic Republic of Iran who has thought about these issues. My argument is that people have cultural rights beside their political and economic rights. The state is not just responsible for providing security, justice and welfare; it also must deliver the cultural rights of its citizens. This I believe constitutes the foundation for state intervention in the field of culture. My second point however, is that the boundaries of state intervention in the field of culture should better be limited to policy-making and supervision. Executive duties and production should be handed to the people, to the private sector. There should be incentives and government support for local production, particularly in costly practices such as film production where the investment of the private sector is not enough. Policy-making and supervision, I must emphasize, should remain the responsibility of the government. Major decisions in the field of culture should not be exclusively determined by the free market, although the government certainly must include and involve the private sector and individuals in the process of policy-making and supervision. Due to my perception of the concept of the intellectual, I am in favor of inclusive policy-making and I think our government would benefit from such an approach. We are currently taking this approach in the Cultural Committee [of the parliament] and we seek to open the field of culture for more active involvement of the private sector. But there are government departments that resist this process. The IRIB [Iranian radio and television organization] is resisting our attempt to legalize the broadcast of [foreign] satellite channels under some kind of local regulation. If they don't accept our argument today, I'm sure their resistance will be broken in the future by public pressure and they will pay a price for it.

You mentioned the long and controversial debate over satellites in Iran. According to official reports today there are millions of satellite dishes just in Tehran. The Cultural Committee of the parliament prepared the legislation to ban satellite in Iran a decade ago. How does the Committee see it today?

In the Cultural Committee we have agreed on a new bill, which will soon be proposed to the parliament for a vote. In it we suggest that satellite television should not be considered a black or white issue: absolutely denied or totally embraced. There are all sorts of satellite channels, which do not in any sense violate our cultural policies. We have no other choice than to engage in dialogue with the contemporary world. We must be more tolerant and lenient and allow cable television to provide useful and decent foreign channels for our people [...]. We hope the parliament will soon pass this bill even though the IRIB is still resisting it. I think the reason behind their resistance is not cultural as they claim it to be. In fact it is economic. They don't want to lose their monopoly in broadcasting commercial advertisement.

This brings me to my final question about the economic aspects of cultural globalization. Do you agree with inviting or allowing foreign investment in national culture industries such as cinema? Some suggest that such investments are vital for strengthening the infrastructures of the film industry, for instance, they refer to the poor conditions of movie theaters in Iran and the decrease in the number of cinema seats, which they suggest indicates a decline in national cinema industry as a whole. Should global companies be given permission to, for example, invest and own cinemas in Iran?

I have no objection to foreign investment and the increase in the number of movie theaters in Iran. My only concern is about policy-making and supervision. We should not allow our cultural production field to be dominated by a global economy of culture that only cares about profits. Of course if we want their investment we should accept them to make profits out of it. But we should be in charge of policy-making and regulation. We don't want the culture of [western] development; rather we would like to have 'cultural development'. Instead of being incorporated in the economy of culture, we prefer a cultural economy. Developmental and economic projects should recognize and respect local and national culture if they are to succeed.

From such a viewpoint we may even have to introduce incentives and subsidies. If foreign investment respects national regulations, we shouldn't mind whatever profit it makes. But this is different from the liberal ideas of cultural globalization. Actually global investment and involvement in national cinema production can sometimes have better outcomes than what is routinely produced by local investments. Some of the Iranian films I have recently seen on television are really banal and disgraceful. I don't think such films will be respected anywhere in the world. When I was a student in England before the revolution we used to screen some Iranian films such as *Gav* (*The Cow*, Daryush Mehrjui, 1969) or *Yek ettefaqe sadeh* (*A Simple Event*, Sohrab Shahid-Sales, 1973). These were really remarkable works. Maybe foreign investment could encourage more quality films to be produced. I must admit however that we also have some brilliant directors such as [Ebrahim] Hatami-kia, who, in my view, is the ground-breaking figure of social critique within the framework of the revolutionary discourse.

But some of your colleagues have been very suspicious and negative toward foreign investments in culture, even when it comes to small measures such as building a cultural center by Shell in Southern Iran, the area where Shell is involved in the oil industry.

I don't see it like that. We shouldn't blame others' for our own weaknesses. If we have the strength to organize a powerful cinema then we should welcome such investments. What some of my colleagues are concerned about is that whether our cultural executives can maintain their authority and supervision over foreign involvements in our cultural field. Some MPs maintain that we aren't even seeing enough supervision over the local and national cultural productions in the country. When even the quality of our national cinema and television productions are not satisfactory, this means we don't have adequate supervision and regulation in place. So how are we going to manage foreign investments and productions? This is their bottom line but I still think we shouldn't rule out the option completely.

Thank you very much.

Thank you. I would be interested to read your thesis when it is finished. Can you send me a copy?

Oh certainly! It would be a pleasure to have your comments.

Appendix IV

Interview with Mohammad-reza Jafari-jelveh

17th August 2006, Tehran.

Iranian authorities were among the first in the 1990s to respond to or react against the homogenizing impacts of cultural globalization, using terms such as 'cultural invasion'. Are there any differences in how you view globalization these days? Is it still seen as a threatening project from the West or are there any opportunities for other cultures?

There are different definitions and interpretations of globalization. Sometimes the top-down project of globalism is called globalization, while at other times globalization is used to refer to a process. These are not the same. When speaking of a project, we imply that there is a program established and maintained by a certain board or body for particular purposes and certain destinies. It means a few people from certain parts of the world are attempting to shape the world according to their interests and ideals. The question here is whether they have a legitimate authority to do this. Do the majority agree with the way

Deputy Minister for Cinema and Audio-Visual Affairs, Ministry of Culture and Islamic Cultivation (2005–9).

the world is being shaped or the destiny they are being led to? At the time being, there is no overarching global project that can claim to be totally true and completely just and fair. Therefore the project of globalization, which involves such claims, should be resisted. I would rather call this globalism or top-down globalization.

However globalization for me is in itself a process, a gradual shift, a natural transformation according to the capacities, capabilities and qualifications of different nations, societies and cultures. Every indigenous culture can and should have a chance through its process of evolution and development to be globalized. Different cultures have delivered valuable things for humanity in the past, and they must have the chance to do so in the future. This is why we argue for the preservation of diverse cultures, in order to let them continue their natural life and possible evolution up to the heights that they potentially can reach. If we look back in history, the diverse sites and origins of influential cultures are quite clear. The nations that have significantly contributed to the world of humanity through their discoveries and innovations in science, art, culture and other human virtues are recognizable. It has not all come from a particular place on the earth.

Human beings are all the same species and come from a single origin, from a single truth. The truth was dispersed within them as they were scattered around the world. Culture, beliefs, rituals and ideas to some extent reflect this dispersed truth. This doesn't mean relativism or different truths. It is one single truth that has been dispersed in diverse nations and cultures. In this respect, national cultures, indigenous cultures, regional cultures, minority cultures and sub-cultures should be protected through a collective global action from being destroyed or obliterated. Of course all thoughts and ideas, cultures and civilizations have their natural and historical rise and decline. But they should have the chance to live their natural lives. If a culture has the resources to establish a civilization, it should not be prevented from doing so.

According to history, even those written by western historiographers, the East has been the origin of the most incredible and magnificent civilizations of the world. The East has also been the origin of fascinating religions, and the Middle East and Iran in particular is the point of convergence of all this. In Iran three cultural heritages come together: the oriental, the religious and the Persian. Throughout history this old culture has been capable of establishing great civilizations, which have been renowned, not for wars and destruction and poverty, but for the knowledge, the art and the goodness that they presented the world with. This culture, we believe, can be productive and constructive again, so protecting or preserving it would not be just in our interest, it would benefit the whole world of humanity. We have much to contribute to the world and make it a better place and therefore we must survive. There may be others who think they, or the world, would be better off without us. They have done their best to deny us, even to wipe off our footprints from history, especially those footprints which indicate the path of knowledge, science and art from the East to the West. This is the evil force that triggers inter-cultural or inter-civilizational conflicts. This is what we mean by cultural invasion: when one culture or one civilization deliberately seeks the obliteration of another. In such circumstances we certainly should be fully aware of what is happening. Sometimes we should block some sorts of cultural flows. At the same time, however, we should initiate our own flows of culture. Resistance in the form of barriers and restrictions would not be sufficient for a new birth [of a civilization]. This ambition requires much more systematic programming and hard effort by us. I'm sure there will be many who would appreciate our cultural products with enthusiasm and excitement. For instance, today inside the United States with all the cultural production and the dominant power they have and despite the constant reproduction of a particular [negative] image of others, there has been such a widespread interest in and admiration for the poems of [Molana Jalal Al-Din] Rumi, the great eastern, Muslim, Iranian poet and master of mysticism. Why is Rumi's book of poems *Masnavi Ma'navi*, which is a deeply oriental, religious and Iranian text finding so many readers in the United States? I think such works open a window to the beauties of the East for the West, they build relations and reduce the tensions between the nations. But definitely those in power will not just sit and watch us.

Iranian cinema is a good example. On the one hand it has opened a window to an eastern cultural heritage and has been admired as a different and new cinema by many people in the West, who truly seek new horizons, and follow up the fresh innovations and movements in the field of art and culture. But on the other hand this cinema is also facing a danger and that is the pitfall of being incorporated and directed toward representing a stereotypical and humiliating image of the East, of Islam and of Iran in the West. So we should be aware of the different intentions in the West toward Iranian cinema.

Your emphasis on the role of national cinema in breaking the stereotype image of the Muslims as the other in western media is important. But some critics also point to the historical formation of nation states and argue that national culture or national identity are not natural or intrinsic phenomena. In fact they have been selectively constructed by nation states and the elite for certain reasons. In this respect, 'national identity' is itself seen as a kind of ideology, which masks the ethnic, religious and linguistic differences within a nation and also could lead to conflicts such as in World War II. The question is why should everyone be committed to it? Wouldn't this limit the freedom or creativity of the artist or film-maker whose work may even influence the general understanding of national identity? Wouldn't such commitments to the past, hinder the birth of the new?

Let's start with your final question. Birth always happens in line with the past. Birth means coming from an origin, from a root, from a cradle. Every birth includes a mother and a child. The new originates from the old. When something comes from no-where-land it can not be named birth. Birth involves continuity and reproduction. Of course every birth also brings novelty through the new. But every newborn inherits some identities, some characteristics and some appearances. We can't be in favor of birth and deny or neglect maternity, identity and embededness […]. Birth does not mean a rupture. I think national identity or even the extreme forms of nationalism and chauvinism should not be considered merely as artificial or fictitious constructs. Such structuring was possible only were real essences and tendencies existed within the nations and they just couldn't be ignored.

German society for example, spoke German, lived German and had German customs and rituals that were different from the French or the English. But of course these differences in language, lifestyles and costumes should not lead to confrontation and the destruction of one another. It was the blind and extreme nationalism that triggered those disasters in World War II. If they had seen their differences as the outcome of the dispersion and diversification of a single truth, they could have recognized their shared values and qualities as well as their differences. There should never be bloodshed on the borders of difference. But the borders of difference can be signals and signifiers that help preserve and protect a heritage, which, in its heyday, could possibly benefit other nations.

If the Germans don't continue life as Germans, how would German values survive for the whole of humanity? If the French don't live as French, if the English don't live as English, and if the Asians – in general terms – don't remain Asian, the Chinese, the Indians and the Iranians; if they don't maintain their particular and beautiful languages and accents and tastes; if they don't preserve their heritage, in which language should they speak? What clothes should they wear? What kind of living should they choose? Who could provide a single universal dress code or language and claim that this is the best […]? As I mentioned in the beginning humanity is not yet at the stage to choose the one who should lead all the others, so we won't argue over who should rule the world or who should have the final word for the time being. Of course some in the West claim such a position for themselves and assert that the world is a single village under one rule, which certainly is 'their' rule and thus American culture and American lifestyles and American power and American hegemony should be dominant everywhere. This is what they say, we are not in such a position. Not that we don't have global ideas for the world. But we think the time is not today because the world should itself come to that moment of desire and decision about the appropriate authority that has the merits and virtues of being at the top and leading the world: the authority that can deliver more advantages to all. The authority can rightfully rule the world that is capable of delivering more justice, more freedom and more tolerance with a healing approach toward others who are in pain. This is a different issue which could be discussed separately.

As I said, we shouldn't fight over the borders of difference. Through recognizing the similarities we have and the values we share, we must find ways of coexisting with others and contributing what we think is good. [In this view] the world becomes a *bazaar* (traditional market) where everyone is allowed to bring and sell or exchange their products with others. In such a safe and free space nobody feels threatened for providing a more valuable or interesting product by the jealous gaze of others. The real world today does not offer such conditions. The unprincipled human wants all the ways exclusively open to himself and closed to others. This is the point of clash and conflict between powers.

The other point I would like to refer to here is the definition of nationality and the national. Limited or degrading definitions can not reveal all what these terms can indicate. In the

Appendix IV

Islamic and Iranian culture, the term *mellat* refers to concepts such as nation, population, people and society. But at the same time it means religion, path, and ritual. So a national view is also a religious view. The national includes common culture, common language, common borders and common interests. If we take a broader understanding, the continuity of national life would not be seen as a threat, it would be an opportunity and a value. It provides a context for the recognition of the new. The new will only survive if it is located within a context; if it has true roots and origins [...]

In response to your question about the contradictions between being committed to national identity and being a free artist, well the point is whether being free necessarily means being rootless? Does being creative mean creating something that belongs to nowhere and doesn't have any identity? The art of an artist is to create something new within his or her own context. We shouldn't lose our language or our accent to say something new. We can recognize creativeness under certain conditions and circumstances. Creativeness makes sense when we are able to compare things. We can't compare oranges and apples and consider one as being creative [...].

Freedom also is meaningful when there is an origin and a destiny. The human being needs freedom to move from one condition to another. Having freedom without having a starting point and a destination would not be freedom, it would be being adrift or astray. Literally it is called wandering. Every rational human wants to reach a destination and certainly would not do so with aimless drifting and wandering. One should be on the track and this is what makes people committed [...]. I think it is clear that preserving identity means supporting the continuity of the colors, the tastes, the characteristics and whatever good [of a nation] that has lasted so long, because it has been worth lasting, and therefore it should remain and last. The function of art is to preserve beauty and to extend it. The beautiful also has an origin and is heading toward a destination.

But it has been suggested that in order to communicate with global audiences an artist or film-maker should apply a 'global language' with less local accents or particular dimensions that may alienate others. Some believe that global appraisal and admiration has been only achievable for those Iranian films that have employed a universal language and ...

... and in fact have been de-localized or de-Iranianized! I think an Iranian physician should have Iranian prescriptions for the pains of humanity. If as an Iranian I prescribe in the European style, why not let a European do it? What's the need for an Iranian citizen with an Iranian name who is living at Iran's historical moment and geographic location to produce an American or European version of something. My version should be something unique if it is to be considered new and different. Actually if as an artist I use the rich Iranian heritage and cultural resources and crystallize them in my work, then I can claim to have produced something new and different for the world. Of course this is a difficult task and those who escape from themselves in order to become globally recognized are refusing to do the hard job and prefer the easy way. They are being lazy and thus for them globalization means de-Iranianization. While as I said we have figures such as Rumi who are deeply Iranian, Muslim and eastern but their work has been able to communicate with western readers and give them spiritual pleasure.

My next question is about your responsibility, but in a broad sense. What do you think about state intervention in culture and the arts, particularly in cinema as an industry that may need government support to survive Hollywood? Some believe the government must decide what people should or should not watch in cinemas in order to protect national culture. Others suggest the people should have the right to choose from diverse cultural products and therefore 'naturally' preserve what they deem worth preserving. How far should government intervention in cinema go and do you think there can be a possible end to it in the future?

Governments are the people's representatives and are elected to govern and regulate social affairs. They have a dual responsibility to preserve [the people's] identity and fundamental values and to guarantee their freedom and free-thinking. This approach – which may be termed as tolerant principalism – can provide a space for art and culture to flourish. It doesn't relinquish the field of culture to whatever may happen to it, particularly where it can be vulnerable. Rather it would attempt to guarantee a continuous and thriving arts and culture sector. Of course culture is not something that the government alone can take care of or preserve. The main responsibility here is of the people themselves and the state must provide the appropriate conditions for the people to participate.

I think imprudent state intervention in the field of culture, particularly with political intentions, is one type of intervention that certainly leads to restrictions and reckless acts by the government that denies the artist the right to free work and creativity. This is the damaging type of intervention that is objected to. But if the government intervenes in a minimal manner and considers itself responsible for the rights of both the public and the artists, and also keeps an eye on the overall conditions and intervenes in areas where there is need for more support, [this would be acceptable]. The government should provide a space that motivates the artist and the audience, or the producer and the consumer to produce and consume national products. We are not saying foreign products should not be consumed at all. There is always a natural cultural interaction among cultures through which we acquire products from others and present our cultural products to them. What we emphasize is that generally national products should be preferred and preserved. The consumption of national products should be considered a pride.

The government is the nation's representative to safeguard this motivating space of production and consumption with proper programs and policies. The artist should create according to his or her personal intentions and beliefs. The extent of his or her connection with the origins and roots, which he or she belongs to, determines how much the produced art can be perceived as a national art piece. The only thing the government should do is to support the survival of a cultural sphere that motivates and encourages national approaches. [The state] should not limit creativity, diversity or choice, but it should be able to recognize what is appropriate [for national culture] and what isn't. Our duty is not just to watch (*nezareh*), it is also to oversee and regulate (*nezarat*). A responsible government cannot just be a spectator.

Given that, cultural regulation must not be considered as the job of a teacher who dictates word by word. It is more like the job of a teacher who gives students subjects for writing a composition. The government should provide a space for creativity, […] it cannot produce or create art itself. Production should be done by producers and artists and writers. Unfortunately at certain times government intervention has been defined as if it should directly engage in the production of art. In my view the government should play an indirect and less visible role in culture […] and I don't see any end to this kind of intervention. It is a permanent obligation of the state because the process of identity production and reproduction is endless. The continuation and flourishing of cultural identity should always be ensured.

One other debate in cultural globalization is about the investment in, and ownership of, local or national culture industries by multinational corporations or generally foreign companies. To what extent do you think foreign companies should be involved in the production, distribution or exhibition of Iranian films inside the country or abroad?

I think whoever is interested in Iranian cinema should be able to invest in it. First of all we have the neighboring nations, which belong to the great family of Iranian or Persian culture and have shared histories, myths and languages. Cooperation with such countries and their investment in our cultural industries is certainly reasonable. The investment of our relatives in the great Islamic family is also definitely desirable. Iran has always been an active member of the Islamic world and at the center of the Islamic civilization. This historical responsibility is still lying on our shoulders. Iranian cinema should have products for the entire Islamic world. Our progress and development is not just good for our sake. It will be advantageous for all those who share a same family and the same origins and destinies with us.

We also belong to a greater Asian family whose members are most welcome to invest in Iranian cinema. In a broader view, the South–South cooperation can be mentioned; nations that have similar sufferings and pains and are taking the same path toward justice and freedom. Today we are witnessing more and more relations and cooperation among these countries, from Latin America to Africa and Asia. And finally even the nations of the west or the north can also invest in Iranian cinema. But we should not forget that such investments should not lead to the investor having absolute control in this cinema. The control of this cinema should be in national hands, in eastern, Muslim, Iranian hands. That is the condition in order to preserve the eastern, the religious and the Iranian taste in Iranian cinema. If we want the investment for the sake of national cinema, then our cinema should remain national with those investments. If it is going to benefit only foreign films, then what will its advantage be for Iranian cinema? Generally I think foreign investment is useful if it helps to improve and advance the production capabilities of a national cinema.

I must admit, however, that we have not yet encouraged and mobilized local and national investment in Iranian cinema adequately, before moving toward inviting foreign investment. I'm not saying they are incompatible tasks, but I think priority should be given to expanding the very small size of public and private investment in Iranian cinema. We should inform and enlighten the local investors – both the decision-making centers of the government and the private sector – so that they realize how crucial and vital this investment is for the country.

Thank you very much for your time.

Thank you.

Bibliography

Abak, H. R., 'Seytareh-ye Liberalism bar khashmha-ye yek armankhah (The Dominance of Liberalism over the Rage of an Idealist)', *Shargh Newspaper*, 10 Mordad 1386 (1st August 2007), <http://www.sharghnewspaper.ir/Released/86-05-10/288.htm>. (Accessed November 2007).
Abdi, A., 'Tanaqozhaye fardi va jam'i (Personal and Collective Paradoxes)', *Film Monthly*, 14: 224, pp. 105.
Abecassis, M., 'Iranian War Cinema: Between Reality and Fiction', *Iranian Studies*, 44: 3 (2011), pp. 387–94.
Abrahamian, E., *The Iranian Mujahedin*, New Haven, Yale University Press, 1992.
Ahmad, A. S. and H. Donnan (eds), *Islam, Globalization and Postmodernity*, Routledge, London, 1994.
Ajudani, M., *Mashroute-ye Irani (Iranian Constitutionalism)*, London, Fasl-e Ketab, 1997.
Albrow, M., *The Global Age*, Cambridge, Polity, 1996.
Altman, R., *Film/Genre*, London, BFI, 1999.
Amiri, N., 'Agar koshteh shavam kare hokoomate Iran ast (If I Get Assasinated, the Iranian Government will be Behind It) Interview with Mohsen Makhmalbaf', *Rooz Online*, 30 Ordibehesht 1386 (20th May 2007), <http://www.roozonline.com/2007/05/post_2311.php>. (Accessed November 2007).
Anderson, B., *Imagined Communities: Reflections on the Origins and Spread of Nationalism*, London, Verso, 1983.
Appadurai, A., 'Disjuncture and Difference in Global Cultural Economy', *Public Culture*, 2: 2 (1990).
—— *Modernity at Large: Cultural Dimensions of Globalization*, Minneapolis, University of Minnesota, 1996.
Avini, S. M., *Ayeneh-ye Jadu (Magic Mirror) Vol.2*, Tehran, Saqi, 1999.
—— *Ayeneh-ye Jadu (Magic Mirror) Vol.3*, Tehran, Saqi, 2001.
Azarm, M., M. Yazdani-Khorram and K. Nikoonazar, 'Hich vaqt kasi ra tahqir nakarde-am (I Have Never Humiliated Anyone)', *Kargozaran*, 25 Mehr 1387 (17th October 2008), <http://www.kargozaaran.com/ShowNews.php?34911>. (Accessed January 2009).
Azimi, S., 'In adamhaye ashena (These Familiar People)', *Film Monthly*, 26: 383 (September 2008), p. 32.
Badley, L., R. Barton Palmer and S. J. Schneider (eds), *Traditions in World Cinema*, Edinburgh, Edinburgh University 2006.
Baharloo, A. (ed.), *Mo'arrefi va shenakht-e Mohsen Makhmalbaf (Introducing and Understanding Mohsen Makhmalbaf)*, Tehran, Qatreh, 2000.
Bani-yaqoob, J., 'A Close-Up View on Mohsen Makhmalbaf's Life in Kabul', *Makhmalbaf Film House Website* (2002a), <http://www.makhmalbaf.com/articles.php?a=384>. (Accessed November 2007).

———— 'Vaqti mokhatab-ha bishtar mishavand ... (When the Audience become Larger ...)', *Makhmalbaf Film House Website*, (2002b), <http://www.makhmalbaf.com/articles.php?a=465>. (Accessed November 2007).

Barber, B., *Jihad vs. McWorld*, New York, Times books, 1995.

Beynon, J. and D. Dunkerley (eds), *Globalization: The Reader*, London, Routledge, 2000.

Carroll, N., 'Art and Globalization: Then and Now', *Journal of Aesthetics and Art Criticism*, 65: 1 (2007), pp. 131–43.

Caryl, C., 'America's Unsinkable Fleet', *Newsweek*, 26th February 2007, <http://www.newsweek.com/id/68465>. (Accessed 16th May 2009).

Castells, M., *The Rise of The Network Society*, Oxford, Blackwell, 1996.

Classen, C. and D. Howes, 'The Dynamics and Ethics of Cross Cultural Consumption', in D. Howes (ed.), *Cross Cultural Consumption*, London and New York, Routlege, 1996.

Crofts, S., 'Reconceptualising National Cinema/s', in V. Vitali and P. Willemen (eds), *Theorising National Cinema*, London, BFI, 2006.

Dabashi, H., *Close Up: Iranian Cinema, Past, Present and Future*, London, Verso, 2001.

———— 'Dead Certainties: The Early Makhmalbaf', in R. Tapper (ed.), *The New Iranian Cinema: Politics, Representation and Identity*, London & New York, I.B. Tauris, 2002.

———— *Iran, A People Interrupted*, New York, New Press, 2007a.

———— *Masters and Masterpieces of Iranian Cinema*, Washington DC, Mage, 2007b.

———— *Makhmalbaf at Large: The Making of a Rebel Filmmaker*, London, I.B. Tauris, 2008.

Danan, M., 'National and Postnational French Cinema', in V. Vitali and P. Willemen (eds), *Theorising National Cinema*, London, BFI, 2006.

Danesh, M., 'Darbareye Mohsene Makhmalbaf: Parvaz ra bekhater bespar ... (On Mohsen Makhmalbaf: Remember to Fly ...)', *Shahrvand-e Emruz*, 2: 17, 8 Mehr 1386 (30th October 2007), <http://shahrvandemroz.blogfa.com/post-273.aspx.>. (Accessed December 2007).

———— 'Cinemaye melli, vijegiha, tarifha, ebhamha: Moshkel hamin jast (National Cinema, Characteristics, Definitions and Ambiguities: The Problem is Precisely Here)', *Film Monthly*, 26: 383, pp. 19–20.

Davari, M. T., *The Political Thought of Ayatullah Murtaza Mutahhari: An Iranian Theoretician of the Islamic State*, London, Routledge Curzon, 2005.

Davoodnejad, A., 'Iranian Filmmaker writes Open Letter to Obama', *Tehran Times*, 3rd March 2009, <http://www.tehrantimes.com/index_View.asp?code=190354>. (Accessed 15th March 2009).

Dirlik, A., 'The Global in the Local', in R. Wilson and W. Dissanayake (eds), *Global/Local*, Durham, Duke University, 1996, pp. 21–45.

Dönmez-Colin, G., *Cinemas of the Other*, Bristol, Intellect, 2006.

Dumont, L., 'The Anthropological Community and Ideology', *Social Science Information*, 18 (1979).

Ďurovičová, N. and K. Newman (eds), *World Cinemas, Transnational Perspectives*, New York, Routledge, 2010.

Edemariam, A., 'The Film Bush Asked to See', *The Guardian*, 26th October 2001, <http://www.guardian.co.uk/film/2001/oct/26/artsfeatures>. (Accessed 27th December 2007).

Edensor, T., *National Identity, Popular Culture and Everyday Life*, Oxford, Berg, 2001.

Egan, E., *The Films of Makhmalbaf; Cinema, Politics and Culture in Iran*, Washington DC, Mage Publishers, 2005.

Elena, A., *The Cinema of Abbas Kiarostami*, London, Saqi, 2005.

Elsaesser, T., *European Cinema : Face to Face with Hollywood*, Amsterdam, NLD: Amsterdam University 2005.

Esfandiary, S., 'National Cinema and Globalisation: Situating the Transnational, National and Islamic Dimensions of Iranian Cinema in Global Context', Thesis submitted to University of Nottingham, 2009.

Eshqi, B., 'Duzakhi ke bar ebrahim golestan shod (The Hell that Turned into Paradise for Ebrahim)', *Film-Negar*, 5: 52, Dey 1385 (January 2006), pp. 58–60.

Eslami, M., 'Az kotak-kari be eesar, az khashm be mehrabani, az gerye be khande (From Fighting to Altruism, From Rage to Compassion, From Weeping to Laughter)', in A. Qarehsheikhloo and M. Vafai (eds), *Daryush Mehrjui, naqd-e asar: az Banu ta Mehman-e Maman (Review of Daryush Mehrjui's Works: From Banu to Mum's Guests)*, Tehran, Hermes, 2006.

Esteva, G. and M. S. Parakash, *Grassroots Post Modernism: Remaking the Soil of Cultures*, London and New York, Zed Books, 1998.

Ezra, E. and T. Rowden (eds), *Transnational Cinema: The Film Reader*, New York, Routlege, 2006.

Falicov, T. L., *The Cinematic Tango: Contemporary Argentine Film*, London, Wallflower Press, 2007.

Farahmand, A., 'Perspectives on Recent (International Acclaim for) Iranian Cinema', in R. Tapper (ed.), *The New Iranian Cinema: Politics, Representation and Identity*, London & New York, I.B. Tauris, 2002.

Fathi, N., 'Despite Hopes of Hollywood Visit, Iran's Leaders Stick to the Same Script', *The New York Times*, 1st March 2009, <http://www.nytimes.com/2009/03/02/world/middleeast/02visit.html>. (Accessed 15th April 2009).

Featherstone, M., *Undoing culture: Globalization, Postmodernism and Identity*, London, Sage in association with Theory, Culture and Society, 1995.

—— 'Islam Encountering Globalisation: An Introduction', in A. Mohammadi (ed.), *Islam Encountering Globalisation*, London, RoutledgeCurzon, 2002.

Ferasati, M. (ed.), *Az Karkhe Ta Rhine (From Karkhe To Rhine)*, Tehran, Isargaran, 1993.

—— (ed.), *Jang Baraye Solh (War for Peace), Vol.2*, Tehran, Association for the Cinema of the Revolution and the Sacred Defense, 2001.

Film Monthly, 'Bargozide-haye nevisandegan va montaqedan-e mahnameh-ye Film (The Choices of *Film Monthly*'s Writers and Critics)', 21: 313, Esfand 1382 (February/March 2004), pp. 70–5.

—— 'Parvandeh-ye yek film: Mehman-e Maman (A Dossier for a Film: Mum's Guests)', 22: 319, Mordad 1383 (July/August 2004), pp. 76–111.

—— 'Behtarin asar-e cinema-ye melli-e se dahe (The Best Works of National Cinema in Three Decades)', *Film Monthly*, 26: 383, Shahrivar 1387 (September 2008), pp. 26–31.

Fletcher, H., 'Mujahadeen-e-Khalq (MEK) (People's Mujahedin of Iran or PMOI)', *Council on Foreign Relations (US)* (2008), <http://www.cfr.org/publication/9158/>. (Accessed 15th January 2009).

Garcia Canclini, N., *Hybrid Cultures: Strategies for Entering and Leaving Modernity*, Minneapolis, University of Minnesota, 1995.

Giddens, A., *The Consequences of Modernity*, Cambridge, Polity, 1990.

—— *Runaway World*, New York, Routledge, 2002.

Golmakani, H., 'Tekke'ei az ayene-ye shekaste (A Piece of the Broken Mirror) Interview with Mohsen Makhmalbaf', *Film Monthly* (1995), Republished in Makhmalbaf Film House Website: <http://www.makhmalbaf.com/articles.php?a=288>, (Accessed 15th August 2007).

—— 'Az khoshoonat va ta'assob ta modara va mehrvarzi (From Violence and Dogmatism to Tolerance and Compassion)', *Kian*, 8: 45, Bahman/Esfand 1377 (February 1999), pp. 188–95.

Gordon, C. (ed.), *Power/Knowledge: Selected Interviews and Other Writings by Michel Foucalt, 1972-1977*, New York, Pantheon, 1980.

Haji-aqa-mohammad, J., 'Majmueh-ye pichideh-ei az ravabet va bavarha (A Complex Set of Relations and Beliefs)', *Film Monthly*, 5: 51, Tir 1366 (June/July 1987), pp. 57–8.

Hall, S., 'The Local and the Global; Globalization and Ethnicity', in A. King (ed.), *Culture, Globalization and the World-system*, London, Macmillan, 1991.

Haqiqat, M., 'Yek padidehye Irani dar faranse (An Iranian Phenomenon in France)', *Film Monthly*, 429, Mordad 1390 (July 2011), <http://www.massoudmehrabi.com/weblog/?id=1311174134>. (Accessed 12th August 2011).

Haqiqi, M., 'Az kotak-kari be eesar, az khashm be mehrabani, az gerye be khande (From Fighting to Altruism, From Rage to Compassion, From Weeping to Laughter)', in A. Qarehsheikhloo and M. Vafai (eds), *Daryush Mehrjui, naqd-e asar: az Banu ta Mehman-e Maman (Review of Daryush Mehrjui's Works: From Banu to Mum's Guests)*, Tehran, Hermes, 2006.

Hardt, M. and A. Negri, *Empire*, Cambridge Massachusetts, Harvard University, 2000.

—— *Multitude*, New York, Penguin, 2004.

Harvey, D., *The Condition of Postmodernity: An Enquiry Into the Origins of Cultural Change*, London, Blackwell, 1989.

Hasani-nasab, N., 'Hads bezan che kasi baraye sham miayad? (Guess Who's Comming to Dinner?)', *Film Monthly*, 22: 319, Esfand 1382 (February/March 2004), pp. 77–9.

Hatami-kia, E., 'Television Interview on Shab-e Shisheh-ei talk show, 24 May 2007', Channel Five Website (2007), <http://tv5.irib.ir/shabe-shishei/matn.asp?id=33>. (Accessed 17th August 2007).

Hayward, S., 'Framing National Cinemas', in M. Hjort and S. MacKenzie (eds), *Cinema and Nation*, London, Routledge, 2000.

—— *French National Cinema*, second edn., London, Routledge, 2005.

Held, D., A. McGrew, D. Goldblatt and P. Perraton, *Global Transformations*, Cambridge, Polity press, 1999.

Higbee, W. and H. S. Lim, 'Concepts of Transnational Cinema: Towards a Critical Transnationalism in Film Studies', *Transnational Cinemas* 1: 1 (2010), pp. 7–21.

Higbee, W. and S. Maty Ba (eds), *De-Westernising Film Studies*, London, Routledge, forthcoming.

Higson, A., *Waving the Flag: Constructing a National Cinema in Britain*, Oxford, Oxford University, 1995.

—— 'The Limiting Imagination of National Cinema', in M. Hjort and S. MacKenzie (eds), *Cinema and Nation*, London, Routledge, 2000.

────── 'The Concept of National Cinema', in A. Williams (ed.), *Film and Nationalism*, New Jersey, Rutgers State University, 2002, pp. 52–67.

Hill, J., 'The Issue of National Cinema and British Film Production', in D. Petrie (ed.), *New Questions of British Cinema*, London, BFI, 1992.

────── 'British Film Policy', in A. Moran (ed.), *Film Policy: International, National and Regional Perspectives*, London, Routledge, 1996.

Hirst, P. and G. Thompson, *Globalization in Question: The International Economy and the Possibilities of Governance*, Cambridge, Polity, 1996a.

────── 'Globalization: Ten Frequently Asked Questions and Some Surprising Answers', *Soundings*, 4 (1996b).

Hjort, M., 'On the Plurality of Cinematic Transnationalism', in N. Ďurovičová and K. Newman (eds), *World Cinemas, Transnational Perspectives*, New York, Routledge, 2010.

Hjort, M. and S. MacKenzie (eds), *Cinema and Nation*, London, Routledge, 2000.

Hobsbawm, E. J. and T. O. Ranger (eds), *The Invention of Tradition*, Cambridge, Cambridge University, 1983.

Holton, R. J., *Globalization and the Nation-State*, New York, Palgrave, 1998.

Huntington, S. P., 'The Clash of Civilizations', *Foreign Affairs*, 72: 3 (1993), pp. 22–8.

Jafari-jelveh, M., *Tarhi bara-ye aknoon: dar masir-e cinema-ye melli (A Proposal for Now: Towards a National Cinema)*, Tehran, Farabi Cinematic Foundation, 2008.

Jameson, F., 'Notes on Globalization as a Philosophical Issue', in F. Jameson and M. Miyoshi (eds), *The Cultures of Globalization*, Durham, Duke University, 1998a.

────── 'Preface', in F. Jameson and M. Miyoshi (eds), *The Cultures of Globalization*, Durham, Duke University, 1998b.

Karimabadi, M., 'Manifesto of Martyrdom: Similarities and Differences between Avini's Ravaayat-e Fath [Chronicles of Victory] and more Traditional Manifestoes', *Iranian Studies*, 44: 3 (2011), pp. 381–6.

Karimi, I., *Abbas Kiarostami filmsaz-e realist (Abbas Kiarostami the Realist Filmmaker)*, Tehran, Nashre Ahoo, 1987.

Khatami, E., 'Iranian Film Industry Thriving, Hollywood Learns', *CNN.com*, 29th March 2009, <http://edition.cnn.com/2009/SHOWBIZ/Movies/03/28/iran.hollywood.cinema/index.html>. (Accessed 16th April 2009).

Khoshchehreh, M., 'Kiarostami dar khala', zamine mohkam zire paye Mehrjui (Kiarostami in Abyss, Mehrjui on Solid Grounds)', *Shahrvand*, 927 (2004), <http://www.shahrvandpublications.com/fa/Default.asp?IS=927&Content=NW&CD=CM&NID=3#3>. (Accessed 15th October 2007).

Khoshkhoo, A., 'Bar labeh-ye hafezeh-ye ma (On the Edge of Our Memory)', *Shahrvand-e Emruz*, 2: 17, 8 Mehr 1386 (30th October 2007), <http://shahrvandemroz.blogfa.com/post-273.aspx.>. (Accessed 1st December 2007).

────── 'Chera jangal ra nadidim? (Why Did We Miss the Forest?)', *Shargh*, 10 Mordad 1386 (1st August 2007), <http://www.sharghnewspaper.ir/Released/86-05-10/288.htm>. (Accessed September 2007).

Kianian, R., 'Bazigardani Shishei (Transparent Supervision of the Cast)', *Film Monthly*, 16: 223, Mordad 1377 (July 1998), pp. 20–4.

—— 'An Roozha (Those Days)', *Film-Negar*, 5: 52, Dey 1385 (January 2006), p. 41.

Kilday, G., 'Q&A: Sid Ganis and Annette Bening', The Hollywood Reporter, 15th March 2009, <http://www.hollywoodreporter.com/hr/content_display/news/e3i68061ff8eae6a637da9e62eb703832be>. (Accessed 16th April 2009).

King, N., 'Going to Movies in the Morning: Fredric Jameson on Film', *Critical Quarterly*, 45 (2003), pp. 185–202.

KOIS, 'Religion (in South Korea)', The Korean Culture and Information Service (KOIS), (2009), <http://www.korea.net/korea/kor_loca.asp?code=U05>. (Accessed 12th May 2009).

Leaman, O. (ed.), *Companion Encyclopedia of Middle Eastern & North African Film*, Florence, KY, Routledge, 2003.

Luard, E., *The Globalization of Politics*, London, Macmillan, 1990.

Makhmalbaf, M., '*Afghan Alphabet*, Director's Note', Makhmalbaf Film House Website, (2001), <http://www.makhmalbaf.com/movies.php?m=32>. (Accessed 16th August 2007).

—— 'Frequently asked Questions and Answers', Makhmalbaf Film House Website, (2005a), <http://www.makhmalbaf.com/news.php?lang=1&n=31>. (Accessed 16th August 2007).

—— '*Sex and Philosophy* Dialogue List', Makhmalbaf Film House Website, (2005b), <http://www.makhmalbaf.com/articles.php?a=449>. (Accessed 14th December 2008).

—— '*Sex and Philosophy*, Credits and Information', Makhmalbaf Film House Website, (2005c), <http://www.makhmalbaf.com/movies.php?m=49>. (Accessed 18th December 2008).

—— '*Scream of the Ants* Dialogue List', Makhmalbaf Film House Website, (2006), <http://www.makhmalbaf.com/doc/070717060853ScreamoftheAnts.doc>. (Accessed 15th December 2008).

Malakooti, B., 'Dayereh-ye tange khak va khoon parasti (The Insular Cycle of Glorifying Land and Blood)', Makhmalbaf Film House Website (2003), <http://www.makhmalbaf.com/articles.php?a=396>. (Accessed November 2007).

Mansoori, M., 'Shadi-ye Zendegi, Gham-e Ensani (Happiness of Life, Sorrow for Humanity), Interview with Mohsen Makhmalbaf', *Cinema Weekly (Accessed at Makhmalbaf Film House Website)*, (1996), <http://www.makhmalbaf.com/doc/shadi.doc>. (Accessed 16th July 2007).

Maqami-kia, H., 'Lotfesh be ine ke faqat ye sarbaz nabinish (The Delicate Point is that You Don't Consider Him Only a Soldier)', *Film-Negar*, 5: 52, Dey 1385 (January 2006), p. 64.

Mehrabi, M., 'Haghighate talkh, maslehate shirin va rastegarie darigh shode (Bitter Truth, Sweet Expedience and the Avoided Emancipation)', *Film Monthly*, 424, April 2011, <http://www.massoudmehrabi.com/weblog/?m=02&y=1390>. (Accessed 15th August 2011).

Miles, A., 'Shocked by Slumdog's Poverty Porn', *The Times*, 14th January 2009, <http://www.timesonline.co.uk/tol/comment/columnists/alice_miles/article5511650.ece>. (Accessed 10th April 2009).

Miller, D., *On Nationality*, Oxford, Oxford University, 1995.

Miller, T., 'The Crime of Monsieur Lang: GATT, the Screen and the New International Division of Cultural Labour', in A. Moran (ed.), *Film Policy: International, National, and Regional Perspectives*, London, Routledge, 1996, pp. 72–84.

Mir-ehsan, A., 'Zaman-e Irani (Iranian Time)', *Film-Negar*, 5: 52, Dey 1385 (January 2006), pp. 42–7.

Mirbakhtyar, S., *Iranian Cinema and the Islamic Revolution*, New York, McFarland & Company, 2006.

Moazzezi-nia, H., 'Mardi ke khod ra be zanu dar avard (The Man Who Wrecked Himself)', *Shahrvand-e Emruz*, 2: 17, 8 Mehr 1386 (30th October 2007), <http://shahrvandemroz.blogfa.com/post-273.aspx.>. (Accessed December 2007).

—— (ed.) *Cinema-Jashnvareh: Cinemaye Iran, Jashnvareh-haye Jahani (Cinema-Festival: Iranian Cinema, Worldwide Festivals)*, Tehran, Soroush, 2009.

Mohammadi, A., (ed.) *Islam Encountering Globalisation*, London, Routledge Curzon, 2002.

—— (ed.) *Iran Encountering Globalization*, London, Routledge Curzon, 2003.

Moosavi, M., 'Goftogooye Kalameh ba Mirhosein Musavi piramun masaele mohemme keshvar (Interview with Mirhosein Mousavi on the important issues of the country)', *Kalameh*, (2009), <http://www.kaleme.com/1388/11/13/klm-10327/>. (Accessed 14 June 2011).

Moosavi, S., 'Gozareshi az jalaseh-ye naqd o barresi *Ejareh neshinha* dar hozeh honary (A Report on the Seminar for Review and Critique of *The Lodgers* held in the Arts Centre)', Gol-Agha Online, (2007), <http://www.golagha.ir/news/2006/Aug/13/528.php>. (Accessed 23rd September 2007).

Morgenstern, J., 'Slumdog Finds Rare Riches in Poor Boy's Tale', *Wall Street Journal*, 14th November 2009, <http://online.wsj.com/article/SB122661670370126131.html>. (Accessed 4th April 2009).

Morley, D. and K. Robins, *Spaces of Identity: Global Media, Electronic Landscapes and Cultural Boundaries*, London, Routledge, 1995.

Mostaghasi, S., 'Hameye ina ro arzoon forookhty! (You Sold Them All Too Cheap)', *Film-Negar*, 5: 52, Dey 1385 (January 2006), pp. 51–6.

Motahhari, M., *Khadamat-e motaghabel-e Islam va Iran (The Mutual Acomplishments of Islam and Iran)*, twelfth edn., Tehran, Sadra, 1983.

Nabavi, E., 'Interview with Mohsen Makhmalbaf', *Soroush*, 388, 20 Tir 1366 (11th July 1987).

Naderi, A., 'The Path I Found …', *Film Monthly*, 24: 346, Ordibehesht 1385/May 2006, p. 20.

Naficy, H., *An Accented Cinema: Exilic and Diasporic Filmmaking*, New Jersey, Princeton University, 2001.

—— 'Islamizing Film Culture in Iran: A Post Khatami Update', in R. Tapper (ed.), *The New Iranian Cinema: Politics, Representation and Identity*, London & New York, I.B. Tauris, 2002, pp. 173–208.

—— 'Iranian cinema', in O. Leaman (ed.), *Companion Encyclopedia of Middle Eastern & North African Film*, Florence, KY, Routledge, 2003a.

—— 'Theorizing 'Third World' Film Spectaorship: The Case of Iran and Iranian Cinema', in A. R. Gunteratne and W. Dissanayake (eds), *Rethinking Third Cinema*, New York, Routledge, 2003b, pp. 183–201.

—— 'Iranian Émigré Cinema as a Component of Iranian National Cinema', in M. Semati (ed.), *Media, Culture and Society in Iran: Living with Globalization and the Islamic State*, London, Routledge, 2008.

Nazer, B., 'Khoshoonate Pak (Innocent violence)', *Kian*, 8: 45, Bahman/Esfand 1377 (February 1999), pp. 196–7.

Ohmae, K., *The End of the Nation-State*, New York, Free Press, 1995.

Paquet, D., 'The Korean Film Industry: 1992 to Present', in J. Stringer and C. Y. Shin (eds), *The New Korean Cinema*, Edinburgh, Edinburgh University, 2005.
Park, S. H., 'Korean Cinema after Liberation: Production, Industry and Regulatory Trends', in F. Gateward (ed.), *Seoul Searching: Culture and Identity in Contemporary Korean Cinema*, Albany, State University of New York, 2007.
Paya, A., 'Recent Developments in Shi'i Thought', in M. Khan (ed.), *Islam and Political Order: Muslim Reflections on Democracy, Secularism and Law*, New York, Rowman and Littlefield, 2005.
Pooria, A., 'Kash eede dashtan kafi bood (If Having an Idea was Enough)', *Shahrvand-e Emruz*, 2: 17, 8 Mehr 1386 (30th October 2007), <http://shahrvandemroz.blogfa.com/post-273.aspx.>. (Accessed 15th December 2007).
Poormohammad, M., 'Du film ba yek belit! (Two Films for One Ticket!)', *Film Monthly*, 5: 53, Shahrivar 1366 (September 1987), p. 85.
Qarehsheikhloo, A. and M. Vafai (eds), *Daryush Mehrjui, naqd-e asar: az Banu ta Mehman-e Maman (Review of Daryush Mehrjui's Works: From Banu to Mum's Guests)*, Tehran, Hermes, 2006.
Qoochani, M., 'Terajedi-ye Mohsen Makhmalbaf (The Tragedy of Mohsen Makhmalbaf)', *Shahrvand-e Emruz*, 2: 17, 8 Mehr 1386 (30th October 2007), <http://shahrvandemroz.blogfa.com/post-289.aspx.>. (Accessed December 2007).
Qookasian, Z., (ed.) *Majmueh-ye maqalat dar naqd va mo'arrefi-ye asare Abbas Kiarostami (A Collection of Essays Criticising and Introducing the Work of Abbas Kiarostami)*, Tehran, Nashre Didar, 1996.
Rahimieh, N., 'Marking Gender and Difference in the Myth of the Nation: A Post-Revolutionary Iranian Film', in R. Tapper (ed.) *The New Iranian Cinema: Politics, Representation and Identity*, London & New York, I.B. Tauris, 2002.
Rantanen, T., 'A Man Behind Scapes: An Interview with Arjun Appadurai', *Global Media and Communication*, 2: 7 (2006), pp. 7–19.
Razi, A., 'Besyar safar bayad ta pokhte shavad khami (One Should Travel Much to Become Mature) ', *Makhmalbaf Film House Website*, (2002), <http://www.makhmalbaf.com/articles.php?a=386>. (Accessed 15th November 2007).
Robertson, R., 'Interpreting Globality', in *World Realities and International Studies Today*, Glenside, PA, Pennsylvania Council on International Education, 1983.
——— 'The Relativization of Societies: Modern Religion and Globalization', in T. Robbins, W. C. Shephard and J. McBride (eds), *Cults, Culture and the Law*, Chico, CA, Scholars, 1985.
——— 'Globalization and Societal Modernization: A Note on Japan and Japanese Religion', *Sociological Analysis*, 47 (1987a), pp. 35–42.
——— 'Globalization Theory and Civilizational Analysis', *Comparative Civilizations Review*, 17 (1987b).
——— 'Globalization, Politics, and Religion', in J. A. Beckford and T. Luckman (eds), *The Changing Face of Religion*, London, Sage, 1989.
——— *Globalization: Social Theory and Global Culture*, London, Sage, 1992.
——— 'Glocalization: Time-Space and Homogeneity-Heterogeneity', in M. Featherstone, S. Lash and R. Robertson (eds), *Global Modernities*, London, Sage, 1995.

Rosen, P., 'History, Textuality, Nation: Kracauer, Burch and Some Problems in the Study of National Cinemas', in V. Vitali and P. Willemen (eds), *Theorising National Cinema*, London, BFI, 2006, pp. 17–28.

Rosenberg, J., 'Globalization Theory: A Post Mortem', *International Politics*, 42 (2005), pp. 2–74.

Saeed-Vafa, M., 'Location (Physical Space) and Cultural Identity in Iranian Films', in R. Tapper (ed.), *The New Iranian Cinema: Politics, Representation and Identity*, London & New York, I.B. Tauris, 2002.

Said, E., *Representations of the Intellectual: The 1993 Reith Lectures*, New York, Vintage, 1996.

Scholte, J. A., *International Relations of Social Change*, Buckingham, Open University, 1993.

Semati, M. (ed.), *Media, Culture and Society in Iran: Living with Globalization and the Islamic State*, London, Routledge, 2008.

Shahabi, M., 'The Iranian Moral Panic over Video: A Brief History and Policy Analysis', in M. Semati (ed.), *Media, Culture and Society in Iran: Living with Globalization and the Islamic State*, London, Routledge, 2008.

Shahrvand-e Emruz, 'Seire so'oodi ta soqoot ya taksire ta'assof bar angize Mohsen Makhmalbaf (Rising Up to the Point of Fall: The Regrettable Replications of Mohsen Makhmalbaf)', *Shahrvand-e Emruz*, 2: 17, 8 Mehr 1386 (30th October 2006), <http://shahrvandemroz.blogfa.com/post-273.aspx.>. (Accessed December 2007).

—— 'Shevaliyeye bi sarzamin dar peye fathe mogholestan khareji (The Homeless Knight in Seek of Conquering Mongolia)', *Shahrvand-e Emruz*, 2: 17 (November 2007), <http://shahrvandemroz.blogfa.com/post-273.aspx.>. (Accessed December 2007).

Shari'atmadari, H., 'Chera Sokut? (Why Silence?)', *Keyhan*, 13 Esfand 1387 (3rd April 2009), p. 2.

Shaw, L. and S. Dennison, *Brazilian National Cinema*, Oxon, Routledge, 2007.

Shin, J., 'Globalization and New Korean Cinema', in C. Shin and J. Stringer (eds), *New Korean Cinema*, Edinburgh University, 2005.

Simpson, J., 'AMPAS Iran Visit Spits In The Face of Gays, Women, Jews and Film', *Digital Journal*, 3rd March 2009, <http://www.digitaljournal.com/article/268391>. (Accessed 16th April 2009).

Sinclair, J., 'Mexico, Brazil and the Latin World', in J. Sinclair, E. Jacka and S. Cunningham (eds), *New Patterns in Global Television: Peripheral Vision*, Oxford, Oxford University, 1996.

Solhjoo, T., 'Daste bolande hadese', *Film Monthly*, 16: 223, Mordad 1377 (July 1998), pp. 9–10.

—— 'Hamase, Arman, Terajedi (Epic, Ideal, Tragedy) A Discussion on the Films of Hatami-kia', *Film-Negar*, 5: 52 (2006), pp. 32–8.

Straubhaar, J., 'Brazil: The Role of the State in World Television', in N. Morris and S. Waisbord (eds), *Media and Globalizatoion: Why the State Matters*, Lanham, Roman & Littlefield, 2001.

Szeman, I., 'Cultural Studies and the Transnational ', in G. Hall and C. Birchall (eds), *New Cultural Studies*, Edinburgh, Edinburgh University, 2006.

Tait, R., 'Hollywood Goes to Tehran – and Is Ordered to Apologise for Its Sins', *The Guardian*, 2nd March 2009, <http://www.guardian.co.uk/world/2009/mar/02/mahmoud-ahmedinejad-arts-film-hollywood>. (Accessed 15th April 2009).

Talebi-nejad, A., 'Hamgam ba Mardom, Hamrah ba Mas'oolan (Along with the People, in Line with the Officials)', *Film Va Cinema*, 2: 8 (1997), p. 13.

—— 'Hamase, Arman, Terajedi (Epic, Ideal, Tragedy) A Discussion on the Films of Hatami-kia', *Film-Negar*, 5: 52, Dey 1385 (January 2006), pp. 32–8.

—— 'Noqteh-ye tahavvol-e yek filmsaz (The Moment of Transformation in a Filmmaker's Career)', *Shargh*, 10 Mordad 1386 (1st August 2007), <http://www.sharghnewspaper.ir/Released/86-05-10/288.htm>. (Accessed 1st September 2007).

Tapper, R. (ed.), *The New Iranian Cinema: Politics, Representation and Identity*, London & New York, I.B. Tauris, 2002.

Tomlinson, J., *Cultural Imperialism: A Critical Introduction*, London, Pinter, 1991.

—— 'Internationalism, Globalization and Cultural Imperialism', in K. Thompson (ed.), *Media and Cultural Regulation*, London, Sage and Open University, 1997, pp. 117–62.

—— *Globalization and Culture*, Cambridge, Polity, 1999.

—— 'The Agenda of Globalization', *New Formations*, 50 (2003), pp. 10–21.

Tracy, M., 'Popular Culture and the Economics of Global Television', *Intermedia*, 16: 2 (1988).

Varzi, R., *Warring Souls: Youth, Media, and Martyrdom in Post-Revolution Iran*, London and Durham, Duke University, 2006.

Vitali, V. and P. Willemen (eds), *Theorising National Cinema*, London, BFI, 2006.

Weber, C., 'Not Without My Sister(s): Imagining a Moral America in *Kandahar*', *Open Democracy* (2005), <http://www.opendemocracy.net/content/articles/PDF/3006.pdf>. (Accessed 15 June 2011).

Willemen, P., 'The National Revisited', in V. Vitali and P. Willemen (eds), *Theorising National Cinema*, London, BFI, 2006.

Williams, A., 'Introduction', in A. Williams (ed.), *Film and Nationalism*, New Jersey, Rutgers University, 2002a.

—— (ed.), *Film and Nationalism*, New Jersey, Rutgers University, 2002b.

Yusof Ali, A., *(Translation of) The Holy Quran*, London, Tahrike Tarsile Quran, 1998.

Zahedi, T., 'Estesna va qa'edeh (Exception and Rule)', *Film Monthly*, 16: 223, Mordad 1377 (July 1998), pp. 12–13.

www.ingramcontent.com/pod-product-compliance
Ingram Content Group UK Ltd.
Pitfield, Milton Keynes, MK11 3LW, UK
UKHW051849210426
5322IPUK00025B/630